European Meetings

Anna Sybilla Bidwell (ed.)

European Meetings

Social and Political Studies

PETER LANG
EDITION

Bibliographic Information published by the Deutsche Nationalbibliothek
The Deutsche Nationalbibliothek lists this publication in the Deutsche Nationalbibliografie; detailed bibliographic data is available in the internet at http://dnb.d-nb.de.

This publication was co-financed from the statutory grant in University of Social Sciences and Humanities, Faculty in Wrocław (NO: BST/WROC/2012/02d) and the National Science Centre (Poland) (No. NN116314839, 2010-2013, The functioning of the parliaments of Central Europe in comparative perspective).

Library of Congress Cataloging-in-Publication Data

European meetings : social and political studies / Anna Sybilla Bidwell (ed.).
    pages cm
    ISBN 978-3-631-64484-3
    1. European Union. 2. European Union countries—Politics and govern-
ment. 3. European Union countries—Foreign relations. I. Bidwell,
Anna Sybilla.
JN30.E855 2013
341.242'2—dc23

                                                                    2013025881

ISBN 978-3-631-64484-3 (Print)
E-ISBN 978-3-653-03309-0 (E-Book)
DOI 10.3726/978-3-653-03309-0

© Peter Lang GmbH
Internationaler Verlag der Wissenschaften
Frankfurt am Main 2013
All rights reserved.
Peter Lang Edition is an Imprint of Peter Lang GmbH.

Peter Lang – Frankfurt am Main · Bern · Bruxelles · New York ·
Oxford · Warszawa · Wien

www.peterlang.de

Contents

Editor's Introduction

The publication is devoted to the discussion of several challenges facing Europe, especially European Union. Scientists who cooperated in producing this volume wrote on topics important to the European society nowadays and in the past, but not always in the main stream. The result is an interesting insight on a number of diverse issues.[1]

One of the most important problems faced by national parliaments in Europe is the democratic deficit in countries belonging to the European Union. The executives gain influence on the decision making process often with little or none reference to their own parliaments. The evolving role of national parliaments in Europe is the focus of Przemysław Paradowski's articles. Understandably most, though not all, of his studies concentrate on the Central and South Europe. The comparison of the changes that took place in the party systems in four Vysegrad countries in the last decade of the XX century and the first decade of the XXI century, gives us an interesting insight into the direction in which the status of parliaments in those countries evolves. The author concentrates on the activity of the parliamentary oppositions in Poland, Slovakia, Czech Republic and Hungary. Paradowski stresses that in the 1990's there was a rather clear left-right division between government and opposition coalitions, whereas the picture in the first decade of the XXI century becomes much more complicated. Then he goes on to discus the case of Montenegro's party system as it developed in the years 1990 – 2006. The system is classified as extremely multiparty, with one party dominating, lacking alternation of power. Interesting proved the comparison of the Montenegro experience in building the party system with that of other countries in the region. For the position of all national parliaments, essential is their role in the European Union decision-making process. An important move was made in the direction of strengthening their status by the Lisbon Treaty, which introduced the early-warning mechanism. The procedure provides the national parliaments with the opportunity to express their views about the draft legislation. The question remains whether the national parliaments can use it to build for themselves an important role vis-a-vis the European Parliament, Commission and the Council.

---

1 The articles by P. Paradowski: Changes in parliamentary opposition..., and: From domination to domination. Comments on the party system development in Montenegro (1990-2011), (Spotkania Europejskie 4/2011), by M. Łukasik-Duszyńska: William Max-Muller..., by S. Michalak: The image of the British secret service... and by J. Marczuk: The situation of a transsexual person... can be found on the internet.

It is worth stressing that Przemysław Paradowski's articles complement each other. Although ever since the 1990's the leaders of the European Union were conscious of the fact that the citizens of all the countries forming this unique organization had not been well informed, this problem is not yet solved. With all the possibilities opened up by information technologies it would seem that both informing and consulting the members of the society should be much easier. According to the research presented by Monika Łukasik-Duszyńska in her article on European communication policy, the Internet pages set up by EU institutions are lacking in all sorts of ways. In consequence instead of a two-way communication she observed that the Internet is being used as a tool for informing not communicating.

The article by Sebastian Michalak on relations between the European Union and Taiwan gives us an interesting insight into the problems of the latter. The EU seems to set a good example for relations between the Republic of China and the Peoples Republic of China in ways of solving long lasting conflicts as well as gaining from cooperation. At the same time it is important that European integration proved that the smaller countries could gain stronger positions in the process. The second article is a study of Taiwanese intelligence agencies, which up till 2008 tended to focus on providing early-warning intelligence or long-term threat assessments. Since then, with the improvement of relations with China, some commentators suggested that the Taiwanese intelligence agencies were ordered to reduce their activity in the mainland China.

Several articles are of historical importance. M. Łukasik – Duszyńska presents the work of the British Envoy, William Max-Müller who in the 1920's worked in Warsaw. We get an interesting insight into the way he collected information that was later sent to the Foreign Office, and learn who influenced the picture of the situation in Poland, as set down in his reports. S. Michalak in his articles concentrates on the functioning of the Polish security service before 1989. He compares ways of recruiting secret collaborators in the 1950's with those in the 1970's and 1980's. In first period they generally were forced to cooperate with the help of compromising materials. But many people enlisted in the later period were persuaded by the government's propaganda and considered it their patriotic obligation. Others were payed for their services. This study is supplemented by Michalak's article presenting the influence of the British secret service's experience on the methods applied by the Polish communist civilian counter-intelligence. In the process we not only learn a lot about the functioning of the Polish counter-intelligence but also get an interesting image of the British intelligence as seen by communist oppression apparatus.

The article by Joanna Matczuk is an attempt to discuss a problem not often analysed. That is the legal aspects surrounding identity in particular in the case of transgender and transsexualism. In the paper the author presents the distinction between formal legal frameworks and the practice that the transsexual community in Poland faces. The conclusion being that there is a need for new and adequate rules of law and regulations, and that the legislator will have to address the problem with deeper understanding of its complexity. Poland is used as a case study, remembering that other countries with similar experience will face the same challenge.

The challenges facing Europe and European Union in particular are manifold. In this volume we address some of them especially the changing position of national parliaments in the contest of their co-operation with the European Union Parliament, but also the way citizens are informed and consulted by the EU institutions, and look at the problems facing security services both now and in the past.

For encouragement and constructive criticism we would like to thank PhD Stuart Shields (University of Manchester UK) and professor Krzysztof Wójtowicz (University of Wrocław).

A. Sybill Bidwell

Changes within parliamentary opposition models in the light of party systems' evolution in Central Europe in the first decade of the 21st century

Przemysław Paradowski

Parliamentary opposition in the Central Europe states could emerge only on the debris of the communist system. The turning point was 1989-1991 period, when the successive states of the region and the Soviet Union were regaining full independence and sovereignty. Formerly before 1989 political opposition in the Central Europe states was illegal and apart from some scarce exceptions it was never a parliamentary one. The aim of the opposition in undemocratic states was resistance against the regime as a whole and changing or overthrowing it. Within the states that were becoming democratised the opposition's role underwent some major changes. It was not anymore just a matter of destroying the system but rather functioning within it on particular terms as well as being ready to replace those in power, that meant in due course taking over the governing of the state.[1] Democratizing the countries of the region concerned was initially a variegated process and was taking place without any obstacles.[2] Therefore the political systems, meaning both party systems and parliaments, were and still are diverse as much as are the resulting models of parliamentary opposition.

Parliamentary opposition is a small yet important part of a broadly understood opposition.[3] It is closely related to democratisation and parliamentarisation of the Central Europe states. Free, competition based elections in the states of the region were possible due to introduction of political pluralism and were a result of parliaments having regained their functions. The parliaments took a central position in forming political systems of the Central Europe states. In democratic systems, parliamentary opposition is a necessary condition and its basic tasks are the control, critique and creating an alternative to government coalition.[4] Besides that, political system can greatly benefit from opposition's presence in parliament. One of the benefits of the well functioning opposition in the democratic systems could be its influence on bettering

---

1 M. Kubát, Politická opozice v teorii a středoevropské praxi (vybrané otázky), Praha 2010, p. 52.
2 P. Lewis, Political Parties in Post-Communist Eastern Europe, London 2000, p. 17-18.
3 E. Zwierzchowski, Opozycja parlamentarna, in Opozycja parlamentarna, E. Zwierzchowski ed., Warszawa 2000, p. 12.
4 E. Zwierzchowski, op.cit., 26.

governmental performance, making democratic system legitimation stronger, moving arguments and conflicts from the streets to parliament and gaining experience to be able to take over the power.[5]

The literature on functioning of the parliamentary opposition in Central Europe is not very rich especially if compared with the numerous works on the opposition in Western Europe or the United States. The researchers have been so far studing to different aspects of parliamentary opposition in Central and Eastern Europe. Kopecky and Spirova analysed parliamentary opposition in Bulgaria, Czech Republic and Hungary accepting as the basis the A. King's typology.[6] Philip Norton mentioned the Central Europe opposition in the conclusion of the collective work edited by L. Helms.[7] Recently a monograph on the opposition in the states of Central Europe by Michał Kubát was also published.[8] He analised the models of parliamentary opposition in Polish literature. A. Antoszewski wrote about parliamentary opposition in post-communist Europe, and S. Bożyk described opposition in the Polish Sejm.[9] All the works mentioned here fill some study gaps on parliamentary opposition in Central and Eastern Europe. But the researchers rather tend to deal with the matters of parliamentary opposition of their own regions in a form of digressions in works devoted to all kinds of issues connected to development of parliaments and party systems in Central Europe.[10]

The environment within which the opposition in the Central Europe parliaments functions and its nature are undergoing changes.[11] Therefore the data pertaining to parliamentary opposition in the first decade of transformation

---

5   R. Holzhacker, The Power of Opposition Parliamentary Party Groups in European Scrutiny, *The Journal of Legislative Studies*, Vol.11, No.3/4, Autumn/Winter 2005, p. 430.

6   P. Kopecký, M. Spirova, Parliamentary Opposition in Post-Communist Democracies: Power of the Powerless, The Journal of Legislative Studies, Vol. 14, Nos. 1/2, March/June 2008, 133-159. See A. King, Modes of Executive-Legislative Relations: Great Britain, France and West Germany, Legislatives Studies Quarterly, 1 (1976).

7   P. Norton, Making Sense of Opposition, in Parliamentary Opposition in Old and New Democracies, ed. L. Helms, Routledge, London/New York 2008.

8   M. Kubát, op.cit.

9   A. Antoszewski, Wzorce opozycji parlamentarnej w Europie postkomunistycznej, in Opozycja w systemach demokratycznych i niedemokratycznych, ed. K. Łąbędź, M. Mikołajczyk, Kraków 2001; S. Bożyk, Opozycja parlamentarna w Sejmie RP, Wydawnictwo Sejmowe, Warszawa 2005.

10   Recently to the Central European parliaments was devoted The Journal of Legislative Studies, Special Issue: Post-Communist Parliaments: Change and Stability in the Second Decade, Vol. 17, No. 2, June 2011, 116-127.

11   A. Antoszewski, op.cit., p. 112.

do not necessarily correspond with the models of the subsequent decade. As stated by A. Antoszewski, parliamentary opposition differs by the extend and level of uniformity, whereas the differentiating factors are variables characteristic for a party system and standards of government forming. The common features of the Central Europe party systems were a high level of competitiveness, which meant a lack of constantly dominating party, and that the majority of a dominating party over a defeated one was not significant, whereas political competition was characterised by a high level of hostility and frequent alternation of power.[12] The above mentioned features had in greater or lesser degree undergone modifications in the second decade of functioning of the Central Europe states' political systems.

As the models of parliamentary opposition I understand a party structure present in a parliament after each elections. The structure of the party system inspires more or less efficient activity of opposition.[13] This is a starting point for using the tools available in the systems of parliamentary democracy for exhibiting functions and reaching goals by opposition parties. Yet on this point, which means determining the extend of fragmentation and polarisation, depends the power of an opposition in relation to a governing coalition.

In this article I try to look into the way parliamentary opposition changed in four Central Europe countries belonging to the Visegrád Group. In a short article it is not possible to present all the tools the opposition in Central Europe such is using. Among others the parliamentary control of the executive, participating in the activities of parliamentary commissions, or influencing the order of proceedings. Since on the parliamentary level the opposition comprises of political parties I analyse it by looking at it through the prism of development and changes of the party systems on the parliamentary level in the above mentioned countries. This approach is justified as in the Central Europe countries dominates a model of party interactions on the parliamentary level.[14] The first part of the article briefly characterises, based on A. Antoszewski's ascertainment,[15] the opposition models of the first decade of transformation. The second part looks into the changes in the party systems after successive elections in the first decade of the 21st century. The following part is devoted to the analysis of the characteristics of the opposition models. As the starting point I accept what has been settled for the first decade of parliamentary opposition

---

12   Idem, p. 113-114.
13   P. Kopecký, M. Spirova, op. cit., p. 138.
14   See P. Kopecký, M. Spirova, op. cit., p. 154.
15   See A. Antoszewski, op.cit., pp. 111-119.

functioning in Central Europe.[16] In the fourth part I characterise the changes in the parliamentary opposition models in the Visegrád Group countries in the first decade of the 21st century.

Parliamentary opposition models in the first decade of transformation

The parliamentary opposition models of the first decade of transformation were described by A. Antoszewski. He linked his analysis to the development of political competition and drew it based on the P. Lewis's concept as the starting point.[17] In this concept four phases of the development of the political competition in East and Central Europe were specified. For the sake of analysing parliamentary opposition models in the Visegrád countries it is important to place these countries' party systems development within the frame of the above mentioned concept.

The beginning phase constituted the first free elections or partly free parliamentary elections in which in most of these countries post-communist parties competed with a broad spectrum of anticommunist formations such as Forum. As belonging to this category should be classified the Czech Civic Forum (Czech: Občanské fórum - OF) and the Slovakian Public Against Violence (Slovakian: Verejnosti proti Násiliu – VPN): the elections were held in both the republics forming Czechoslovakia; as well as the Polish Civic Committees (Polish: Komitety Obywatelskie – KO). Hungary does not fall within the frame of this typology since the pluralistic party system started to form there already in 1987 and during the first free elections in the spring of 1990 the previously formed political parties were competing.[18] A characteristic aspect of this phase was electoral victory of the afore mentioned organisations such as Forum or – as it happened in Hungary – anticommunist parties, and forming by them a government. The exception in this regard were the Polish "contract elections." As a result of decisions made by the Round Table the representatives of the communist party and its satellite parties were able to secure for themselves most of the Sejm's mandates. This contract determined

16   Idem.
17   P. Lewis, op.cit., p. 74-78; A. Antoszewski, Wzorce..., pp. 115-116.
18   P. Lewis, op.cit., p. 19. On forming Hungarian political parties see L. Benda, System partyjny Węgier, in ed. A. Antoszewski, P. Fiala, R. Herbut, J. Sroka, Partie i systemy partyjne Europy Środkowej, , Wydawnictwo Uniwersytetu Wrocławskiego, Wrocław 2003, pp. 63-69.

the anticommunist opposition to have created a government with the participation of the communist party representatives.

The second phase of the party systems development was characterised by fragmentation or transformation of the organisations such as Forum into political parties. The extend of fragmentation was very big in Poland, but smaller in the Czech Republic and Slovakia. In all the Central Europe states the "left" wing of the party realm was consolidated within the communist parties. To some extend special was the Czech party system in which on the basis of the left, besides the functioning communist party, formed a stronger Social Democracy with anticommunist roots.[19]

The third phase was characterised by authority alternation, that means taking over (regaining) the control by the post-communist parties, which won the parliamentary election. That happened in Poland and in Hungary. Whereas the Czech Republic again falls outside of this pattern since there the power was maintained by the right-wing Civic Democratic Party (Czech: Občanská demokratická strana – ODS). Similar was the situation in Slovakia where the control over the state, apart from a break lasting just few months, was in the hands of V. Mečiar's populist party.

The last phase of party competition was determined by P. Lewis as the second half of 1990s[20]. It was characterised by the stabilization of the interparty competition patterns, which in most of the Central Europe states meant rivalry between strong post-communist parties and the right and centre-right groups.[21] Among the Visegrád Group this tendency can be noted in Poland's and Hungary's party systems. In Poland after the 1997 elections the Democratic Left Alliance (Polish: Sojusz Lewicy Demokratycznej – SLD) lost the parliamentary majority it had in 1993-1997, and formed a strong and uniform opposition. Also in Hungary the Hungarian Socialist Party (Magyar Szocialista Párt – MSZP) that ruled the country in the 1994-1998 period, as a result of the 1998 elections, took over the role of a strong and uniform opposition. In Slovakia though the post-communist Party of the Democratic Left (Slovakian: Strana demokratickej l'avice – SDL) having returned to the parliament after absence between 1994-1998, entered a broad, ruling coalition known as the Slovak Democratic Coalition (Slovakian: Slovenska demokraticka koalicia – SDK) comprised of parties ideologically diverse – but united by an opposition against V. Mečiar's Movement for a Democratic Slovakia (Slovakian: Hnutie za demokratické

---

19 W. Sokół, System polityczny Czech, in Systemy polityczne państw Europy Środkowej i Wschodniej, ed. W. Sokół, M. Żmigrodzki, Lublin 2005, p. 235.

20 P. Lewis, op.cit., p. 78.

21 A. Antoszewski, Wzorce…, p. 116.

Slovensko – HZDS). In the Czech Republic the Communist Party of Bohemia and Moravia (Czech: Komunistická strana Čech a Moravy – KSČM) won 11% (1996) and 12% (1998) of the mandates was isolated and did not play any important role in the rivalry between the Czech Social Democratic Party (Czech: Česká strana sociálně demokratická – ČSSD) and the ODS.

A. Antoszewski distinguishes four variants of parliamentary opposition that were characteristic to the first decade of post-communist countries transformation in Europe: a uniform (integrated) left-wing opposition, fragmented left-wing opposition, integrated right-wing opposition and fragmented right-wing opposition. As for the four countries being the object of my discussion in Hungary and Poland functioned the patterns of integrated left-wing opposition and fragmented right-wing opposition, in Czech Republic fragmented left-wing opposition and integrated right-wing opposition, whereas in Slovakia both the left-wing and the right-wing oppositions were fragmented.[22] These observations were in great part supported by M. Kubát, although the left-wing and right-wing oppositions in Czech Republic as well as the right-wing opposition in Hungary and the left-wing in Poland were graded as slightly fragmented.[23]

Party systems changes in the second decade of transformation

The analysis of changes in parliamentary opposition models in the second decade of transformation should be preceded by a review of changes in the Visegrád Group countries' party systems. Party systems in Central and East Europe, as A. Antoszewski commented, remain in the transformation phase.[24] This remark also concerned the Visegrád Group countries, although it should be noted that the Hungarian and Czech party systems were regarded as the most stable in the region. The subsequent elections, especially these held in 2010, confirmed the A. Antoszewski's constatation. Within the last ten years party systems in all the Visegrád countries had been remodeled.

In the first decade of the 21st century in three out of the four Visegrád countries parliamentary elections were held in 2002, 2006 and 2010, whereas in Poland alone in 2001, 2005 and 2007. As a result of these elections the party systems underwent a further evolution and, the models of parliamentary opposition were also altered. These transformations can be described by using

---

22   A. Antoszewski, Wzorce..., p. 118 (Table 1) and 119.
23   M. Kubát, op.cit., p. 98.
24   A. Antoszewski, Wzorce..., p.117.

A. Siaroff's scheme which in Poland was adopted by W. Sokół in his article on the transformation in the Central and East Europe countries.[25]

The author proposed adopting quantitative criteria which allow to classify party systems in democratic countries. These criteria included the number of parties which achieved at least the number of places in the parliament equal to 3% (Parties with 3 Percent of the Seats: P3%S); total number of the mandates gained by the biggest two parties (Two-Party Seat Concentration: 2PSC); distance between the mandates number of the biggest two parties (Seat Ratio First to Second Party: SR1:2); analogical distance between the second and third party (Seat Ratio Second to Third Party: SR2:3); as well as the effective number of parties in the parliament (Effective Number of Parliamentary Parties: ENPP).[26] A. Siaroff classified two-party systems (P3%S not greater than 3; 2PSC at least 95%; ENPP close to 2.0; small difference SR1:2; big difference SR2:3), two-and-half-party systems (P3%S between 3 and 5; 2PSC 80-95%; SR1:2 not greater than 1.6; SR2:3 1.8 or more), moderately multi-party systems with one dominating party (P3%S from 3 to 5; SR1:2 1.6 or more), moderately multi-party system with two dominating parties (P3%S from 3 to 5; SR1:2 below 1.6; SR2:3 1.8 or more), extremely multi-party system with one dominating party (P3%S above 5; SR1:2 1.6 or more), extremely multi-party systems with two main parties (P3%S above 5; 2PSC 55-75%; SR1:2 below 1.6; SR2:3 1.8 or more), extremely multi-party with balance between the parties (P3%S above 5; 2PSC below 60%; SR1:2 below 1.6; SR2:3 below 1.8).[27] Based on the afore given criteria W. Sokół classified the Central and East European countries' party systems until the 2002 elections.[28] Taking into account the earlier data gathered by e.g. W. Sokół, A. Antoszewski and M. Kubát[29] I will try to take a closer look at the party systems evolution in the Visegrád countries in the subsequent years and to outline the consequences these changes brought for the parliamentary opposition models.

---

25 W. Sokół, Transformacja ustrojowa państw Europy Środkowej i Wschodniej – próba bilansu, in Systemy polityczne państw Europy Środkowej i Wschodniej, ed. W. Sokół, M. Żmigrodzki, Lublin 2005, p. 64-66; A. Siaroff, Comparative European Party Systems. An Analysis of Parliamentary Elections since 1945, New York and London 2000.

26 A. Siaroff, op.cit., p. 69-70; W. Sokół, Transformacja..., p. 62-66.

27 A. Siaroff, op.cit., p. 70-71; W. Sokół, Transformacja..., p. 62-64.

28 W. Sokół Transformacja..., p. 64-66, Table 25.

29 W. Sokół, Transformacja..., p. 59-69; A. Antoszewski, Wzorce..., p. 111-119; M. Kubát, op.cit., p. 89-110.

Table 1. Characteristics of the Visegrád countries' party systems in the first decade
of the 21th century

	P3%S	2PSC	SR1:2	SR2:3	ENPP	P3%S	2PSC	SR1:2	SR2:3	ENPP
	2002					2006				
Czech Republic	5	64.00	1.20	1.41	3.81	5	77.50	1.09	2.84	3.09
Slovakia	7	42.70	1.29	1.12	6.12	6	54.00	1.61	1.55	4.81
Hungary	3	94.80	1.06	8.54	2.21	3	90.70	1.13	9.10	2.41
	2001					2005				
Poland	6	61.10	3.33	1.22	3.60	6	62.60	1.17	2.37	4.26

	P3%S	2PSC	SR1:2	SR2:3	SR2:3
	2010				
Czech Republic	5	54.50	1.05	1.29	4.51
Slovakia	6	60.00	2.21	1.27	4.01
Hungary	4	83.40	4.46	1.25	1.48
	2007				
Poland	4	81.50	1.26	3.14	2.82

Source: Own calculations

The Hungarian party system evolved from the two-and-half-party system
tending towards two-party system in 2002 to moderately multi-party system
with one dominating party in 2010 (Figure 1). The dominating party in the 2010
elections won not only the absolute but also constitutional majority in the
parliament.

In the 2002 elections some other parties present on the parliamentary level at
the beginning of transformation did win enough votes to enter the Assembly. In
2002 the Independent Smallholders' Party (Hungarian: Fuggetlen Kisgazdapart –
FKgP) disappeared from the parliamentary scene, and the Hungarian
Democratic Forum (Hungarian: Magyar Demokrata Fórum – MDF) entering the
elections in coalition with the Fidesz. Thus only four parties entered the
parliament. Four years later the status quo was maintained. This stable system
was turned upside down after the 2010 elections. Apart from the Parliament
having been dominated by the Fidesz and the Christian Democratic People's
Party (Hungarian: Kereszténydemokrata Néppárt – KDNP), as well as the
failure of the MSZP for the first time since the beginning of transformation, the

members of two parties: the Alliance of Free Democrats (Hungarian: Szabad Demokraták Szövetsége – SzDSz) and the MDF did not enter the parliament. The posts of these two parties were taken by two new in the parliamentary realm parties: the nationalistic Movement for a Better Hungary (Hungarian: Jobbik Magyarországért Mozgalom – Jobbik) and the liberal party sympathising with the Hungarian Green Movement: the Politics Can Be Different (Hungarian: Lehet Más a Politika – LMP).[30]

The result of dominating the party system on the parliamentary level by a big Fidesz party in a coalition with a small KDNP, put together with the elections failure of the previously ruling left-wing party, is an unprecedented in Hungary weakness of the parliamentary opposition which has neither any real chances to influence those in power, nor to conduct destructive actions. Is then the Hungarian party system to be described as a dominating party system? Taking into consideration the variables and factors characterising a one dominating party system it is too early to say.[31] Above all it is hard to predict the results of the future elections. Yet if the tendency persists it will be possible to determine that the Hungarian system is heading towards one dominating party. However considering the instability of the electorate in Central Europe it is more likely that the system will come back to its moderately multi-party form with two main parties leading the way.

The Czech party system after the 2002 elections was put into a category of the moderately multi-party systems with two main parties. After the subsequent elections in 2006 the Czech party system can be described as extremely multi-party with two main parties. More radical change took place after the 2010 elections when the majority of the two main parties in comparison with the other ones decreased to such a degree that it could be considered an extremely multi-party system with balance between the parties. At the beginning of the 21st century similarly like in Hungary the system seemed to be stabilised. After the 2002 elections the makeup of the parliament was preserved. In 2006 from the parliamentary level the Freedom Union–Democratic Union (Czech: Unie Svobody–Demokratická unie – US-DEU) was excluded, and its place was taken by the Czech Green Party (Czech: Strana Zelených – SZ). More substantial changes occurred after the 2010 elections. Besides the above mentioned decrease in support for the two main parties the first time from the beginning of

---

30 M. Kuta, Parlamentní volby v Maďarsku 2010, Vybraná Témata 7/2010, Parlament České republiky, Kancelář Poslanecké sněmovny, Parlamentní institut, p. 4-7.

31 M. Bankowicz, Opozycja polityczna w systemie partii dominującej, in Opozycja w systemach demokratycznych i niedemokratycznych, ed. K. Łabędź, M. Mikołajczyk, Kraków 2001, p. 180.

transformation no mandates were acquired by the Christian and Democratic Union– Czechoslovak People's Party (Czech: Křesťanská a demokratická unie - Československá strana lidová – KDU-ČSL). The Czech Green Party turned to be an ephemeron whose encounter with the parliament ended after one term. But in the Chamber of Envoys appeared, with quite a big support, two new parties: the Tradition Responsibility Prosperity 09 (Czech: Tradice Odpovědnost Prosperita 09 – TOP 09) and the Public Affairs (Czech: Věci veřejné – VV). The system tailored after the 2010 elections on the parliamentary level requires the coalition to be formed from a greater number of parties. Presently the coalition comprises of three parties, out of which two (ODS and TOP 09) hold a comparable power in the parliament. Actually in the previous term the coalition was also formed by three parties, but the ODS gained a substantial advantage over its partners. The difference is that in the present term the opposition holds less mandates than it did in the previous term which lessens its ability to influence those in power, e.g. in the present term it cannot (without one of its partners withdrawal from the coalition) efficiently pass a motion of no confidence as it was possible during the 2006-2010 term.

The Slovakian party system had no stability period unlike the Czech and Hungarian ones. Here the changes were more frequent although it is worth to note that during the 2002-2006 and 2006-2010 terms the core of the National Council was formed by the same five groups. On the parliamentary level after the 2002 and 2006 elections the system could be assessed as extremely multiparty with balance between the parties. Nevertheless in 2006 noticeable was gaining greater advantage, in comparison with the elections held four years earlier, by one group, the Direction–Social Democracy (Slovakian: Smer–sociálna demokracia – Smer), over the other parties. The advantage was not yet significant enough to consider the system as multi-party with one dominating party. Further changes occurred, this time similarly as in the Czech Republic and Hungary, after 2010 elections. This time Smer gained enough advantage over the other parties for the party system to be considered extremely multi-party with one dominating party. The Smer's domination was not by absolute majority, therefore the other parties formed the coalition forcing the dominating party to enter the opposition.[32] This phenomenon is neither new in Central Europe nor in Slovakia.[33] The consequence of this

---

32 G. Mesežnikov, Post-election Slovakia. The first half-year of center-right government, KAS International Reports 4/ 2011, p. 109-111.

33 The 1998 elections were narrowly won by the HZDS, but having no partner besides SNS to form a majority coalition entered the opposition. See L. Kopeček, Słowacki system..., p. 183.

situation is the weakness of the ruling majority formed by many parties and strengthening of the uniform opposition holding nearly half of the mandates. Besides securing a dominating position (combined with moving to the opposition) in the parliament by the social democrat, tending towards populism Smer party, from the parliamentary level were removed the parties which were present in the National Council nearly from the beginning of transformation: the populist HZDS and the Party of the Hungarian Coalition (Slovakian: Strana maďarskej koalície – SMK). The former lost its mandates to Smer and to a new on the parliamentary level party, the Freedom and Solidarity (Slovakian: Sloboda a Solidarita – SaS). The SMK was thus replaced by a new party, the Most-Hid.[34]

The Polish party system after the breakup and failure of the Solidarity Electoral Action (Polish: Akcja Wyborcza Solidarność – AWS) evolved from a moderately multi-party system with two main parties (after the 1997 elections) in the direction of extremely multi-party system with one dominating party (after the 2001 elections).[35] The main party after four years of being in the opposition turned to be again the SLD, that means a post-communist party. In the subsequent elections held in 2005 the greatest number of mandates was gained by two parties created after the AWS's breakup: the Law and Justice (Polish: Prawo i Sprawiedliwość – PiS) and the Civic Platform (Polish: Platforma Obywatelska – PO). The system modeled after these elections can be classified as extremely multi-party with two main parties. The parliament was entered by two parties considered to be extremist:[36] the Self-Defense of the Republic of Poland (Polish: Samoobrona Rzeczpospolitej Polskiej – abbreviated as Samoobrona) and the League of Polish Families (Polish: Liga Polskich Rodzin – LPR), which initially granted a "silent" support to a minority government formed by PiS, only to form together with this party a majority coalition a few months later. After dissolution of the Sejm and holding the 2007 elections the system underwent further changes. Two anti-system parties did not cross the threshold and found themselves outside the parliament. The Sejms' mandates were won by only four parties out of which two acquired a significant advantage over the remaining parties. According to A. Siaroff's classification the system could be described as two-and-half-party. Characteristic for the Polish party system in the first decade of the 21st century is the formation and functioning of two big parties with anti-communist roots

---

34   M. Kuta, Parlamentní volby na Slovensku 2010, Vybraná Témata 12/2010, Parlament České republiky, Kancelář Poslanecké sněmovny, Parlamentní institut, p. 4-7.

35   W. Sokół, Transformacja..., p. 65.

36   M. Kubát, op.cit., p. 137-140.

as well as a great decrease in support for the post-communist party. It seems that the Polish party system became stable, at least for the time being, and there are no indications that the efforts to enter the parliamentary level by some new parties would prove successful.

Figure 1. *Party systems classification on the parliamentary level in the Visegrád countries after the elections held in the 21ˢᵗ century*

One dominating party	Slovakia 2010, Poland 2001	Hungary 2010		
Two dominating parties	Poland 2005, Czech Republic 2006	Czech Republic 2002	Poland 2007, Hungary 2002 Hungary 2006	
Balance between the parties	Czech Republic 2010 Slovakia 2002, 2006			
	Extremely multi-party	Moderately multi-party	Two-and-haf-party	Two-party

Source: Own

After having reviewed the party systems' changes in the Visegrád countries two important questions are to be raised. Firstly, the parliament level having been vacated by some parties which had been present in this realm since the beginning of transformation as well as having it entered by some new parties in Hungary, the Czech Republic and Slovakia alike, confirm the established by A. Antoszewski fact of constant political system transformation in the region. As a result of the elections, especially those held in 2010, the changes underwent also the Czech and Hungarian party systems which were considered stable.[37] Political stability index for the Czech Republic equal to 0.69, for Hungary equal to 0.77,[38] was brought respectively down to 0.37 and 0.43, that means closer to the results of the less stable Slovakian and Polish systems.[39]

Secondly, worth noticing is an observation that the parties which fall out of the parliamentary level in the countries of the region usually do not find their way back to the parliament, and moreover they leave a political arena altogether. This fact has been confirmed by the examples from all the four countries. This

---

37   See A. Antoszewski, Parties and Party Systems..., p. 329.
38   A. Antoszewski, Parties and Party Systems..., p. 329-330.
39   Compare A. Antoszewski, Parties and Party Systems..., p. 330.

may be a sign of the Central Europe parliaments still playing an important role as places of forming and modeling political parties as well as recruiting the elites, as it was some years ego noted by D. Olson.[40]

Characteristics of parliamentary opposition in the Central Europe states

A characteristic feature of the party systems of the Central and East Europe countries was the ability of the post-communist parties to systematically increase their support and reach for power.[41] In the Visegrád countries such a situation occurred in Poland and Hungary. In both the countries the post-communist parties after a period of time spent in opposition mobilized the electorate and as a result of the 1993 elections in Poland and 1994 elections in Hungary were able to form a majority (in Poland) and oversized (in Hungary) coalitions to stay in power for the next four years. In the subsequent elections both the SLD and MSZP formed a strong, in both cases holding 35% of the mandates, opposition so that after four years they could again reach for the power and form the majority coalitions. In each of these countries though the regaining of the power by the post-communist countries took place in a different situation. The SLD in Poland came back to power in a great degree due to the weakness of the right and centre-right-wing parties' coalition, the AWS, which broke apart even before the end of the term. While in Hungary the post-communist party competed with a strong centre-right party Fidesz which despite having won the elections remained in the opposition. In the second decade of the transformation both parties lost the elections (in Poland after one term in 2005, and in Hungary after two terms in 2010). The SLD acquired in the 2005 elections 12% of the mandates and did not rise in the subsequent ahead-of-term elections held in 2007 reaching the score of 11%. Whereas the MSZP gained in the 2010 elections 15% of the mandates. These results were unprecedented and pushed away both the parties into a deep and weak opposition. It is worth noting that these two big post-communist parties in a great degree contributed to their marginalisation. The situation of these post-communist parties was determined in Poland by the Rywin Affair, and in Hungary by prime minister Gyurcsány's comment on distorting the information about the condition of the Hungarian economy as well as his having signed a controversial gas agreement with

---

40 D. M. Olson, Demokratyczne instytucje legislacyjne. Ujęcie porównawcze, przełożył Jerzy S. Kugler, Warszawa 1998, p. 131, 141.
41 A. Antoszewski, Wzorce..., p. 117. Partie nazywane postkomunistycznymi są mocno zróżnicowane. See A. Antoszewski, Parties and Party Systems..., p. 92-93.

Russia.[42] The MSZP did not even help to pass the motion of no confidence against its prime minister in 2009. From the beginning of transformation the situations of the post-communist parties in Czech Republic and Slovakia were different. The Czech KSČM systematically winning seats in the Chamber of Deputies (from 11 to 20% of mandates) was from the beginning of transformation isolated in the parliament and remained in the opposition. The left-wing electorate in the Czech Republic was taken over by the ČSSD and it is the only case of a strong, not connected with communists, social democratic party so far noted in the Visegrád countries. Whereas in Slovakia the post-communist parties from the beginning of the transformation were weak and only sporadically entered their members to the National Council, although it should be mantioned that during the 1998-2002 term the SDL joined a broad coalition. In the subsequent elections though, it lost all its seats. Its place in the parliament was taken with 7% of the mandates by the Communist Party of Slovakia (Slovakian: Komunistická strana Slovenska – KSS) which after four years also found itself outside of the parliament. Neither did both of these parties come back to the National Council in 2010. In Slovakia the strong position of the post-communist parties was taken over by populist parties, first by the HZDS and then by the Smer.

In the 1990s, which was concluded by A. Antoszewski in his article, in Central Europe the rule was the post-election principle of power alteration[43] (maintaining the power after the 1996 elections by the ODS in the Czech Republic was just an exception to this principle). But in the following decade the alternation ceased to be the rule in the Visegrád countries. The ČSSD maintained the power after the 2002 elections, the MSZP in coalition with the SzDSz after the 2006 elections, and the ODS after the 2010 elections (although in this case with some other members of the coalition). It should be noted that the right-wing coalition, although in a partly changed composition, maintained the power in Slovakia after the 2002 elections. Thus some big parties that were remaining in the opposition longer than one term, such as the Fidesz and Smer, utilised that time to secure their dominating positions within the opposition parties' realm and to increase its support. The principle of the alternation of power was each time followed in Poland. As a result of the 2001 elections the power was taken over the post-communist party, and after four years by the

---

42   Especially the comment of the prime minister. See Hloušek, Kopeček, Origin, ideology and transformation of political parties. East-Central and Western Europe compared, Ashgate 2010, p. 191.

43   A. Antoszewski, Wzorce..., p. 114; F. Millard, The Czech Republic, Hungary and Poland, in Developments the Central and Eastern European Politics, ed. Stephen White, Judy Batt and Paul G. Lewis, Basingstone New York: Palgrave Macmillan 2007, p. 39-40.

right-wing party. The SLD failed in these elections and did not manage to regain the power after the following, ahead-of-term elections in 2007. After this year again the alternation of power took place, in which the power was taken from the PiS by the PO in coalition with the PSL.

In the first decade of the 21st century the political systems in Central Europe are characterised by a high, although apparently slightly lower than in the preceding decade, level of competitiveness, which means a lack of a constantly dominating party. The level of competitiveness decreased in the Czech Republic (ODS and ČSSD) in 2002 and 2006 and in Hungary (MSZP and Fidesz) in 2002, 2006 and 2010. In the Czech Republic the level of competitiveness increased after the 2010 elections. The advantage of the two dominating parties was substantially reduced. A high level of competitiveness was noted in Poland in 2001 and 2005 as well as in Slovakia in 2002, 2006 and 2010. In Poland the level of competitiveness dropped down in 2007 and, as shown in opinion polls, it will be maintained on that level in 2011.[44] A characteristic feature for the countries of the region remains the hostility in the competition between the parties. In Hungary and in the Czech Republic it survived between post-communists vs. anti-communists; in Slovakia between centre-right parties vs. populist parties, whereas in Poland the enmity between the post-communists and the right-wing transformed into the enmity between two main parties of anti-communist background.

In the second decade of transformation no changes occurred as far as the cabinet forming standards are concerned. In the post-communist countries in the 1990s the cabinets were usually formed by majority or by coalition.[45] It should be also mentioned that the ruling coalitions were usually winning by just several seats. This applies also to the countries belonging to the Visegrád Group. The exception to this rule were the minority governments first of the centre-right coalition composed of the ODS, KDU-ČSL and ODA, and later of the ČSSD, in the Czech Republic with a "silent" support based on "opposition agreement" of the biggest right-wing party ODS in 1998-2002.[46] Another exception was the oversized coalition in Hungary in the 1994 elections, when the post-communist MSZP having gained the absolute majority of over 54% of the mandates in the Assembly formed a coalition with the SZDSZ.[47]

---

44   The opinion polls conducted by the biggest Polish public opinion survey institutions the OBOP, CBOS, GFK Polonia indicate that after the 2011 election on the parliamentary level will remain only four parties already present in it and the domination of the two parties: the PO and the PiS will be sustained.

45   A. Antoszewski, Wzorce..., p. 117.

46   Na temat umowy i kontrowersji wokół jej interpretacji zob. M. Kubát, op.cit., p. 105-107.

47   L. Benda, op.cit., p. 87-88.

In the first decade of the 21st century the results of the elections forced to form majority coalitions often achieved by a minimum advantage. The distance between the coalition forming a government and the opposition would fall within the range of 1.02 (the Czech Republic in 2002) and 1.31 (Slovakia in 2006) [Table 2]. The exceptional situation took place after the 2006 elections in the Czech Republic, when a deadlock occurred in the Chamber of Deputies. The parliament broke into two blocks: the left-wing with the ČSSD and KSČM and the centre-right with the ODS and KDU-ČSL accompanied by a small Green Party (SZ), which because of the economic liberalism was closer to the ODS than to the ČSSD. Thus the two blocks controlled 100 mandates each in a 200-person Chamber of Deputies. The deadlock resulted in a crisis lasting half-a-year. The first minority government of the ODS formed by Mirek Topolánek lost the confidence motion. The second government of the ODS, this time a coalition one, won the confidence motion because of two ČSSD deputies absence during the voting.[48] This cabinet is hard to classify since it fulfilled neither the criteria of a majority nor a minority government. Therefore it might be appropriate to call it a nonminority government.[49] The exception was also a short lived minority government of PiS with a silent support of two smaller parties (Samoobrona RP and LPR) in Poland after the 2005 elections. After a few months this silent coalition was formalised and the government supported by the majority coalition was formed. A much bigger change took place as a result of the 2010 elections in Hungary which is another exception to the rule: the Fidesz in electoral coalition with a small KDNP party gained not only the absolute majority but also a constitutional one. The distance between the coalition and the opposition was 2.14 [Table 2].

The majority coalitions winning by a minimum advantage mean that the opposition remaining in the minority still holds an important position in parliament, usually close to half of the mandates. The acknowledgement of this fact is not tantamount to the real strength of the opposition. Its actual position in a parliament depends on many other factors, which include its fragmentation and polarisation. A. Antoszewski noted that the left-wing opposition was more uniform in the post-communist countries when in the system existed one strong post-communist party and more fragmented opposition of the centre-right parties.[50] This interrelation could be observed in the systems with one big post-communist party (e.g. Poland and Hungary). After the elections in 2005 and

---

48 L. Linek, Czech Republic..., p. 936; V. Havlik, L. Kopeček, Kształt i stabilność..., p. 67-68.
49 V. Havlik, L. Kopeček, Kształt i stabilność..., p. 69.
50 A. Antoszewski, Wzorce..., p. 118.

2007 in Poland, as well as in 2006 and 2010 in the Czech Republic, Slovakia and Hungary, the situation changed to some extend. This change occurred due to the weakening of the post-communist parties which within the parliamentary opposition are just one of the few clubs of a similar strength, like in the Hungarian National Assembly, or they give room to some other opposition party, like in the Polish Sejm. In the Czech republic the parliamentary opposition remained, similarly to the previous term, to be the left-wing side (ČSSD i KSČM), but with a smaller number of mandates. In Slovakia though the opposition was entered by the previously ruling left-wing-populist Smer, which provides a uniform and strong opposition to the broad ruling coalition.

In the first decade of the 21st century not all the majority coalitions were able to sustain the power throughout the whole term. This fact apparently does not confirm a proposed for the western countries thesis concerning a big stability of the coalitions characterised by a minimum advantage.[51] The stability of the coalitions was hindered by their makeup. The ruling coalitions comprised of many often ideologically diversified parties, like e.g. in Slovakia in 2002 and 2006 in the Czech Republic in 2002, in Hungary in 2002 and 2006, and in Poland in 2005 they were very unstable, which resulted in breakups of some coalitions. Also after the 2010 elections very unstable proved the coalitions in Slovakia and the Czech Republic. In both cases the conflict between the coalition partners arise.[52]

Table 2. *Distance between the ruling coalition and the opposition after the elections in the Visegrád countries in the 21st century*

Slovakia				Czech Republic			
	coalition	opposition	distance		coalition	opposition	distance
2002	52.00%	48.00%	1.08	2002	50.50%	49.50%	1.02
2006	56.67%	43.33%	1.31	2006	50.00%	50.00%	1.00
2010	52.70%	47.30%	1.11	2010	59.00%	41.00%	1.44

---

51 A. Siaroff, op.cit., p. 113.
52 See Rok po wyborach na Słowacji: oceny rządów koalicji. http://www.wyszehrad.com/slowacja/aktualnosci/rok-po-wyborach-na-slowacji-oceny-rzadow-koalicji (13.06.2011). Czechy: Konflikt w koalicji trwa. http://www.wyszehrad.com/czechy/aktualnosci/czechy-konflikt-w-koalicji-trwa (28.06.2011). Największy sukces rządu Nečasa – to, że nadal istnieje. http://www.wyszehrad.com/czechy/aktualnosci/najwiekszy-sukces-rzadu-necasa-ze-nadal-istnieje (2011-07-11).

Hungary				Poland			
	coalition	opposition	distance		coalition	opposition	distance
2002	51.30%	48.70%	1.05	2001	56.74%	43.92%	1.29
2006	52.85%	47.15%	1.12	2005	53.26%	46.74%	1.14
2010	68.13%	31.87%	2.14	2007	52.17%	47.83%	1.09

Source: Own

Changes in the opposition patterns in the first decade of the 21st century

The results of the parliamentary elections in Hungary in 2002 and 2006 resulted in changes to the opposition patterns. The right-wing remaining for the whole two terms (during the rule of the left-wing MSZP in coalition with the Fidesz) in the opposition became unified. In the 2002 elections the MDF stood for elections together with the Fidesz. But the remaining in the ruling coalition with the Fidesz for the 1998-2002 term FKgP and the Hungarian Justice and Life Party (Hungarian: Magyar Igazsag es let Partja – MIÉP) did not enter their candidates to the parliamentary level. In the subsequent elections held in 2006 both parties did not come back to the parliamentary level. The winner amongst the right-wing parties turned to be again the Fidesz entering its 164 members to the parliament. As a result of the coalition with the Fidesh marginalised was the MDF, which in 2006 after standing up alone for the election entered only 11 members to the National Assembly. The evolution continued after the 2010 elections. In the opposition remained: an extremist right-wing party – the Jobbik; a left-wing party, the previously ruling MSZP; and a new liberal party sympathising with the Green Movement which was formed in 2009 – the LMP. Among these three opposition parties the Jobbik represents the extremist and anti-system opposition. The opposition after the 2010 elections can be described as fragmented and three-sided which makes it highly polarised. It is therefore hard to speak about the cooperation within a frame of the parliamentary opposition. Any positive cooperation of the Jobbik and LMP clubs' delegates with the MSZP representatives is considered by them impossible. Similar is the state of affairs as far as the Jobbik-LMP relation is concerned.[53] But there is

---

53 See: LMP wyklucza jakąkolwiek formę współpracy z Gyurcsánym http://www.wyszehrad.com/wegry/aktualnosci/lmp-wyklucza-jakakolwiek-forme-wspolpracy-z-gyurcsanym (26.05.2011). Węgierska opozycja nie zamierza współpracować. http://www.wyszehrad.com/wegry/aktualnosci/wegierska-opozycja-nie-zamierza-wspolpracowac (13.07.2011).

possible a joint – although not necessarily coordinated before hand – voting against the ruling coalition.[54] The result of the oppositions weakness and dominating the party system on the parliamentary level by the Fidesz with participation of the KDNP are criticised both in Hungary and in the whole European Union "muzzle" laws and the new constitution. Already in the first year after the elections in Hungary could be noticed clear negative results of gaining such a great majority by one political party present in the parliament.[55] Preserving this state of affairs may lead to merging the dominating party with the state institutions and consequently evolving in the direction of authoritarianism.[56]

After the Czech parliament elections in 2002 in the opposition remained the right-wing ODS and the communist KSČM. Whereas the ruling coalition was formed by three parties: the left-wing ČSSD, the centre US-DEU and the centre-right KDU-ČSL. After four years in 2006 in the opposition remained two left-wing parties: the ČSSD and KSČM, which means the left-wing opposition was poorly fragmented but polarised. It should be noted though that both the parties were in some crucial moments able to cooperate, like while passing the motion of no confidence against the government. The coalition was again formed by three parties: the right-wing ODS, the centre-right KDU-ČSL and the left-wing Czech Green Party. In both terms the ruling coalitions were very diversified which was not favourable to the government stability. But the opposition was fragmented and polarised. In the 2002-2006 term the opposition was two-sided and it was hard to coordinate the activities of the right-wing ODS and the communist KSČM. In the next term it was easier for the Social Democrats to cooperate with the KSČM than it had been before with the ODS. In the 2010 elections two parties cooperating with the ODS did not enter their members to the parliament, and the ODS itself gained 28 mandates less than in 2006. The places of these parties both in the parliament and in the government were taken by two new parties: the TOP 09 and the VV. But the opposition remained a left-wing (ČSSD and KSČM), fragmented and polarised.

In Slovakia after the 2002 elections the left-wing opposition remained fragmented. Next to the populist HZDS came up two new on the parliamentary

---

54 Opposition parties unite in rejection of Fidesz proposal for single-round, mixed election system.   http://www.politics.hu/20110711/all-opposition-parties-reject-fidesz-proposal-for-single-round-mixed-election-system/ (11.07.2011).

55 See the discussions by E. Bojtára, J. Kisa, L. Rajka and G. A. Tótha w Debacie „Gazety". Grozi nam węgierska epidemia? „Gazeta Wyborcza" 2011, No. 123, p. 27.

56 M. Bankowicz, op.cit., p. 185-186.

level left-wing parties: the SMER[57] and the KSS. The ruling coalition was
formed by four right-wing and centre-right parties. After four years the
alternation of power occurred. In the fragmented opposition remained two right-
wing parties, and a controversial government coalition was formed by the
HZDS, SMER and the nationalist Slovak National Party (Slovakian: Slovenská
národná strana – SNS). After the 2010 elections to the opposition moved,
despite of its clear advantage, the Smer. The government formed four small
parliament clubs which were united by the aversion towards the populist-
nationalist ruling coalition of the previous term. Thus the opposition is uniform
(SMER holds 41.33% of the mandates) and poorly polarised (the other
opposition party was the nationalist SNS which was previously ruling together
with the Smer, controlling 6% of the mandates).

    In Poland after the 2001 elections the parliamentary opposition was
composed of four groups of comparable power (ranging from 14% to 8% of the
mandates). Three of these parties (PO, PiS and LPR) had been formed just
before the elections as a result of breakup of the broad centre-right coalition –
the AWS, only one of them (Samoobrona RP) functioned before, but was not
able to cross the threshold. The opposition was thus strongly fragmented and
polarised which resulted in difficulties with coordinating the activities of the
opposition on the parliamentary level and efficient influence on the ruling
majority. The situation was altered by the Rywin affair, which was skillfully
used by the opposition to weaken the ruling party during the proceedings of the
Sejm's special investigative committee. After this affair the confidence in the
SLD was hindered and the party definitely lost the parliamentary elections. The
parliamentary opposition after the subsequent elections held in 2005 was formed
by three parties: the centre-right, the populist, and the post-communist, which
means it was fragmented. In 2007 only by four parties entered the Sejm, but two
of them formed a majority coalition, and the remaining two: the right-wing and
the post-communist left-wing remained in the opposition which is still
fragmented and polarised.

    In classifying the parliamentary opposition in Central Europe the researchers
adopted a division into the left-wing and the right-wing poles.[58] It seems though
that this approach was adequate in the analysis of the parliamentary opposition
in the 1990s, although one can find the systems such as the Slovakian one,

---

57 It is hard to explicitly define the ideological profile of the Smer. At the beginning it was a
    populist party tending towards being anti-systemic, then it presented itself as Social
    Democrat party to finalny in the coalition with the HZDS and SNS take on a tinge of
    nationalism. See Hloušek, Kopeček, op.cit. p. 33.
58 See M. Kubát, op.cit., p. 89-98.

which do slip out of this classification.[59] At that time the rivalry between the political parties to a great extend matched the division into the left, which was usually integrated (especially in those systems where the post-communist parties led the way), and the right, which was usually fragmented. In case the elections had been won by the left the fragmented right remained in the opposition and the other way around: when the right-wing parties had been able to form a coalition, the integrated left remained in the opposition. In the subsequent decade it is hard to capture such a division. After the 2002 in the Czech Republic in the opposition remained the communist KSČM and the right-wing ODS. In Slovakia after the 2002 elections the opposition was formed by the parties considered anti-systemic: the populist HZDS, the left-populist Smer and the communist KSS; and from 2010 the Smer and the nationalist SNS. In Hungary since 2010 in the opposition have been remaining the post-communist MSZP, the nationalist Jobbik and the liberal LMP. Whereas in Poland after the 2007 elections in the opposition remained the post-communist SLD and the right-wing PiS. These examples prove, in my opinion, that one ought to analyze the opposition as a whole without dividing it into strictly left or right fractions. Such a division only fogs the diversity within the opposition.

Table 3.   Parliamentary opposition classification in the first decade of the 21st century according to its fragmentation and polarisation

Parliamentary opposition	Unified	Poorly fragmented	Fragmented
Unpolarised	Hungary (2002, 2006)		
Poorly polarised	Slovakia (2010)	Poland (2005), Slovakia (2002)	
Polarised		Poland (2007), Czech Republic (2002, 2006, 2010)	Poland (2001), Slovakia (2006), Hungary (2010)

Source: Own

---

59 L. Kopeček, System partyjny Słowacji, in Partie i systemy partyjne Europy Środkowej, ed. A. Antoszewskiego, P. Fiali, R. Herbuta, J. Sroki, Wydawnictwo Uniwersytetu Wrocławskiego, Wrocław 2003, p. 216-218.

Conclusions

In this article I attempted to outline the problem of parliamentary opposition in Central Europe. Although some works have been published concerning this issue, the result is negligible, especially when compared with the abundant literature on West European parliamentary opposition, explored comprehensively and applying comparative methodology.

The models of parliamentary opposition are determined by the results of the parliamentary elections as well as the changes and stabilisation of the party systems on the parliament level. The party systems in Central Europe, despite some periods of stabilisation in the Czech Republic and in Hungary, are still undergoing changes. Throughout the whole period of transformation the party system in Slovakia is unstable, and consequently the models of parliamentary opposition in the National Council are constantly being adjusted.

In the 21st century the opposition is no more only left-winged (the exception is the Czech Republic) or only right-winged. It is diversified, two- or even three-sided, which depends on the model of the parliamentary system and the result of the elections. It would be too simple to apply to the current situation the basic division into a left and right wing opposition. In the Hungarian and Polish parliaments there are three- and two-sided oppositions which undoubtedly hinders the cooperation of the polarised political parties, and simultaneously weakens the possibility to exhibit by the parliamentary opposition its functions. Obstructed, although not impossible, is influencing the legislative processes and control over the ruling majority.

The coalition cabinets composed of three or more parties are unstable. But their weakness and the occurring sometimes coalition breakups are not the outcome of the strength of the opposition. They are rather a result of coalition's weakness in the realms that are often an object of conflict. The opposition may exercise a substantial influence on the parliamentary arena when a ruling coalition is unstable and opposition parties are able to cooperate.[60]

Translated by Iwona Szuwalska

---

60   See P. Kopecký. M. Spirova, op.cit. p. 155.

Development of the party system in Montenegro (1990-2012)

Przemysław Paradowski

Montenegro has got a long history, yet not much of it were periods of statehood with full sovereignty and independence. For ages Montenegrins had been struggling with Turks who were trying to subjugate their land. Independence came only in the second half of XIX century. Beginning with the 1910, king Nikola I Petrović-Njegoš considerably strengthened the state structures by establishing the constitution (1905) and creating new institutions the most important of which was the National Assembly (Skupština).[1] Although at that time parliamentary elections were not fully democratic they still facilitated Montenegrins with the freedom of choice and resulted in the first political parties having come into being in the history of Montenegro.

During the first plena the Skupština deputies were divided into two fractions: the pro-princely (later pro-royalist) fraction and the opposition. In the first Skupština the opposition deputies formed the Club Party (Klubaška stranka, KS), which later became the basis of the first political party to be formed in the history of Montenegro, the People's Party (Narodna stranka, NS). In response the True People's Party (Prava narodna stranka, PNS) was formed by the pro-princely fraction.[2] But the development of parliamentarism and party system did not last for long, since already in November 1918 Montenegro lost its independence to Serbia. In the Kingdom of Serbs, Croats and Slovenes (SHS) she was not a separate province, but became an integral part of Serbia and her role was marginalised.[3] The development of political parties in the Kingdom of SHS undergoing a centralisation process, and then in Yugoslavia, was obstructed, and the rivalry was centred mainly around the issue of Montenegro's status within the new state.[4] Similar was the situation after the World War II when Montenegro became one of the republics of the Socialist Federal Republic

---

1 Š. Rastoder, "A short review of history of Montenegro, Montenegro in Transition," Problems of Identity and Statehood, ed. by F. Bieber, Nomos Verlagsgesellschaft, Baden-Baden, 2003, 124-125.

2 Ž. Andrijašević, Š. Rastoder, The History of Montenegro: from ancient time to 2003, Podgorica: Montenegro Diaspora Centre, 2006, 129-130.

3 Š. Rastoder, op.cit., 133.

4 Zob. I. Banač, The national question in Yugoslavia: origins, history, politics, Cornell University Press, New York, 1988, 289-290; J. R. Lampe, Yugoslavia as history: twice there was a country, Cambridge University Press, 2000, 139.

of Yugoslavia (SFRY) and just like in other republics only one party could exist
on its territory, the communist one.

The situation in Montenegro changed only during 1989–1991, when as a
result of the communist Yugoslavia's breakup, just like in other republics, the
political pluralism was introduced. Yet Montenegro did not announce her
independence, but on the contrary, after the referendum she became, along with
Serbia, a part of the Federal Republic of Yugoslavia (FRY) proclaimed in April
1992.[5] Although the federal constitution defined the new state as the federation
of two equal republics in fact, because of Montenegro's lesser potential, there
was no chance for her to match the status of Serbia's.[6]

The first decade of transformation in the post-communist Montenegro was
divided by S. Darmanović into two periods.[7] The first one began with "anti-
bureaucracy revolution" in January 1989. This "revolution" was marked by
removing the old communist elites from power and taking it over by the new
ones. Yet characteristic was the fact that the coup took place within the structure
of the communist party and all the leaders of the "revolution" were the members
of the League of Communists of Montenegro (Savez komunista Crne Gore,
SKCG).[8] These changes opened a period S. Darmanović described as a semi-
authoritarian regime dominated by one party, the successor of SKCG: the
Democratic Party of Socialists (Demokratska Partija Socijalista, DPS).[9]

The second period of transformation was initiated by the conflict within the
successor party after the elections won by it in 1996. The argument that cast its
shadow on the whole internal policy of the republic was connected to the
support, or the lack of it, for the policy of the federation's president S.
Milošević. After several years of entanglement in military, domineering policy
of S. Milošević, Montenegrins changed their mind by ending their firm support
for the relationship with Serbia expressed in the 1992 referendum. The society

---

5   P. Simic, "Yugoslavia at the crossroads: reforms or disintegration?," Is southeastern
     Europe doomed to instability?, eds. Dimitri A. Sotiropoulos and Thanos Veremis,
     London: Frank Cass & Co. Ltd., 2002, 200.
6   Ž. Andrijašević, Š. Rastoder, op.cit., 262; see M.F. Goldman, Revolution and change in
     Central and Eastern Europe. Political, economic and social challenges, New York: M.E.
     Sharpe, Inc., 1997, 309.
7   S. Darmanović, "Duga tranzicija u Crnoj Gori – od polukompetitivnih izbora do
     izborne demokratije," eds. V. Pavićević, S. Darmanović, O. Komar, Z. Vujović, Izbori
     i izborno zakonodavstvo u Crnoj Gori 1990-2006, Centar za Monitoring – CEMI,
     Podgorica, 2007, 83.
8   O. Komar, Z. Vujović, Europeanisation of National Political Parties and Party System:
     Case Study of Montenegro, Politics in Central Europe 3 (2007), 53. See Ž. Andrijašević,
     Š. Rastoder, op.cit., 260-261.
9   See S. Darmanović, op.cit., 84-89.

was divided, into the advocates of its continuation and those who were opposed to it.[10] Furthermore, in consequence of M. Đukanović's victory in presidential elections in Montenegro, the conflict between Podgorica and Belgrade escalated. This "cold war," expressed in many aspects of coexistence within one country, contributed to the corrosion of federal institutions and disintegrated the very structure of federation.[11] The phase concerned being a transitional period leading to consolidation of electoral democracy ended according to S. Darmanović with Milošević's fall in October 2000.[12]

The subsequent period lasting till independence referendum in May 2006, characterised as a period of democratic system's consolidation, was dominated by an argument whether to remain – even in a lose – relationship with Serbia or to gain independence.[13] On 14 March 2002 the governments of Serbia and Montenegro signed the Belgrade Agreement negotiated under the influence of the European Union representative (High Representative for Common Foreign and Security Policy) Javier Solany, which dissolved the FRY.[14] On 29 January 2003 Montenegro's Skupština voted the dissolution of the FRY and to establish the free union of Serbia and Montenegro. Few days later on 4 February the Constitutional Charter starting the State Union of Serbia and Montenegro was passed by majority of votes in both Federation Assembly's chambers.[15] From the beginning of existence of the State Union of Serbia and Montenegro (SUSM) there was present a political struggle between Đukanović's government and the opposition parties, both about the position and the future of Montenegro. The conflict is related to an over-century-long problem of Montenegrins being divided into those who seek a close relationship with Serbia and those who strive for Montenegro's full sovereignty and independence.[16]

On 2 March 2006, based on Article 25 of the Constitutional Charter of the State Union of Serbia and Montenegro which offers the possibility of starting

---

10   M.F. Goldman, op.cit., 331.

11   See P. Simic, op.cit., 201.

12   O. Komar, Z. Vujović, op.cit., 55. For a wider perspective see S. Darmanović, op.cit., 89-93.

13   See S. Darmanović, op.cit., 83 and 93-97.

14   M. Braniff, Intergrating the Balkans. Conflict resolutions and the impact of the EU expansion, New York, 2011, 141. For a wider perspective see W. van Meurs, "The Belgrade Agreement: Robust Mediation between Serbia and Montenegro," Montenegro in Transition. Problems of Identity and Statehood, ed. F. Bieber, Baden-Baden: Nomos Verlagsgesellschaft, 2003, 63-82. S. Darmanović, op.cit., 97.

15   R. Bideleux, I. Jeffries, The Balkans: a post-communists history, New York: Routlege, 2007, 499-500. In Skupština 55 voted in favour whereas 7 against.

16   On the division issue see J. Dzankic, Bipolar worlds of nation and state in Montenegro, CEU Political Science Journal, issue: 2/2007, passim.

the procedure on changing the status of the state union, including parting of
Serbia and Montenegro, the Skupština issued a decision to call on a referendum
"on the state-status of Montenegro."[17] On 21 May 2006, in compliance with that
decision after a generally peaceful campaign, the citizens of the Republic of
Montenegro entered the ballot boxes and voted with a slight majority (from 55.5
to 44.5%) for independence with a full legal international recognition of their
country. Attendance reached 86.5%.[18] Although nearly 88 years earlier
Montenegro parted from Serbia, the problem of the society division into
supporters of the independent existence and those who advocated maintaining
the relationship with Serbia persisted. During the preparation for the referendum
on independence the EU representatives proposed that the results should be
considered valid if the support for the Montenegro's independence exceeded
55% threshold. Both sides, that means the supporters of independence and the
advocates of remaining in the relationship with Serbia, agreed to that proposal.
As the results showed the independence was passed by minimum majority and
the adversaries of independence articulated the accusations that the government
employed dishonest means to reach the threshold required in the elections.[19]

The development of the party system

Montenegro as a part of communist Yugoslavia was one of the six republics, and
the ruling SKCG was, just like in other republics, a branch of a communist
party. A transition from one-party system to multi-party one took place in 1990
through entering amendments to the Constitution of the Socialist Republic of
Montenegro, which opened the possibility to form political parties and to
associate.[20] This amendment was preceded by changes within the SKCG itself as
in 1989, owing to the "anti-bureaucratic revolution," the control over the party
was taken by young party activists such as Momir Bulatović, Milo Đukanović or
Svetozar Marović who saw the need of reforms. The leadership over the SKCG

17 Odluku o raspisivanju republičkog referendum o državno-pravnom statusu Republike
    Crne Gore, SU-SK Broj 01-178/2, Podgorica, 2 March 2006 http://www.skupstina.me/
    index.php?strana=fiksna&id=401&menu_id=1.0 (28.08.2011)
18 Izvještaj o rezultatu glasanja na referendumu o državno-pravnim statusu republkie Crne
    Gore održanom 21. Maja 2006. godine. http://www.skupstina.me/ (1.09.2011)
19 P. Hockenos, J. Winterhagen, "A Balkan Divorce that Works? Montenegro's Hopeful
    First Year," *World Policy Journal*, Summer 2007, 39. On the referendum see
    S. Darmanović, op.cit., 97-100.
20 V. Pavićević, "Analiza normativne structure i efekata sistema," eds. V. Pavićević,
    S. Darmanović, O. Komar, Z. Vujović, Izbori i izborno zakonodavstvo u Crnoj Gori
    1990-2006, Centar za Monitoring – CEMI, Podgorica, 2007, 13-14.

took M. Bulatović.[21] The following year the Union underwent many changes, simultaneously absorbing smaller socialist groups and organisations, and on the Congress in June 1991 its name was changed into the Democratic Party of Socialists of Montenegro (DPS). The term "communist" was formally discarded.[22]

In 1990 new political parties without communist background started to form. Amongst them should be mentioned these which played lesser or greater role in political life of Montenegro. In January 1990 the Liberal Alliance of Montenegro (Liberalni savez Crne Gore, LSCG) was formed as the first party appealing to the principles of the European liberalism and emphasising the importance of Montenegrin culture and historical tradition. In the period of Yugoslavia's breakup the LSCG clearly supported the independence of Montenegro. In the spring of 1990 the communist elites of Montenegro were divided giving life to smaller parties, e.g. the Independent Communist Organisation which did not accept the nationalist rhetoric of S. Milošević's supporters. Whereas in July 1990 the Party of Socialists and the Socialist Party were formed. In the same year the conservative centre-right NS was formed emphasising a strong Serbian national identity and drawing on the tradition of the People's Party of 1906. Along with political pluralism the national issues that were formerly suppressed by the communist were given new attention. So there started to appear some parties whose aim was the protection of minorities' rights. The rights of Muslims were claimed by the Party of National Equality, and in September 1990 the first party of Albanian minority was formed: the Democratic League of Montenegro (Demokratski Savez u Crnoj Gori, DSCG).[23] There was also active the Union of Reform Forces (Savez reformskih snaga Jugoslavije, SRSJ) gathering the supporters of the union's prime minister Ante Marković.[24]

The structure of the party system was influenced (at different times and in various degrees) by four factors, which were the arguments concerning several important issues: the type of political system, independence and federalism, ethnic divisions, and disagreements between the left and right.[25]

---

21 J. Bugajski, "Political Parties of Eastern Europe. A Guide to Politics in the Post-Communist Era," The Center for Strategic and International Studies, New York, 2002, 496; J. Dzankic, op.cit., 197; Ž. Andrijašević, Š. Rastoder, op.cit., 261.

22 J. Bugajski, op.cit., 496; Ž. Andrijašević, Š. Rastoder, op.cit., 263.

23 Zob. Ž. Andrijašević, Š. Rastoder, op.cit., 262-263.

24 J. Wojnicki, "System partyjny Czarnogóry," eds. K. Krysieniel, J. Wojnicki, Partie I systemy partyjne w państwach byłej Jugosławii, Pułtusk, 2009, 115.

25 V. Goati, Političke partije i partijski sistemi, Centar za monitoring – CEMI, Podgorica, 2007, 272.

From the beginning the main political issues being simultaneously the axis
dividing the parties were the future of the Union State and the relationships
with Serbia.[26] It should be taken under consideration though that before the
break-up in the DPS, that is until 1997-1998, the parties supporting the idea
of loosening the relations with Serbia and full sovereignty of Montenegro
remained in minority.

On 9 December 1990 the opening elections were conducted. The
amendments to the Constitution of the Socialist Republic of Montenegro
allowed the elections to be competitive, direct, and secret.[27] It should be noted
that it was SKCG that had the greatest influence on introducing the changes
leading to the development of multi-party system.[28] Unarguable victory was won
by the communist SKCG attaining over 56.2% support and 66.4% of mandates
in the Republican Assembly. To the parliament were also elected candidates of
some of the above listed new parties but they obtained only a dozen or so per
cent support (the coalition between the SRSJ and LSCG achieved 14.5% of the
mandates, and the NS 15.3%). The mandates were also gained by ethnic
minority party the Democratic Coalition – Albanians Together (Demokratska
koalicija, DK) [Table 4]. The results clearly showed that the communist were
the most trusted by the Montenegrins who shared their view on Montenegro's
remaining in the relationship with Serbia. The SKCG achieved, during these
first since the Kingdom of Montenegro competitive elections, a dominating
position in the developing party system.[29]

Changes in the party system between 1992 and 2002

Since 1992, shortly after establishing the FRY, the dissonance between the two
republics started to deepen on many levels, which amongst others was expressed
by the new Constitution of the Republic of Montenegro kept aloof from the
nationalist rhetoric of the Serbian Constitution. Noticeable were also the
divisions within the DPS, which were expressed by rivalry between two of its
members M. Bulatović and Branko Kostić in presidential elections. There were
also visible, at that time still temporary, disagreements between the DPS and
Serbia's successor party the Socialist Party of Serbia (Socijalistička partija

---

26   J. Wojnicki, op.cit., 116.
27   V. Pavićević, op.cit., 14.
28   V. Goati, op.cit., 287.
29   Compare F. Bieber, "Montenegrin politics since the disintegration of Yugoslavia,"
     Montenegro in Transition. Problems of Identity and Statehood, ed. by F. Bieber, Baden-
     Baden: Nomos Verlagsgesellschaft, 2003, 16-17.

Srbije, SPS). Despite the occurring tensions the relations between Montenegro and Serbia were still good.[30] During elections conducted in 1992 and 1996 the dominating position on the political arena maintained the DPS, a party succeeding the SKCG. In compliance with the Republic's new constitution passed in October 1992 the Skupština's deputies were chosen on the basis of direct secret voting in general and equal elections. The ratio was one deputy to 6 thousand citizens. The details of the election law were regulated by an act.[31] In the first of the above mentioned elections the DPS gained 42.7% of the votes, which made 54.12% of the Assembly mandates. Amongst the remaining parties a 12% support, which made a dozen or so mandates, gained the LSCG and the NS. Another two parties, the Radical Party of Serbia (Srpska radikalna stranka, SRS) and Social Democratic Party of Montenegro (Socijaldemokratska Partija Crne Gore, SPCG) gained a few mandates each. [Table 4]

After the subsequent elections in 1996 [Table 4] the DPS gained 49.9% of the votes, which made 63.38% of the Parliament mandates. This way the post-communist party increased its domination on the Montenegro's political scene. As the researchers emphasise, the DPS using its power increased its share by gerrymandering.[32] Not much above 26% of the mandates gained the NS and LSCG entering the elections as a coalition. Both parties, forming an unusual and difficult because of the different approach to Montenegro's independence issue coalition, were hoping to move the DPS from power.[33] As a result they actually lost since in the coalition they reached almost 5% less seats in Skupština than the sum of both the parties' mandates in the 1992 elections. The dethroning of the DPS despite of cooperation and forming a coalition did not come off successful. Apart from the mentioned groups, single mandates achieved the Bosnian's Party of Democratic Action (Stranka demokratske akcije, SDA) and the Albanian DSCG, as well as the Democratic Union of Albanians (Demokratska unija Albanaca, DUA). As a result of setting an election threshold on the level of 4% calculated not on the basis of national support but in relation to a general number of voters who had voted in a given constituency, the two parties – the Social Democratic Party of Montenegro (Socijaldemokratska partija Crne Gore, SDP) and the Party of Serbs Radicals (Stranka srpskih radikala, SSR) – despite exceeding the threshold on the

---

30   See F. Bieber, op.cit., 22-26.
31   V. Pavićević, op.cit., 15. For broader perspective on the electoral law see: ibidem, 16-20.
32   O. Komar, Z. Vujović, op.cit., 54.
33   Ibidem, s. 54.

national level remained without mandates.[34] The elections confirmed a stable dominating position of the DPS, and for the opposition parties despite of rather long-lasting support brought about failure.[35]

After the 1996 elections, especially in the face of the accusations of electoral fraud and mass demonstrations in Serbia, the conflict within the biggest party of Montenegro escalated.[36] Its key role in the republic's internal policy was visible in the DPS's domination in parliament and in consequence taking over the most important posts in the republic. The governments prime minister from the beginning of 1990s was Milo Đukanović gaining ever bigger support. Momir Bulatović supported by Slobodan Milošević, was appointed president of the Republic. The two charismatic politicians who had been cooperating since the late 1980s turned against each other in few important questions, the key of which was the future of Montenegro. According to Đukanović loosening the bound with Serbia was necessary. He remained aloof from the Milošević's policy leading e.g. to the conflict in Kosovo, and assumed that the only way of Montenegro's development was its independence. Whereas Bulatović remained loyal to the leader of Serbia and opted for maintaining the status quo, for which he gained an overall support of the Federations president S. Milošević.[37] The conflict escalated in 1997. In July the DPS broke up into two fractions and then both politicians rivalled to win the presidency of Montenegro. In 1997 elections the Montenegrins chose for the presidential post M. Đukanović.[38] The presidential elections were the struggle for influence on the policy and bigger support might have been a great stimulus and could influence the results of the following parliamentary elections. The conflict resulted in a split of these two politicians. M. Đukanović remained in the DPS whereas M. Bulatović together with supporting him party members formed in March 1998 a new party named the Socialist People's Party of Montenegro (Socijalistička narodna partija Crne Gore, SNP).[39]

This situation introduced changes into political rivalry in the Republic of Montenegro. The following three elections conducted in 1998, 2001 and 2002 were characterised by competition between two parties (blocs): the DPS of M. Đukanović and the SNP of M. Bulatović created as a result of the DPS's break-up. The remaining parties such as the LSCG received the results below 10%, or

---

34 V. Pavićević, op.cit., 25-26.
35 F. Bieber, op.cit., 29.
36 Ibidem.
37 V. Goati, op.cit., 274.
38 J. Bugajski, op.cit., 498.
39 P. Simic, op.cit., 201; J. Bugajski, op.cit., 498.

formed electoral coalitions together with two biggest entities on the political arena. And thus during all the three above mentioned elections the SDP remained in electoral and parliamentary coalition with the DPS, supported by a coalition with NS in 1998 and the Civic Party of Montenegro (Građanska partija Crne Gore, GPCG) in 2002. In the elections of 2001 and 2002 into the coalition with the SNP entered the Srpska narodna stranka (SNS, eng. Serb People's Party) and the NS.

After the 1998 elections, also in the context of nationalist policy of S. Milošević in Kosov, the conflict between the powers of Serbia and Montenegro escalated. M. Đukanović initiated a policy aiming at secession of Montenegro from the FRY, and in response to it S. Milošević isolated the smaller republic.[40] As a result of the DPS's policy Milošević introduced in the Federal Assembly in July 2000 changes to the Constitution of the Federal Republic of Yugoslavia. These changes were not consulted with any institutions representing Montenegro. This specific constitutional coup d'état resulted in unifying the state and Montenegro was reduced, from being a republic that was at least formally equal to Serbia, to a status of one of the electoral regions of the unified Yugoslavia.[41] The elections in 2001 were conducted right after the overthrowing S. Milošević's rule, which plunged them in still different political circumstances. These were the only elections in which the DPS did not achieve (together with its coalition) the majority of mandates in the Parliament. The solution for the situation was broadening of the coalition but the only potential partner, the LSCG, refused to join the ruling coalition with the DPS. Therefore the DPS created a minority government, supported by the LSCG, which predictably was not stable.[42] After a few months another elections were held in which the coalition formed by the DPS gained the absolute majority and remained in power for the whole term. During this term a political situation had changed. After the fall of Milošević the terms of the relationship between Serbia and Montenegro were negotiated. The negotiations between the prime ministers Z. Đinđić and M. Đukanović with the participation of a EU representative led to acceptance of compromise solutions and signing the Belgrade Agreement by the virtue of which the State Union of Serbia and Montenegro was established.

---

40   See F. Bieber, op.cit., 33-34.
41   Ž. Andrijašević, Š. Rastoder, op.cit., 269-270.
42   Ibidem, 270.

Table 1.   The Montenegro's party system on the parliamentary level.

	P/C3%	2PSC	SR1:2	SR2:3
1990	4	80.00	4.88	1.31
1992	5	70.59	3.29	1.08
1996	3	90.14	2.37	6.33
1998	3	91.03	1.44	5.80
2001	3	89.61	1.09	5.50
2002	3	92.00	1.30	7.50

Source: the table prepared based on own calculations following the pattern proposed by A. Siaroff.[43]

All the three elections had been won by coalitions formed by the DPS although the distance between the two biggest parties (together with their coalitions) on the electoral level was moderate in 1998 (1.37) and 2002 (1.25), and very small in 2001 (1.03). Similar situation was present on the parliamentary level on which the distance after the subsequent elections equalled 1.44, 1.09 and 1.3 [Table 1]. In terms starting after the elections of 1998 and 2002 the DPS together with its coalition gained the absolute majority in the Parliament with 53.85% and 52% of the mandates respectively. With 46.75% of the mandates he had to look for a coalition partner. V. Goati, drawing on the theory of J. Blondel and taking into consideration the electoral coalitions, concluded that the party system during that period reminded the two-and-half-party one. However he noted that it was an illusion since the coalitions had been formed by several parties.[44] Considering a small distance between the biggest two parties (and taking into account that their coalition partners gained a minimum number of mandates) and a very big distance between the second and the third parties reaching 5.8 in 1998, 5.5 in 2001, and 7.5 in 2002, as well as a high level of the coalition's discipline noted by V. Goati, and the fact that the political life at the time was a two-party one,[45] the party system may be classified as two-and-half party tending towards a two-party system. The previously dominating DPS,

---

43   I conducted the calculations for the parties and electoral coalitions, which brought their candidates into Skupština. P3% - Parties/Coalitions with 3 Percent of the Seats; 2PSC – Two-Party Seat Concentration; SR1:2 – Seat Ratio First to Second Party; SR2:3 – Seat Ratio Second to Third Party. A. Siaroff, Comparative European Party Systems. An Analysis of Parliamentary Elections since 1945, New York/London, 2000, 27-33.

44   V. Goati, op.cit., 281. See J. Blondel, Comparing Political Systems, Wiltshire, Trowbridge: Weidenfeld and Nicolson, 1973.

45   V. Goati, op.cit., 281.

despite having had suitable rival – the SNP – still was not dramatically weakened by the 1997–1998 break-up[46] and maintained its position as a governing party. The system at the time was strongly polarised.[47] The main parties – DPS and SNP – differed as for the approach to the key issues related to the future of the Republic and her relationship with Serbia, views on democratisation, free market or accession to the European Union. Above that, as established by V. Goati, the SNP was at the time an anti-system party (discrediting legibility of the DPS) and irresponsible (e.g. it blocked actions related to gaining international economical support).[48]

Although the election law in 1990s was based on the principles of freedom, universality, directness, equality, and secrecy,[49] according to Ž. Andrijašević and Š. Rastoder, during 1990-1998 Montenegro was a pseudo-democratic country. The turning point were the 1998 elections, which in their opinion were "free and fair."[50] Although historians stated in the conclusion that the parliamentary elections held during 1990-2002 only in a slight degree fulfilled the standards of democracy. "All parliamentary elections in Montenegro were characterized by political strife, large-scale politicization of society, the use of all means available to woo voters' support, the involvement of the state apparatus in the election campaigns and the predominance of general topics, such as the issues of statehood, national integrity or Montenegro's general prospects in the current state framework" – they wrote in 2006.[51] Whereas O. Komar and Z. Vujović, considering the elections at that time were "free and fair," noted that the opposition had no chance to take over the power. Simultaneously the DPS won the elections by the will of the electors, and its position was a result of the monopoly inherited from the SKCG, which was connected to adopting the control mechanisms of the different aspects of state's functioning. The DPS was from the beginning presented as a "state party,"[52] which was a result of its inheritance.

---

46 See P.G. Lewis, Political parties in post-communist Eastern Europe, Routlege/ London/New York, 2000, 137.
47 F. Bieber, op.cit., 36.
48 V. Goati, op.cit., 282-283. In his study on polarisation of the system the author draws on G. Sartori's theory. See G. Sartori, Party and Party Systems, A Framework for Analysis, Volume I, Cambridge: Cambridge University Press, 1976.
49 V. Pavićević, op.cit., 17.
50 Ž. Andrijašević, Š. Rastoder, op.cit. 269.
51 Ibidem, 271.
52 O. Komar, Z. Vujović, op.cit., 54.

Party system of independent Montenegro

One-chamber Skupština, in compliance with the Constitution of Montenegro passed on 19 October 2007, numbers 81 deputies (the former constitution of 1992 had not specified the number of deputies) chosen in five-adjective elections: general, free, equal, direct and secret (Article 45). Active and passive electoral rights hold the citizens of Montenegro who are over 18 years of age and have been living on the territory of Montenegro for minimum two years.

General rules of the electoral law are particularised by the Act on the election of councillors and deputies of 8 February 1998 as amended.[53] In parliamentary elections Montenegro constitutes one electoral region covering her entire area from which 76 deputies are chosen. The candidates for the remaining 5 seats are chosen from a special constituency which covers the area inhabited by an Albanian minority. Minority nations are entitled to "authentic" representation in the Parliament of the Republic of Montenegro (Article 79). This general statement is especially important since Montenegro is a country of highly diversified ethnicity. As per 2011 its territory is inhabited by over 620 thousand people, 44.98% of who are the Montenegrins. Amongst other ethnical groups the biggest are Serbs (28.73%), Bosnians (8.65%), and Albanians (4.91%).[54] Interesting are though the data concerning the languages used by the inhabitants of Montenegro. Most of them declare Serbian as their language (42.88%), and the second position holds Montenegrin (36.97%). Above 5% of them declares as their languages Bosnian and Albanian.[55] Amongst numerous minorities only Albanians are guaranteed the parliament mandates. Other minorities must compete on the same basis as Montenegrin parties. This fact causes the parties of Croatian, and during the last elections also Bosnian, minority to form an elective and parliamentary coalition with the DPS.

Deputy candidates can be proposed by the parties, coalitions of parties, and groups of electors. They shall present the lists of candidates for the national as well as special constituencies. The lists are closed. The elective system is proportional and the parliament seats are calculated based on the highest

---

53   Zakon o izboru odbornika i poslanika. Službeni List Republike Crne Gore 4/98, 5/98, 17/98, 14/00, 18/00, 9/01, 41/02, 42/02. http://www.crnvo.co.me/docs/regulativa/Zakon_ o_izboru_odbornika_i_poslanika.pdf (4.10.2011)

54   Popis stanovništva, domaćinstava i stanova u Crnoj Gori 2011. godine, Crna Gora, Zavod za Statistiku, Saopštenje, Broj 83, Podgorica, 12. 07. 2011. godine, Table 4a, 8. http://www.monstat.org/userfiles/file/popis2011/saopstenje/saopstenje(1).pdf (26.07.2011)

55   Ibidem, Table 5a, 12.

averages with the use of d'Hondt's method. The election threshold is set at 3% on the national level.

The Montenegro's electoral law complies, although with many objections, with the basic principles of the democratic electoral law. Freedom House awards them 3.25 points on its 1–7 points assessment scale, which makes an average of the Balkan states.[56] These reports assess the independent Montenegro's elections, both those of 2006 and 2009, as "free and fair".[57] Nevertheless a high level of distrust between the governing and the opposition parties was emphasised. The opposition parties accused the governing ones of dishonesty and expressed a lack of trust that the election process would ever allow an alternation of power. Freedom House criticised the deputies of the governing parties for ignoring the recommendations of international organisations, amongst others OSCE, which could help to better the election process.[58] According to a non-governmental organisation Matica Crnogorska conducting studies on the condition of democracy in this country suggests that the biggest obstacle in development of democracy are the long-set relations between the unchanging government and the permanent opposition.[59] The debate on amendments to the electoral law was a long one. The changes introduced were in accordance with the instructions of international institutions, at the same time they were the conditions to be fulfilled by Montenegro on her way to accession to the European Union.[60]

After the independence referendum in the Montenegro's party system both the changes and some elements of continuation have been observed. The referendum on the independence issue held in March 2006 has shown that the division into the supporters of the independent country and the advocates of maintaining the relationship with Serbia is still present. This division axis still present since 1990 has been confirmed by the first parliamentary elections of the independent Montenegro held in the autumn 2006. In these elections along with

---

56 Nations in Transit 2011, table 2, 40. http://www.freedomhouse.org/images/File/nit/
    2011/NIT-2011-Tables.pdf (04.09.2011)
57 Nations in Transit 2010, Montenegro by Draško Đuranović,
    378.http://www.freedomhouse.org/images/File/nit/2010/NIT-2010-Montenegro-proof-
    II.pdf (04.09.2011)
58 Nations in Transit 2007, Montenegro by Lisa McLean. http://www.freedomhouse.org/
    inc/content/pubs/nit/inc_country_detail.cfm?page=47&nit=431&year=2007&pf
    (04.09.2011)
59 http://www.balkaninsight.com/en/article/survey-suggests-montenegrins-are-dissatisfied-
    with-progress (27.08.2011)
60 The new elective law was passed on 8 September 2011 http://www.balkaninsight.com/
    en/article/montenegro-government-passes-landmark-electoral-law (12.09.2011)

formerly existing parties such as DPS, SDP, and SNP appeared some new parties or coalitions of the parties. In June 2006 from a formerly active non-governmental organisation the Group for Changes (Grupa za promjene, GP) was formed the Movement for Changes (Pokret za promjene, PZP). The Group remained neutral during the campaign preceding the 2006 referendum. The party continued the activities of the Group and its principal goal was still a critique against any exploitation on the part of the governing coalition as in its opinion the DPS's rule was undemocratic. In the elections held in the independent Montenegro also participated three parties representing minority nations. In 2006 the elections were successfully entered by a coalition the Serb List (Srpska Lista, SL) which was formed by the People's Socialist Party of Montenegro (Narodna socijalistička stranka Crne Gore, NSS) and the SNS with the participation of several other smaller Serbia-oriented parties and organisations. In the subsequent elections stood the New Serb Democracy (Nova srpska demokratija, NOVA or NSD) formed by the NSS and SNS joined together in January 2009. In 2003 the Croatian minority was represented by the Croatian Civic Initiative (Hrvatska građanska inicijativa, HGI), and the Bosnian one by Bosniak Party (Bošnijačka stranka, BS) formed in 2006. From the scene disappeared the liberal party LSCG, and its successor the Liberal Party of Montenegro (Liberalna Partija Crne Gore, LPCG) did not exceed the election threshold and did not enter the parliament.

For the elections the lists were presented by 12 parties and electoral coalitions, which included four of the Albanian minority. Again the coalition of the DPS and SDP turned out successful with the participation of the HGI, gaining 48.9% of the votes and 50.62% of the mandates. Clearly weaker result than four years earlier achieved the SNP in coalition with the NS and Democratic Serb Party (Demokratska srbska stranka, DSS), which received only 13.58% of the mandates. Exactly the same number of deputies was entered to the Parliament by the new on the Montenegrin political scene PZP, but it was a success for this organisation. One mandate more than the above mentioned parties gained the SL. Three mandates won the BS. The three groups representing the Albanian minority – the DSCG, DUA and Albanian Alternative (Albanska Alternativa, AA) achieved one mandate each.[61]

The most important task for the new government and parliament was passing a new constitution of the already independent country. Achieving a qualified majority of 54 votes in the Parliament against the resistance of the most of the opposition proved the efficiency of the DPS and M. Đukanović

---

61   Konačne rezultate izbora za poslanike u Skupštinu Republike Crne Gore. Republička izborna komisija. Broj 323. Podgorica, 20. septembra 2006. godine. http://www.skupstina.me/ (3.09.2011)

himself. Some kind of popularity poll for the political parties were the 2008 presidential elections. They were won with nearly 52% of the votes by the current president and the candidate supported by the DPS Filip Vujanović. The presidential elections confirmed a safe position of the DPS in the Montenegro's party system and the weakness of the other parties including the SNP which had been very strong at the turn of XX and XXI centuries.

The subsequent elections were held in 2009. It was a pre-term election which was the result of passing the new Constitution of the Republic of Montenegro. The lists were announced by 16 parties and electoral coalitions, including 4 parties (coalitions) of the Albanian minority. The elections confirmed the domination of Đukanović's party. The coalition of the DPS, SDP, HGI, joined by the BS gained 59.26% of the Parliament mandates. The SNP slightly increased its result (19.75% of the mandates) standing for the elections on its own. The SL and the PZP lost some support gaining respectively 9.88% and 6.17% seats in Skupština. The parties and coalitions representing the Albanian minority entered to the Assembly four deputies: the DSCG, DUA, New Democratic Power (Nova Demokratska Snaga, FORCA) and the Albanian Coalition (Albanska Koalicija, Perspektiva). This time the NS and DSS coalition did not enter the Parliament gaining 2.9% of the votes. A similar result gained the LPCG and DC coalition, as well as the Party of Pensioners and Disabled People (Stranka Penzionera i Invalida Crne Gore, SPICG).[62]

The last pre-term elections were held in 2012 as a result of the decision made by the ruling party. DPS authorities have decided to shorten the term of parliament and hold early elections in October 2012 (instead of in the spring of 2013). The reason for the decision was the fact that Montenegro started membership talks with the EU. „Early elections were needed for the next steps in the EU accession process, which must be dealt with by a new government over a full term in office" said Caslav Vesovic, DPS spokesperson.[63] The lists were announced by 13 parties and electoral coalitions. Coalition European Montenegro (Koalicija Evropska Crna Gora – Milo Đukanović) containing DPS, SDP and LPCG won the election (39 mandates), but failed to win an absolute majority in Skupština. "European Montenegro" has signed coalition with the HGI (1 mandate) and BS (3 mandates), which made up together 53% seats in parliament. In opposition stayed SNP (only 11,1% seats in parliament) and two new parties:

---

62 Konačne rezultate izbora za poslanike u Skupštinu Republike Crne Gore. Državna izborna komisija. Broj 328. Podgorica, 10. aprila 2009. godine. Službeni List Crne Gore 27/2009. http://www.sllistcg.me/ (3.09.2011).

63 M. Milosevic, Montenegro Ruling Party Plans Early General Election, BIRN, Podgorica, 18 Jul. 2012. http://www.balkaninsight.com/en/article/parliamentary-elections-in-montenegro-in-sight (8.08.2012).

Democratic Front (Demokratski Front) with 24,7% seats and Positive Montenegro (Pozitivna Crna Gora) with 8,6% seats. The parties and coalitions representing the Albanian minority entered into the Assembly only two deputies.[64]

The party system of the independent Montenegro can be classified as extremely multiparty with one dominating party. After the period of relentless rivalry of the two big parties, and more precisely speaking the blocs of the 1998-2002 period, the system came back to the 1990s model.

Table 2.   *The Montenegro's party system on the electoral level.*

	P3%	2PVC	ENEP	EFRG
2006	5	63.50	3.36	0.298
2009	4	67.57	3.35	0.301
2012	5	68,40	3,56	0.281

Source: the table prepared based on own calculations in accordance with the model proposed by A. Siaroff.[65]

In comparison to the beginning of 1990s there are more parties on the parliamentary level. After the 2006 and 2009 elections the advantage of the winning party over the second one was respectively 2.84 and 2.25, and the second over the third only 1.09 and 1.78. After the elections in 2012, the situation has changed. The difference between the first and the second party in parliament decreased to 1.50, and between the second and the third increased to 2.22. 7 and 6 parties achieved above 3% of the parliament seats, and the effective number of parliamentary parties equalled from 4.24 (2006) to 3.80 (2009) and 4.32 (2012). [Table 3]

Table 3.   *The Montenegro's party system on the parliamentary level.*

	P3%	2PSC	SR1:2	SR2:3	ENPP	PFRG
2006	7	56.77	2.84	1.09	4.24	0.236
2009	6	63.94	2.25	1.78	3.80	0.263
2012	7	61,73	1,50	2,22	4,32	0.231

Source: the table prepared based on own calculations in accordance with the model proposed by A. Siaroff.[66]

---

64 Izvještaj o rezultatima izbora za poslanike u Skupštinu Crne Gore. Državna Izborna Komisija. Broj 912. Podgorica, 25. oktobar. 2012 godine.http://www.skupstina.me/ (9.02.2013).

65 P/C3% – Parties/Coalitions with 3 Percent of the Votes; ENEP – Effective Number of Electoral Parties; EFRG – Electoral Fragmentation. A. Siaroff, op.cit., 27-33.

The differences between the entities which rose above the threshold clause entering their deputies to the parliament and the number of parties forming parliamentary clubs was a result of some parties grouping into two- or more-entity electoral coalitions. After elections the members of coalitions started to form their own parliamentary clubs. From the beginning of 1990s such a steady electoral coalition has been formed by the DPS and SDP. Similar was the situation with other emergency electoral coalitions such as the SNP-NS-DSS of 2006. So in 2006 the electoral threshold was exceeded by 5 entities (coalitions and parties), and 7 parliamentary clubs were opened. Whereas in 2009, 4 coalitions and parties exceeded the threshold, and there were 6 clubs formed in the Assembly.

The coalition bargains characteristic for the most of the party systems of the Middle and South Europe are not present in the Montenegro's parliamentary system. The system is indeed multi-party, but the elections has been being won by the absolute majority by the DPS-SDP-HGI coalition (in 2009 joined by the BS) and this is by that coalition that the government is formed. The electoral coalition is transforming into the ruling coalition. In the past the bargains would take place only during the 2001 elections (the only elections during which the coalition formed by the DPS had not achieved the absolute majority in the parliament) and ended with the failure. The DPS and SDP formed a minority cabinet just to bring about the pre-term parliamentary elections. In 2012 coalition of the DPS, SDP and LPCG did not win absolute majority but Milo Đukanović has signed an agreement with the previous coalition partners, the BS and HGI.

∗∗∗

In Skupština deputies can group and form parliamentary clubs in the first session of the new parliament. Formal requirement for the formation of the club is a group of at least three deputies. In 2006 after the first elections in the independent Montenegro the deputies formed seven parliamentary clubs: DPS, SDP, BS, SN, SNP, PZP and SL, and three Albanian deputies remained non-associated. The biggest club was formed by the DPS deputies (34 members including a HGI deputy). The biggest opposition club was formed by the SL deputies (12 members). After the 2009 elections six parliamentary clubs were formed. Three of them were formed by the parties constituting a ruling coalition of the DPS, SDP and BS. The clubs were also formed by the SNP, NSD and

---

66   P3% – Parties with 3 Percent of the Votes; 2PSC – Two-Party Seat Concentration; SR1:2
– Seat Ratio First to Second Party; SR2:3 – Seat Ratio Second to Third Party; ENPP –
Effective Numbers of Parliamentary Parties; Parliamentary Fragmentation. A. Siaroff,
op.cit., 27-33.

PZP. A HGI deputy entered the DPS club just like three years earlier. Albanian groups' deputies remained non-associated until 2011, and then two of them created the Albanian club. The biggest of all the clubs remains the DPS with its 36 deputies. Among the opposition clubs the biggest is the SNP with 16 members.[67] After the 2012 elections seven parliamentary clubs were formed. The biggest club traditionally was formed by DPS (30 members). Coalition clubs formed SDP, BS and Albanian minority with HGI and LPCG. Opposition clubs were formed by DF, SNP and PCG[68].

The parliamentary level, similarly to the electoral one, is dominated by the DPS and its smaller coalition partner the SDP. The representatives of these parties monopolised the Skupština's cabinet. Its chairman is R. Krivokapić (SDP) who has been continuously holding that position since 2003. The opposition does not have its vice-chairman in the Skupština. After the 2006 elections an opposition candidate had been presented but did not receive a sufficient support from the chamber. Therefore the opposition parties gave up further efforts to take over one of the vice-chairmen positions. Also after the 2009 elections the opposition parties did not present their vice-chairman candidate. This situation definitely diminishes the importance of the opposition in Skupština.[69]

The majority coalition dominated also the parliamentary commissions. In the 2009-2012 as many as 10 out of 12 commission chairmen belong to the DPS and SDP. The majority in these commission also have the deputies of the ruling coalition. It is worth to mention that the biggest commission after the 2006 elections, that means the constitutional commission, was dominated by the representatives of the coalition who took 9 out of 17 seats, and its chairman became the Skupština's chairman R. Krivokapić.[70]

***

The rivalry between the parties is basically the competition between the dominating DPS – supported by the SDP and every now and then some smaller minority parties such as the HGI and BS – and the Serb parties (e.g. NOVA)

---

67 Izvještaj o radu Skupštine Crne Gore 23 saziva za period 2. oktobar 2006 – 31. decembar 2007 godinu, Skupština Crne Gore, Podgorica, 2008, 17; Izvještaj o radu Skupštine Crne Gore za 2009. godinu, Skupština Crne Gore, Podgorica, 2010, 17; Polugodišnij izvještaj o radu 1. januar 20011 – 30. jun 2011 godine, Skupština Crne Gore, Podgorica, 2011, 7.

68 See www.skupstina.me/ (9.02.2012).

69 Izvještaj o radu Skupštine Crne Gore 23 saziva za period 2. oktobar 2006 – 31. decembar 2007 godinu..., 10; Izvještaj o radu Skupštine Crne Gore za 2009. godinu..., 8.

70 Izvještaj o radu Skupštine Crne Gore za 2009. godinu... , 16; Izvještaj o radu Skupštine Crne Gore 23 saziva za period 2. oktobar 2006 – 31. decembar 2007 godinu..., 16.

remaining in the permanent opposition or the socialists (SNP) who support closer relations with Serbia. On the marginal position remain the liberal parties or the change parties such as the PZP. This status quo has been maintained since the break-up of the DPS during 1997-1998 despite of unrests and transformations related to the Montenegro's status first as a part of the Yugoslavian Federation, later as a state remaining in a lose relationship with Serbia, and presently as an independent country. On the arena of rivalry between the parties there rarely come up any new entities, and even if they do, they are thrown back to a marginal position. Some of them, such as the PZP, raised great hopes for the changes, but in the following elections they would lose much of their importance. More often the new parties are being formed by joining together the previously existing ones such as the NSD (NOVA).

The specificity of the party system is a fact that since 1990 the same political formation has been winning the elections. It received the biggest support in 1990 still as the SKCG (56.2%), and in the following elections it oscillating between 42-51% of the valid votes [see Chart 1]. Characteristic are a lack of alternation of power and high, except for the 1998–2002 period, and the distance between the winning party and the second party. This proves a low level of competiveness in the Montenegro's party system. This opinion is supported by a fact that since 1990 only one party – the DPS – has been constantly present in the Parliament. The DPS is the longest continuously ruling party in Europe. Even the president Alexander Lukashenko in Belarus had not been in office that long.

Chart 1.   The votes and mandates gained by the DPS in the following elections.

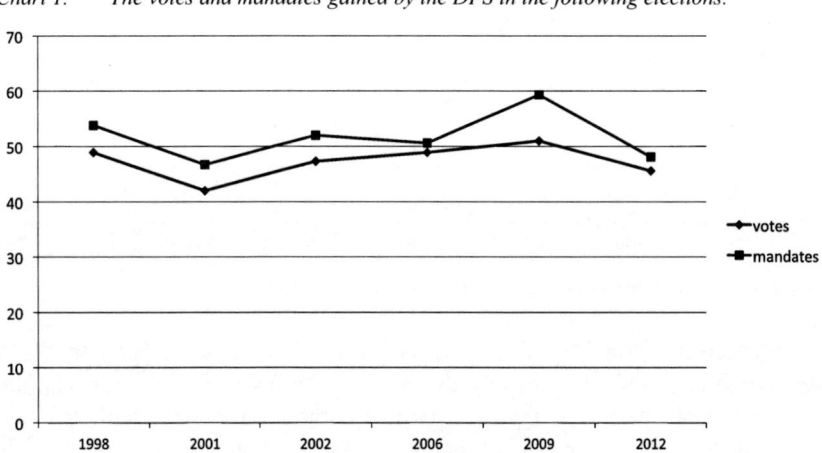

Source: own chart prepared based on data presented in Table 4.

The DPS (by itself or in an electoral coalition) apart from a single case from 2001 gained over 50% of the mandates in the Skupština. In all the electoral coalitions the DPS was a clearly dominating party. Although each of the coalition partners in the Parliament formed its own parliamentary club, they remained in the ruling coalition with the DPS. By the way it is worth noting that the coalition parties on their own would have great difficulties with exceeding the 3% electoral threshold.

The main rival party for the DPS was the SNP beginning with its formation in 1998. After the 1998–2002 the SNP made a strong opposition to the ruling party. It lost much of the support after the 2006 referendum lost by the advocates of remaining in the relationship with Serbia. The SNP was reduced to a role of one of the several opposition parties holding the same (low) number of the Parliament mandates. After the 2009 elections the party regained the status of the second power in Skupština, but the number of the mandates was more or less twice as smaller than during 1998-2002. [see Chart 2] After the 2012 elections SNP lost the status of the main opposition party in Skupština for DF.

Chart 2.   The support and number of the mandates (in percents) gained by the DPS and SNP.

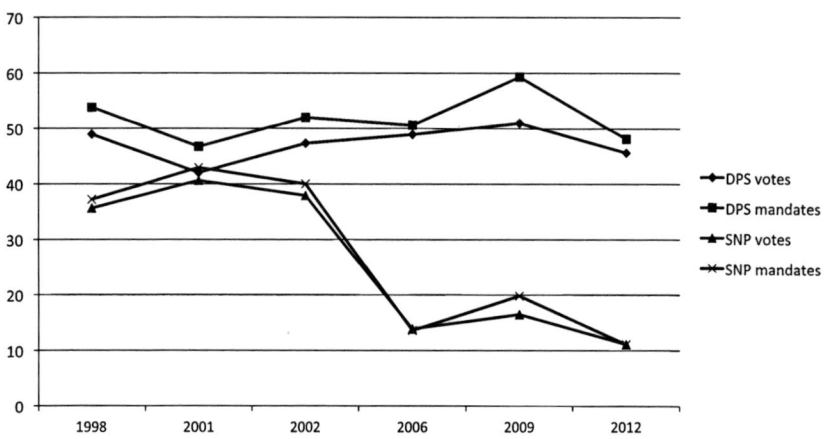

Source: own chart prepared based on data presented in Table 4.

After the elections in 2006 the success of the new progressive party the PZP. This group achieved 11 mandates, the same as the SNP, and one less than the SL. The new party wedged in between the constantly conflicted the independence and the pro-Serbian parties. Some observers of the Montenegro's political scene took this fact at face value expressing the hopes for shattering, in the following elections, the ossified party system. Things turned different though. The PZP in the 2009 elections received 5.9% of the votes and only 5 mandates in the Parliament.

Conclusions

The Montenegro's party system may be classified as multi-party with one dominating party the Milo Đukanović's DPS. This domination, unchanging since the beginning of 1990s, is independent of the form of the state and of the Montenegro's status. The characteristic of the party system is a lack of alternation of power; since the opening elections of 1990 the DPS has been ruling independently or in coalition with the SDP. Characteristic is also the fact that the dominating party is the successor party. In fact in Central and South Europe the rule of the successor parties was nothing unusual, yet it was nowhere else seen that such a group maintained the power continuously since the opening elections. The specificity of this situation is increased by the fact that the very same roots belong to the second political power of Montenegro, the SNP. Therefore the parties of non-communist roots play in Montenegro a marginal role.

As a result of the domination of one political party, except for the 1998-2002 period, some smaller entities were trying their hand at coalitions formed between them, or since 1998 with one of the two strong political parties. This first solution was applied in the opening elections and brought neither the desired result, which was victory, nor forming any strong opposition against the SKCG. Similar lack of the desired effect was seen with the NS and LSCG in 1996. The second type of coalition, the cooperation with the stronger partner, has been taken to for several reasons. One of them was the weakness of the individual parties. The SDP, after the success in the 1992 elections, suffered a defeat and did not exceed the election threshold in 1996. Two years later it formed a coalition with the strong DPS and that allowed it to bring few of its deputies to the parliamentary level. In the subsequent elections it was a steady coalition partner of the DPS, and its deputies are present both in Skupštinie and in the government.[71] The SDP chairman R. Krivokapić is, because of that loyal cooperation and the support of the DPS, a long-term chairman of the National Assembly.

The Montenegro's party system is characterised, except for the 1998-2002, by a low level of competitiveness, and the parliamentary opposition seems weak and conflicted with the ruling camp. Steady element are the accusations on the part of the opposition parties against the ruling DPS concerning the interfering

---

71   See J. Wojnicki, op.cit., 117-118.

with the results of the elections. These accusations, although much exaggerated, are not entirely unfounded, which has been confirmed by the OBWE reports. The Montenegro's political parties are strongly centralised,[72] and the leader figures play a key role in their structure. They are – just like M. Đukanović in the DPS, R. Krivokapić in the SDP, and before M. Bulatović – some kind of bind uniting the parties. One may conclude that these are the "leadership" type parties, similarly to many parties of the Central Europe states.

The Montenegro'e party scene is polarised. The main division axis, had been relations with Serbia, confirmed in the subsequent elections. Nevertheless the referendum and elections results were satisfying for the advocates of the independent Montenegro, according to V. Goati, made that issue less important. The parties are also diversified by a whole range of social and economical issues, including the ways of fighting the economic crises. The reason for the polarisation of the party scene still remains the questions of the ethnic background.[73] An important dividing issue is also an attitude towards the former prime minister and the president M. Đukanović, the crucial figures on political scene of Montenegro. But the issue on which consensus has been reached is a positive approach towards the integration with Europe. It is agreed on, although under certain conditions, by the Serbian parties such as the SSR after the 2006, and presently the NSD. It is a great achievement that throughout the years of the existence of the FRY, as well as the union of Serbia and Montenegro, it was one of the most important problems polarising the Montenegro's party scene.[74] The party system changed after the 2006 elections from the extremely polarised into the moderately polarised one.[75]

Montenegro's party system in the mid 1990s developed as multi-party system with one dominating party (the SKCG, and since 1991 the DPS). The successor of the communist party, holding onto the traditional values of the communist heritage, but gradually moving towards the free market and European positions. After the transitional period brought about by the break-up within the DPS and multi-party system with two main parties, after the 2006 elections the system came back to the 1990s model. In the changed political and economical situation, the DPS with its transformed programme again took a dominating position in the Montenegro's party system. The 2009 elections only strengthened its status.

Translated by Iwona Szuwalska

---

72   V. Goati, op.cit., 262.
73   V. Goati, op.cit., s. 263-264.
74   See V. Goati, op.cit., 264.
75   See also V. Goati, op.cit., 284.

Table 4.   *Results of the elections for Skupština of the Republic of Montenegro (the FRY and Serbia and Montenegro parts) during 1990-2002 and the independent Republic of Montenegro in 2006 and Montenegro in 2009 and 2012.*

Political parties	1990		1992		1996		1998		2001		2002		2006		2009		2012	
	%	Seats	%	Seats	%	Seats	%	Seats	%	Seats	%	Seats	%	Seats	%	Seats	%	Seats
Demokratska Partija Socijalista Crne Gore (DPS)	56.2	83	42.7	46	49.9	45	48.9	42	42.0	36	47.3	39	48.9	41	51.0	48	45.6	39
Socijalistička narodna partija (SNP)	-	-	-	-	-	-	35.6	29	40.6	33	37.9	30	13.9	11	16.5	16	11.1	9
Liberalni savez Crne Gore (LSCG)	SRSJ*	-	12.0	13	NS*	-	6.2	5	7.9	6	5.8	4	BS*	-	-	-	-	-
Stranka srpskih radikala (SSR)	-	-	7.6	8	4.3	-	1.2	-	1,2	-	2.8	-	-	-	-	-	-	-
Demokratska koalicija – albanci zajedno (DKAZ)	-	-	-	-	-	-	-	-	-	-	2.4	2	-	-	-	-	-	-
Sosijaldemokratska partija (SDP)	-	-	4.1	4	5.5	-	DPS*		DPS*		DPS*		DPS*		DPS*		DPS*	
Građanska partija Crne Gore (GPCG)	-	-	-	-	-	-	-	-	-	-	DPS*		-	-	-	-	-	-
Srpska narodna stranka (SNS)	-	-	-	-	-	-	1.9	-	SNP*		SNP*		-	-	-	-	-	-
Narodna stranka (NS)	12.8	13	12.7	14	24.9	19	DPS*		SNP*		SNP*		SNP*		2.9	-		
Demokratski savez u Crnoj Gori (DSCG)	-	-	3.9	-	-	-	1.8	2	1.6	1	-	-	1.3	1	0.9	1	DP**	
Demokratska unija Albanaca (DUA)	-	-	-	-	1.3	2	1.0	1	1.2	1	-	-	1.1	1	1.5	1	-	-
Stranka demokratske akcije (SDA)	-	-	3.4	3	0.6	-	-	-	-	-	-	-	-	-	-	-	-	-

Albanska alternativa (AA)												0.8	1	DSCG*	-	-	
FORCA												0.6	-	0.9	1	1.4	1
Albanska koalicija – perspektiva (AK-P)														0.8	1	-	-
Savez reformskih snaga Jugoslavije (SRSJ)	14.1	17															
Demokratska koalicija (DK)	10.1	12															
Hrvatska građanska inicijativa (HGI)												DPS*		DPS*		0.4	1
Bošnjačka stranka (BS)												3.6	3	DPS*		4.2	3
Demokratska srpska stranka (DSS)												SNP*		NS*		-	-
Srpska lista												14.6	12	-	-	-	-
Nova srpska demokratija (NSD; NOVA)														9.1	8	-	-
Pokret za promjene (PZP)												13.0	11	5.9	5	-	-
Pozitivna Crna Gora (PCG)																8.2	7
Demokratski Front (DF)																22.8	20
Demokratska Partija (DP)																1.1**	1
Liberalna Partija (LPCG)																DPS*	
Others	3.8	-	17.0	-	8.9	-	3.0	-	6.1	-	4.8	-	2.2	-	9.1	-	5.2	-
Seats	-	125	-	85	-	71	-	78	-	77	-	75	-	81	-	81		81

DPS: Democratic Party of Socialists (1990: Savez komunista Crne Gore, eng. League of Communists of Montenegro); SNP: Socialist People's Party; LSCG: Liberal Alliance of Montenegro; SSR: Serbian Radical Party (2002: Patriotic Coalition for Yugoslavia, PKJ); DKAZ: Democratic Coalition-Albanians Together; SDP: Social Democratic Party of Montenegro (1992: Social Democratic Party of Reformists, SPR); GPCG: Civic Party of Montenegro; SNS: Serbian People's Party; NS: People's Party (1996: Coalition People's Unity, KNS); DSCG: Democratic Alliance in Montenegro; DUA: Democratic Union of Albanians; SDA: Party of Democratic Action; AA: Albanian Alternative; FORCA; AK-P: Albanian Coalition – Perspective; SRSJ: Union of Reform Forces of Yugoslavia; DK: Democratic Coalition; HGI: Croatian Civic Initiative; BS: Bosniak Party; DSS: Democratic Serb Party; Serbian List; NSD (NOVA): New Serbian Democracy; PZP: Movement for Changes; PCG: Positive Montenegro; DF: Democratic Front; LPCG: Liberal Party; Source: http://www.parties-and-elections.de/montenegro2.html   (10.07.2011);   www.supstina.me (02.12.2012). * In coalition. ** In coalition Albanska Koalicija.

Is the role of national parliaments being strengthened in the EU? Early warning system after the Lisbon Treaty having come into force

Przemysław Paradowski

Introduction

"National parliaments are important, but they are not equal partners in the EU's decision-making process" – noted the President of the Bundestag, Norbert Lammert, in response to the question whether the national parliaments are important partners in EU decision-making processes at the Conference in Ljubljana in 2008.[1] The statement of the Bundestag's President is, as it seems, closer to reality than enthusiastic words of Jaime Gama, the President of the Assembly of the Portuguese Republic, who two years later during the fourth inter-parliamentary meeting on the future of Europe held in Brussels stated that "national parliaments are the greatest winners of this new Treaty."[2] The above quoted statements express the differences in perceiving the role of national parliaments in the EU.

Before the Lisbon Treaty had come into force the national parliaments would have few possibilities of exercising their influence on the integration processes. The most important, but still indirect, means to effect the decisions of the EU institutions seemed to be state's control in the area of their EU policy as well as inter-parliamentary cooperation under the Conference of Parliamentary Committees for Union Affairs (COSAC). Initiated in 2006 by the president of the European Commission José Barroso an informal political dialogue known as the "Barroso Initiative" was also there to serve launching national parliaments into the orbit of decision-making processes. In the Treaty of Lisbon the spectrum of national parliaments influence on decision-making processes was broadened, and its most important solution appears to be a new procedure referred to as an early-warning mechanism (system). The parliaments had been granted the rights of "upholders" of the subsidiarity principle in the draft EU

---

1   The role of national parliaments in EU decision-making processes: a collection of papers presented at the Conference "The Role of National Parliaments in EU Decision-Making Processes" organised by the Jože Pučnik Institute in Ljubljana on 11 January 2008, edited by Mateja Jančar, Ljubljana: Inštitut dr. Jožeta Pučnika, 2008, p. 26.

2   National parliaments' role in EU affairs improved by new Treaty, EP Press release, 4 December 2007, http://www.europarl.europa.eu/sides/getDoc.do?pubRef=-//EP//TEXT+ IM-PRESS+20071203IPR14219+0+DOC+XML+V0//EN

Constitution, but after its rejection in referenda they were included in the Lisbon Treaty after some slight amendments.

As soon as these rights had been entered into the EU draft Constitution the question arose as to how the new mechanism would work. Amongst the researchers dominated the opinion that they would not have any substantial influence on strengthening parliaments' position in the EU's decision-making processes. As it was commented by T. Raunio: "This mechanism was mainly introduced in response to legitimacy concerns, and it is very likely that its will remain modest."[3] The COSAC Secretariat took trouble to conduct pilot checks on chosen draft legislative acts as for their adherence to the subsidiarity principle. The results of this COSAC undertaking seems, although not explicitly, to confirm the view of limited impact of the early warning mechanism on the strengthening of the national parliaments' role in decision-making processes.[4] Yet the real test of the early warning mechanism started with the moment the Lisbon Treaty came into force. The early warning mechanism can indeed exhibit a strengthening effect on national parliaments' participation in the EU's decision-making processes and simultaneously eliminate democracy deficit. In order to achieve the above ends it is necessary to fulfil one condition, which is an efficient implementation of the mechanism. Without proper engagement of the parliaments in implementing of the early warning mechanisms, strengthening of national parliaments role in the EU's decision-making processes will be an illusory. Two years have passed since the Lisbon Treaty entered into force one can try to find an answer to the key question, whether the early warning system has indeed strengthened the position of national parliaments in decision-making processes. Being aware of the fact that two years is far too short period to present an exhaustive answer to the question, I have attempted to analyse the problem of implementing the rights to monitor the adherence to the subsidiarity principle. The results of the analysis will at least to some extend provide answers to some constituent questions. Firstly, to what extend do the parliaments take advantage of the rights they have been granted? Secondly, what problems occur in implementing the early warning mechanism? And thirdly, was the democracy deficit due to it at least to some extend diminished?

---

3 T. Raunio, Destined for Irrelevance? Subsidiarity Control by National Parliaments, Area: Europe Working Paper 36/2010, Real Instituto Elcano, p. 11. http://www.realinstitutoelcano.org/wps/portal/rielcano_eng/Content?WCM_GLOBAL_C ONTEXT=/elcano/elcano_in/zonas_in/europe/dt36-2010, On this matter see a.o. T. Raunio, Much Ado About Nothing? National Legislatures in the EU Constitutional Treaty, European Integration online Papers, vol. 9, no. 9, 2005. http://eiop.or.at/eiop/ texte/2005-009a.htm; I. Cooper, The Watchdogs of Subsidiarity: National Parliaments and the Logic of Arguing in the EU, Journal of Common Market Studies, 44(2) 2006.

4 See COSAC Reports: http://www.cosac.eu/en/info/earlywarning/.

In the first part of this article I present some observations on strengthening the national parliaments' role in the integration processes. In the second part I describe the Lisbon Treaty decisions on national parliaments, and especially the procedures of subsidiarity control. In the last part I analyse some chosen aspects of implementing the early warning mechanism after the Lisbon Treaty has entered into force.

From the process of strengthening national parliaments

The EU integration processes have been dominated by the executives of the member states, and the influence on the community matters, especially decision-making processes of the member states' parliaments and the European Parliament was none, or insignificant. This phenomenon was termed as democracy deficit. The process of parliamentarisation of the communities started in the 1980s and has been going on since then. Although the position of the European Parliament was strengthened during that time and the institution itself was promoted to "the A-players category" as far as legislation process was concerned,[5] the role and importance of national parliaments change a lot slower.

The national parliaments have been significantly weakened as a result of the European integration. First of all they have lost all sorts of legislative powers as they were transferred to the EU level. The marginalisation could hardly be overestimated as the national parliaments from being the only legislators in their states moved to being forced to share their power with the transnational institutions. The loss of the position was not compensated by any valuable instruments, which would allow the parliaments to influence legislation on the European level.[6]

---

5   See R. Corbett, F. Jacobs, M. Shackleton, The European Parliament, 7th edition, John Harper Publishing, London, 2007, pp. 3-7.

6   So far there were many researchers who dealt with the problem of national parliaments. See among others, National Parliaments and the European Union: The Constitutional Challenge for the Oireachtas and Other Member State Legislatures, ed. G. Barrett, Dublin: Clarus Press, 2008; Kiiver, P. The National Parliaments in the European Union: A Critical View on EU Constitution-Building, The Hague: Kluwer Law International, 2006; A. Maurer, W. Wessels, National Parliaments on their Ways to Europe: Losers or Latecomers? Baden-Baden: Nomos 2001; National Parliaments within the Enlarged European Union: From 'victims' of integration to competitive actors?, eds. J. O'Brennan, T. Raunio, Abingdon: Routledge, 2007; T. Raunio, The Gatekeepers of European Integration? The Functions of National Parliaments in the EU Political System, Journal of European Integration, Vol. 33, No. 3, May 2011, pp. 303-321; A. Cygan, National parliaments within the EU polity – no longer losers but hardly victorious, ERA Froum (2012) 12, pp. 517-533.

The processes that led to weakening and in fact to marginalisation of national parliaments in the European Communities resulted at the end of 1980s in increased activity of the national parliaments representatives in the area of strengthening their positions in common Europe. National parliaments representatives took up an informal collaboration, which was soon to transform into institutionalised inter-parliamentary cooperation under the Conference of Speakers of the European Union Parliaments and the Conference of Parliamentary Committees for Union Affairs of Parliaments of the European Union (COSAC).[7] The effect of dealing with the issue of national parliaments during the conference preparing a new treaty was included in the Maastricht Treaty's two declarations: on the national parliaments in the EU and on the Conferences of Parliaments. The declarations were not in any way binding, yet they contributed to providing the parliaments with more effective information procedures regarding the EU issues as well as tightening their cooperation with the European Parliament. As a result of the inter-governmental commission's works on the subsequent treaty the position of the national parliaments in the EU has been significantly strengthened. There have been two protocols attached to the Amsterdam Treaty in which the rules pertaining to the parliaments' access to information, documents, and draft legislative acts have been set, and the platform of inter-parliamentary cooperation, which for many years has already been the COSAC, has been sanctioned. The issues included in the protocols have become a part of primary legislation and on their basis the national parliaments took part in union matters until the Lisbon Treaty had entered into force.[8] Another effort to strengthen the parliaments, unsuccessful because of the treaty having been rejected in referendums, was made during the Convention preparing a new constitution for Europe. There were two groups working on the role of the national parliaments in the EU: Working Group I – on the Principle of Subsidiarity, and Working Group IV on the Role of National Parliaments.[9]

---

7   See M. Knudsen, Y. Carl, COSAC – its Role do Date and Potential in the Future, National Parliaments and the European Union. The Constitutional Challenge for Oireachtas and Other Member State Legislatures, ed. G. Barret, Dublin: Clarus Press, 2008, passim.

8   See J. Karlas, Národní parlamenty a kontrola evropskich záležitostí. Komparativní analýza, Praha: Karolinum 2011, pp. 27-41; P. M. Kaczyński, Paper tigers or sleeping beauty? National Parliaments in the post-Lisbon European Political System, CEPS Special Report, February 2011, pp. 2-3; E. Popławska, Rola parlamentów narodowych w świetle Traktatu z Lizbony, Przegląd Sejmowy 5(100)/2010, pp. 159-162; Compare P. Paradowski, Kompetencje utracone, uprawnienia zyskane. Z procesu europeizacji parlamentów państw Europy Środkowej, Spotkania Europejskie 2 (2009), pp. 85-97.

9   On the works of Convention see among others P. Kiiver, The National Parliaments in the European Union...; R. Grzeszczak, Parlamenty państw członkowskich w Unii Europejskiej, Wrocław 2004, pp. 216-229. See also T. Raunio, The Gatekeepers..., pp. 309-312.

National parliaments in the Lisbon Treaty

The changes introduced in the Lisbon Treaty pertaining to strengthening the role of the national parliaments in the EU were a result of the evolution of parliaments meaning that had been taking place since the beginning of the 1990s, and especially proposals worked out by the Convention and included in the Treaty Establishing Constitution for Europe. J. Barcz noted even that "strengthening the position of the national parliaments (...) is one of more significant EU system reforms."[10]

An important novelty as for strengthening the position of national parliaments was the emphasising of their role in the Treaty itself.[11] Article 10 acknowledges responsibility of an executive representing a country in the European Council and the Council before the parliaments or the citizens. Article 12 states that "National parliaments contribute actively to the good functioning of the Union" and further there are listed six aspects of their possible influence on the functioning of the Union. Thus the parliaments could help the Union with proper functioning: "through being informed by the institutions of the Union and having draft legislative acts of the Union forwarded to them;" "by seeing to it that the principle of subsidiarity is respected;" "by taking part, within the framework of the area of freedom, security and justice, in the evaluation mechanisms for the implementation of the Union policies in that area..., and through being involved in the political monitoring of Europol and the evaluation of Eurojust's activities;" "by taking part in the revision procedures of the Treaties;" "by being notified of applications for accession to the Union;" and "by taking part in the inter-parliamentary cooperation between national Parliaments and with the European Parliament."[12] This provision undoubtedly strengthens national parliaments in the European Union, although – as J. V. Louis has noted – mainly in the symbolic sphere.[13]

Article 12 is extended in other articles of the Treaty as well as in two protocols: "on the role of national parliaments in the European Union," and "on the

---

10   J. Barcz, Zasadnicze reformy strukturalne ustroju Unii Europejskiej, Traktat z Lizbony. Główne reformy ustrojowe Unii Europejskiej, red. naukowa Jan Barcz, Urząd Komitetu Integracji Europejskiej, Warszawa 2008, p. 65.

11   T. Raunio, Destined for Irrelevance..., p. 3.

12   Consolidated versions of the Treaty on European Union and the Treaty on the Functioning of the European Union. Official Journal of the European Union 2010/C 83.

13   J. V. Louis, National Parliaments and the Principe of Subsidiarity – Legal Options and Practical Limits, European Constitutional Law Review, Volume 4, Issue 03, October 2008, p. 133.

application of the principles of subsidiarity and proportionality."[14] The quoted protocols have replaced the above mentioned protocols attached to the Amsterdam Treaty. The content of the protocols has been already discussed in the literature.[15] Their most important resolution was obligatory forwarding consultation documents, annual legislative programme, documents on legislative planning and policy strategy, as well as legislative acts projects by EU institutions' to national parliaments.[16] In short, national parliaments receive fuller EU information and documentation in comparison with the former situation. Extended to 8 weeks (except for emergency situations) was the period from forwarding a legislative project to national parliaments to signing it into the initial agenda in order to accept it or taking a stance within a legislative procedure.[17] Thus national parliaments have more time to discuss and evaluate the project, and if needed to issue an opinion or take a stance. Parliaments are also informed about agendas and results of the European Councils' meetings, as well as protocols from meetings of the Council voting on draft legislative acts. The Court of Auditors is obliged to sent its annual reports for information purposes to the parliaments. Protocol 1 outlines also general framework of inter-parliamentary cooperation in the EU.[18] An access to the fuller information enables national parliaments: 1. to exhibit based on Article 1 of the Lisbon Treaty control of EU parliamentary policy by member states; and 2. to assess draft legislative acts as for adherence to subsidiarity principle.[19]

---

14 Protocol (No 1) on the role of national parliaments in the European Union; Protocol (No 2) on the application of the principles of subsidiarity and proportionality (Protocol 2). Official Journal of the European Union 2010/C 83.

15 See among others J. V. Louis, National Parliaments..., pp. 138-142; R. Grzeszczak, Subsydiarna demokracja. Rola parlamentów narodowych w Unii Europejskiej w Traktacie z Lizbony, Rapporte der Konrad-Adenauer-Stiftung, Nr 10, 2009, pp. 9-15; E. Popławska, Rola parlamentów narodowych..., pp. 166-172; J. Jaskiernia, Rola parlamentów narodowych w Unii Europejskiej w świetle Traktatu z Lizbony, Księga pamiątkowa profesora Marcina Kudeja, Katowice 2009, pp. 225-230; R. Balicki, Parlament narodowy w systemie decyzyjnym Unii Europejskiej (po wejściu w życie postanowień Traktatu z Lizbony), Instytucje prawa konstytucyjnego w dobie integracji europejskiej. Księga jubileuszowa dedykowana prof. Marii Kruk-Jarosz, red. J. Wawrzyniak, M. Laskowska, Warszawa 2009, pp. 340-342.

16 Protocol (No 1), articles 1 and 2.

17 Protocol (No 1), article 4.

18 Protocol (No 1), articles 5, 7, 9, and 10.

19 See Protocol (No 1). After presenting the early warning mechanism for the European Constitution the COSAC ran pilot programmes assessing the functioning of the mechanism on the chosen draft legislative acts. See http://www.cosac.eu/en/ info/earlywarning/. On pilot programmes see: M. P. Kaczyński, Paper tigers..., pp. 6-8.

It is worth stressing that the parliaments' rights in the Treaty have a framework form. They do not impose any particular obligations nor do they specify any means by which the parliaments could implement their rights. The organisational and procedural forms of exercising the "EU function" by the parliaments are to be decided upon by an internal law. This aspect is connected to respecting national identity of the member states by the Union included in Article 4 of the Lisbon Treaty.[20] It is worth mentioning that the question of state law regulating the way of executing rights granted to parliaments in the Treaties is nothing new and such regulations, e.g. in the area of parliamentary control of the states in EU matters, do exist.[21]

Early warning mechanism in the Lisbon Treaty

There have already been issued some publications on control of adherence to the principles of subsidiarity and proportionality in the EU. Articles devoted to this issue are mostly theoretical analyses of legal changes and parliaments' acquiring new rights. The authors of those studies try to predict, in some cases on the basis of pilot programmes run by the COSAC, how parliaments would benefit from such rights.[22] Many researchers are sceptical, and consider this procedure as a mere pretence. Nevertheless the procedure has its advantages and, as P. Kiiver assures, there are reasons to strive for considering and implementing the early warning system.[23]

The foundation of the principles of subsidiarity and proportionality is Article 5 of the Lisbon Treaty and defined therein principle of conferral, which determines the limits of EU's competences. According to that principle "Under the principle of conferral, the Union shall act only within the limits of the competences conferred upon it by the Member States in the Treaties to attain the

---

20 See E. Popławska, Rola parlamentów narodowych..., pp. 157-158.
21 See Karlas, Národní parlamenty..., pp. 32-35.
22 See among others P. Kiiver, The onduct of Subsidiarity Checks of EU Legislative Proposals by National Parliaments: Analysis, Observations and Practical Recommendations (December 5, 2011). ERA Forum (2012) 12, pp. 535-547; E. Popławska, Parlamenty narodowe..., p. 171; D. Král, V. Bartovic, The Czech and the Slovak Parliaments after the Lisbon Treaty, Prague 2010, pp. 70-71; J. Jaskiernia, Rola parlamentów..., pp. 225-230. See also last monograph by P. Kiiver The Early Warning System for the Principle of Subsidiarity. Constitutional theory and empirical reality, London and New York; Routledge, 2012.
23 P. Kiiver, The Early-Warning System for the Principle of Subsidiarity: The National Parliament as a Conseil d'Etat for Europe, European Law Review, Issue 1, 2011, pp. 100-101.

objectives set out therein. Competences not conferred upon the Union in the Treaties remain with the Member States."[24]

As for the above statement the subsidiarity principle determines that in areas which do not belong to the Union exclusive competence the Union is to take action "only if and insofar as the objectives of the proposed action cannot be sufficiently achieved by the Member States, either at central level or at regional and local level, but can rather, by reason of the scale or effects of the proposed action, be better achieved at Union level". As far as the principle of proportionality is concerned, the Treaty states that "the content and form of Union action shall not exceed what is necessary to achieve the objectives of the Treaties."[25]

The institutions of the Union are obliged to adhere to the principles of subsidiarity and proportionality based on the Protocol on the application of these principles, and the control of adherence to the subsidiarity principle was also assigned to national parliaments.[26] Questions related to parliamentary control over adherence to the subsidiarity principle are specified in the protocols – generally in the first one, and in details in the second one. Draft legislative acts presented to the parliaments by the EU Commission, Parliament and Council can be subjected to a control as for their adherence to the principles of subsidiarity and proportionality. The parliaments have eight weeks for such a control beginning from transmission of a draft legislative act to entering it into the meeting agenda of the Council in order to accept it or to take a stance within the framework of legislative procedure. During those eight weeks the parliaments have a full comfort of work on the draft because in this period no decisions can be made on the legislative act that was sent to parliaments. After conducting a control the parliaments can present to the presidents of the European Parliament, Council, and Commission a substantiated opinion on the drafts adherence to the principle of subsidiarity.[27]

---

24 Official Journal of the European Union 2010/C 83.
25 Consolidated versions of the Treaty on European Union and the Treaty on the Functioning of the European Union. Official Journal of the European Union 2010/C 83. On the subsidiarity principle see R. Schütze, Subsidiarity after Lisbon: reinforcing the safeguards of federalism? Cambridge Law Journal, 68(3), November 2009, pp. 525-536; P. Craig, Subsidiarity: A Political and Legal Analysis, Journal of Common Market Studies Vol. 50. No S1. pp. 72-87; Z. Czachór, Parlament państwa członkowskiego Unii Europejskiej a badanie zgodności projektów aktów prawa wspólnotowego z zasadą subsydiarności, Studia Europejskie 1/2006, pp. 41-45.
26 Art. 5. Official Journal of the European Union 2010/C 83.
27 See Protocol (No 2).

Control procedure of the adherence to the subsidiarity principle known as the early warning system is in fact a control ex-ante, that means still before a proposal with a draft legislative act is sent to legislative institutions. The EU institutions pass on to the parliaments drafts and amended drafts of legislative acts: the Commission and Parliament their drafts, and the Council those coming from the groups of member states: the Court of Justice, European Central Bank and European Investment Bank. Also resolutions of the Parliament and positions of the Council after accepting thereof are presented to the national parliaments.[28] The drafts must be reasoned with regard to the principles of subsidiarity and proportionality in such a way that would facilitate the assessment of their adherence to both these principles. Justification should contain some data necessary to assess financial consequences of the draft, and in case of the directive its consequences for regulations introduced by the member states including their influence on regional legislation. Decision whether an objective can be better reached on the Union level should be based on quality indicators, and where possible on the quantity ones.[29]

Presented draft legislative act falls under control of the national parliaments or their chambers which are entitled to present to the presidents of the Parliament, Commission and Council an opinion containing reasons for which a given project is considered inconsistent with the subsidiarity principle. Parliaments/chambers are to consult, if necessary, the regional parliaments holding legislative powers.[30] A reasoned opinion has been given a negative character. It is passed by a parliament/chamber exclusively in cases of deciding that a draft legislative act was not adhering to the subsidiarity principle.[31]

The Union institutions after receiving reasoned opinions should take under consideration objections presented therein.[32] Whereas a draft must be reviewed in case of reasoned opinions on non-compliance with the subsidiarity principle represent at least one-third of all the votes allocated to the national parliaments or one-forth of all the votes in case of a draft legislative act concerning the area of freedom, security and justice based on Article 76 of the Treaty on the functioning of the EU, known as the yellow card. In the procedure of counting votes for the purposes serving the early warning system every parliament has two votes with a condition that in case of two-chamber parliaments each

---

28 Protocol (No 2), article 4.
29 Protocol (No 2), article 5.
30 Protocol (No 2), article 6.
31 P. Kiiver, The Early-Warning System..., p. 103.
32 Protocol (No 2), article 7.1; Compare B. Pawłowski, Kontrola przestrzegania zasady pomocniczości przez parlamenty narodowe państw członkowskich Unii Europejskiej, Zeszyty Prawnicze Biura Analiz Sejmowych, Rok IV 2 (18) 2008, p. 51.

chamber holds one vote.[33] After the review the Commission, another institution, or a group of countries (depending on where the draft comes from) may decide to maintain, amend or withdraw the draft, and the decision must be justified.[34]

Similar is the situation within a regular legislative procedure, although here reasoned opinions on draft legislative act proposal's non-compliance must constitute common majority of the votes allocated to the parliaments – the orange card procedure. After the review the Commission may uphold or withdraw the proposal. In case the Commission decides to uphold the proposal it is obliged to present a reasoned opinion explaining the reasons behind the proposals adherence to the principle of subsidiarity. All the reasoned opinions, of the national parliaments as well as the EU Commission, are passed on to legislative institutions – that means the European Parliament and the Council. Both institutions, taking into consideration the reasoned opinions, assess the compliance of the legislative proposal with the subsidiarity principle before the first reading takes place. If the legislator decides by 55% majority of the Council members' votes or majority of votes given in the Parliament, that the proposal complies with the principle of subsidiarity, then it will not be subjected to further reviewing.[35]

A parliament/chamber has also possibility of ex-post control, which means the right to lodge a complaint with the Court of Justice against the violation of the subsidiarity principle by the legislative act (right after passing thereof). But the competent entity in this regard is a member state (and in some particular cases the Committee of the Regions), therefore a parliament can file a complaint only through its government.[36]

The early warning system definitely did not make the national parliaments co-legislators in the European Union. This conclusion confirms the law as well as the practice. The Treaty on the Functioning of the European Union clearly defines the legislative institutions of the Union, which are the Parliament and Council. (Article 294 TFEU) The procedure gives the national parliaments an opportunity to express themselves about draft legislative acts, but nothing more than that, because reasoned opinions and other views are not binding for the EU institutions. They are not binding to such extend that even the yellow or orange card

---

33 Protocol (No 2), art. 7. Among 27 national parliaments in the European Union 13 are two-chamber parliaments therefore the control can be exhibited by 14 one-chamber parliaments and 26 chambers of the two-chamber parliaments, therefore maximum votes in the control of the adherence to the subsidiarity principle equals 54.

34 Protocol (No 2), article 7.2; See P. M. Kaczyński, Paper tigers..., p. 4; P. Kiiver, The Early-Warning System..., p. 100.

35 Protocol (No 2), article 7.3; see P. M. Kaczyński, Paper tigers..., p. 4; see also A. Cygan, National parliaments..., pp. 523-524.

36 Protocol (No 2), article 8.

procedure does not change anything if the Commission, Parliament or Council are opposed. Yet the Commission while not taking under consideration reasoned opinions is still obliged to justify its decision. Thus one can agree that the voice of the national parliaments in the early warning system is an advice one. P. Kiiver, noticing similarities with the advice body functioning at the French government, compared the early warning system to a kind of *Conseil d'Etat* for Europe.[37]

How does it look in practice? Remarks on complying with the early warning system

The current provisions of the Treaties and Protocols grant the national parliaments greater rights than it was previously seen as far as the control of the EU legislative processes is concerned. Nevertheless from the beginning all the researchers would agree that the real value of these articles could be seen in practice. Therefore there have been many questions as to whether the parliaments would be willing to take advantage, and if yes, then to what extend, of the instruments facilitating their influence on the EU's legislation. It has been emphasised that the efficiency will depend on cooperation between individual parliaments and parliamentary chambers. The COSAC and a platform for the exchange of information and best practice, which is IPEX, were justly seen as the arena of such cooperation.[38] How thus after two years have passed since the Lisbon Treaty, and at the same time all the above described instruments and procedures, having entered into force are they taken advantage of by the national parliaments? To what degree are the parliaments engaged in the early warning system? And does this mechanism bring forth any results? What are the problems with implementing the protocol's provisions?

Trying to find answers to the above stated questions I have conducted the analysis of some chosen aspects of control procedure of the draft legislative acts adherence to the subsidiarity principle, which included especially reasoned opinions as well as other remarks and opinions of the parliaments/chambers sent to the presidents of the Commissions, Parliament, and Council. I have drawn on the data presented on the IPEX platform as well as on chosen national parliament's websites; I have looked into the European Commission's reports and data, as well as reports of the COSAC. One must remember that the data resources presented on the IPEX and European Commission websites are

---

37 P. Kiiver, The Early-Warning System..., pp. 101-102.
38 See R. Grzeszczak, Subsydiarna demokracja, pp. 18-19; E. Popławska, Parlamenty narodowe..., pp. 173-174.

incomplete.[39] Therefore the results of the quantitative research are not 100 per cent precise. Nevertheless they undoubtedly express the tendencies present within the framework of applying the early warning mechanism.

Internal mechanisms of parliamentary control of compliance
with the subsidiarity principle

Changes concerning the role of national parliaments introduced in the Lisbon Treaty resulted in necessity (or rather a possibility) of changing internal subsidiarity control mechanisms. Control of compliance with the subsidiarity control ex ante requires efficient internal mechanisms allowing to assess the adherence of a draft legislative act to the subsidiarity principle.[40] More than half of the parliaments/chambers have introduced the changes, although their range is greatly varied. Whereas other parliaments/chambers decided that the so far applied mechanisms are at least satisfying, and have not introduced, or are just planning to introduce, this kind of modifications.[41]

Internal changes have been introduced on many levels. Some of the states have changed particular provisions in their constitutions (e.g. Germany, France and Austria) and/or in the acts regulating parliaments' cooperation with their governments in matters related to EU membership (e.g. Germany, Ireland, Spain, Poland), in a way that would allow them to execute their tasks.[42] Most of

---

39   Analysis of parliaments' activity in the area of compliance with the principle of subsidiarity was conducted on the basis of fragmentary data by P. M. Kaczyński, Paper tigers..., pp. 1-13. The author used the data available on the IPEX platform in the period from the Lisbon Treaty having entered into force to 2 November 2010. Comparing data presented in Kaczyński's report to the same period COSAC report one can see that the IPEX did not provide many information about reasoned opinions sent to the Commission by the national parliaments. These gaps were filled in later. The problem of providing data on the IPEX platform by national parliaments has been mentioned in the COSAC report. See Sixteenth Bi-annual Report: Developments in European Union Procedures and Practices Relevant to Parliamentary Scrutiny, Prepared by the COSAC Secretariat and presented to: XLVI Conference of Parliamentary Committees for Union Affairs of Parliaments of European Union, 2-4 October 2011 Warsaw, COSAC Secretariat, Brussels, p. 32. Presently the data are definitely more precise and any gaps that cannot be excluded do not have any major impact on the overall vision of the functioning of the early warning system.

40   See Král, V. Bartovic, The Czech and Slovak Parliaments..., p. 31.

41   Sixteenth Bi-annual Report..., p. 46.

42   Thirteenth Bi-annual Report: Developments in European Union Procedures and Practices Relevant to Parliamentary Scrutiny, Prepared by the COSAC Secretariat and presented to: XLIII Conference of Parliamentary Committees for Union Affairs of Parliaments of

the changes though have been entered in the parliaments' or chambers' rules of procedure, as well as in procedures followed so far. These changes resulted in regular meetings of the European Union Affairs Committee or sub-Committee (e.g. the National Council of Austria) as well as closer co-operation between and branch committees (e.g. the Senate in Romania). Taking into account the EU institutions agendas allows better planning of parliamentary works (e.g. Bulgaria). In some parliaments the rights to assess the compliance of draft legislative acts were passed to branch committees (both chambers of Ireland's parliament) or new committees have been established (House of Representatives of the Netherlands).[43] Most of the changes were introduced in order to enable the parliaments, or in their name the specialised committees, to conduct subsidiarity checks for a draft legislative act as well formulating, passing and forwarding a reasoned opinion to the EU Commission.

The most important organs of the parliaments/chambers controlling the draft legislative acts are in most cases the European Affairs Committees. A supporting role, although not less important, play branch committees, which receive the drafts to issue opinions. In some parliaments/chambers branch committees hold an exclusive mandate (e.g. the Camber of Deputies and Senate in Belgium, National Assembly in France, or Bundestag in Germany). Opinions, positions, and resolutions on a draft are usually passed by the European Affairs Committee and/or branch committees. In many parliaments/chambers the procedure involves also plenary sessions on which resolutions passed on the level of committees are voted, and in particular reasoned opinions.[44] In some parliaments neither internal mechanisms nor procedures have been introduced for parliamentary control of adherence to the principles of subsidiarity and proportionality. Some of these parliaments do not rule out such changes in the future.[45]

In accordance with the above mentioned framework the characters of national parliaments' rights, internal procedures used in subsidiarity control are different. Such differentiation is wholly accepted by the European Commission. Every parliament/chamber has worked out, or is still in a process of building, its own mechanisms and procedures of participation in implementing of the early warning system. Apart from similarities, such as engagement of committees specialised in the European Union affairs, there are also many differences, such as the level of branch committees engagement, government representatives or

European Union, 31 May-1 June 2010 Madrid, COSAC Secretariat, Brussels, pp. 12-14; Sixteenth Bi-annual Report..., pp. 46-48.

43   Sixteenth Bi-annual Report..., pp. 46-48; Thirteenth Bi-annual Report..., pp. 14-15.
44   Sixteenth Bi-annual Report..., pp. 46, 48-49; Thirteenth Bi-annual Report..., p. 18.
45   Sixteenth Bi-annual Report..., p. 49.

experts involvement, or finally passing an opinion that has been reasoned only by specialised commission and on a plenary session. (see examples in Table 1)

Table 1.   Examples of the procedures applied in chosen parliaments

Example 1: Assembly of the Republic of Portugal
In the Assembly of the Republic of Portugal draft legislative acts receives the European Union Affairs Committee and then sends them to a competent branch committees for information or issuing opinion. In case of decision about issuing a report or opinion on the draft legislative act, it must be executed by a competent branch committee within six weeks. A report or opinion is then forwarded to the European Union Committee, which must examine a draft legislative act within two weeks. It must look into the legal basis and adherence to the subsidiarity principle of the act. The European Affairs Committee passes a written opinion together with a report and an opinion of a branch committee to the president of the Assembly, who passes it to the EU institution. In case of establishing a violation of the subsidiarity principle the European Affairs Committee presents on a plenary meeting a draft act which, if passed, will be send as a reasoned opinion to the presidents of the EU institutions.[46]
Example 2: Polish Sejm
To draft opinions on EU draft legislative acts and acts passed on the basis of Article 352 paragraph 1 of the TFEU the government attaches information concerning adherence with the subsidiarity principle. If the Committee decides that the subsidiarity principle has been violated, accepts the opinion in this respect. Draft resolution on violation of subsidiarity principle may be introduced either by the European Affairs Committee or at least 15 deputies. Debate and a first reading of a draft take place at the European Affairs Committee, and a second at the plenary sitting. A passed reasoned opinion and cover letter signed by the Sejm marshal are sent by e-mail to the EU Commission, Parliament and Council.[47]
Example 3: Danish Folketing
The European Affairs Committee without any undue delay forwards all important conclusions to competent sector committees. Sector committees can present to the European Affairs Committee initial recommendations within five weeks, if according to their opinion the subsidiarity principle has been violated. Then within eight weeks the European Affairs Committee accepts a final content of a reasoned opinion. In case of discrepancy between recommendations of a sector committee and opinion of the European Affairs Committee a meeting of both committees is called on. Immediately after being adopted, a reasoned opinion is sent to the EU Commission, Council and Parliament.[48]

---

46 Annex to the Sixteenth Bi-annual Report: Developments in European Union Procedures and Practices Relevant to Parliamentary Scrutiny: Replies of National Parliaments and the European Parliament, Prepared by the COSAC Secretariat and presented to: XLVI Conference of Parliamentary Committees for Union Affairs of Parliaments of European Union, 2-4 October 2011 Warsaw, COSAC Secretariat, Brussels, p. 173.

47 Annex to the Sixteenth Bi-annual Report, p. 161.

48 Third draft report on consideration of EU matters by the Folketing in relation to subsidiarity checks. Report issued by the European Affairs Committee on 24 December 2009, Folketinget 2009-10. http://www.cosac.eu/en/info/earlywarning/countryspecific/ denmark/ (On the same webpage see also Report of 24 December 2009).

Parliaments/chambers participation in subsidiarity control procedure

The parliaments/chambers to various degrees engage themselves in subsidiarity control. In principle they choose the draft legislative acts that for some reasons are considered by a parliament or governing circles controversial or important from a given country's policy point of view.[49] Parliaments' activity in implementing the early warning mechanism is a part of informal political dialogue between the parliaments and the European Commission and therefore it is hard to explicitly assess the engagement of different parliaments/chambers. For that reason I have chosen only the activity that is directly connected to the control of compliance with the subsidiarity principle.

The most measurable fruit of the control are the reasoned opinions which, filed in an adequate number, may force the Commission and other institutions to review the draft. By the end of September 2012 the parliaments/chambers have sent 155 reasoned opinions. From amongst 40 parliaments/chambers 32 have formulated a reasoned opinion. The biggest number, that is as many as 27, of reasoned opinions was sent by Swedish Riksdag, by Polish Sejm and Senat, French Senat and Luxembourg Chamber of Deputies 10 each, Cortes Generales 8. Other parliaments/chambers sent less reasoned opinions, and among those there were 13 that sent only one or two reasoned opinions.[50] As for most of the draft legislative acts the parliaments/chambers did not send reasoned opinions. In one case a required number of votes was achieved in order to initiate the procedure of the yellow card. It was a proposal of the Council regulation known as the Monti II.[51]

---

49 See Thirteenth Bi-annual Report..., p. 17.

50 The data come from the IPEX platform. http://www.ipex.eu/IPEXL-WEB/search.do (30.09.2012) For 2010 compare: Report from the Commission on subsidiarity and proportionality, Brussels 10.06.2011, COM (2011) 344, p. 11 (Annex), http://ec.europa.eu/ governance/better_regulation/documents/com_2011_0344_en.pdf (27.05.2012)

51 COM(2012) 130 final Proposal for a Council regulation on the exercise of the right to take collective action within the context of the freedom of establishment and the freedom to provide services. http://www.ipex.eu/IPEXL-WEB/dossier/document/COM20120130.do# (10.10.2012). See D. Adamiec, Pierwszy wypadek zastosowania mechanizmu żółtej kartki – opinie parlamentów dotyczące rozporządzenia Monti II, Zeszyty Prawnicze, Biuro Analiz Sejmowych, nr 3(35) 2012, s. 23-40.

Chart 1.   Number of reasoned opinions sent to the EC by the end of September 2012.

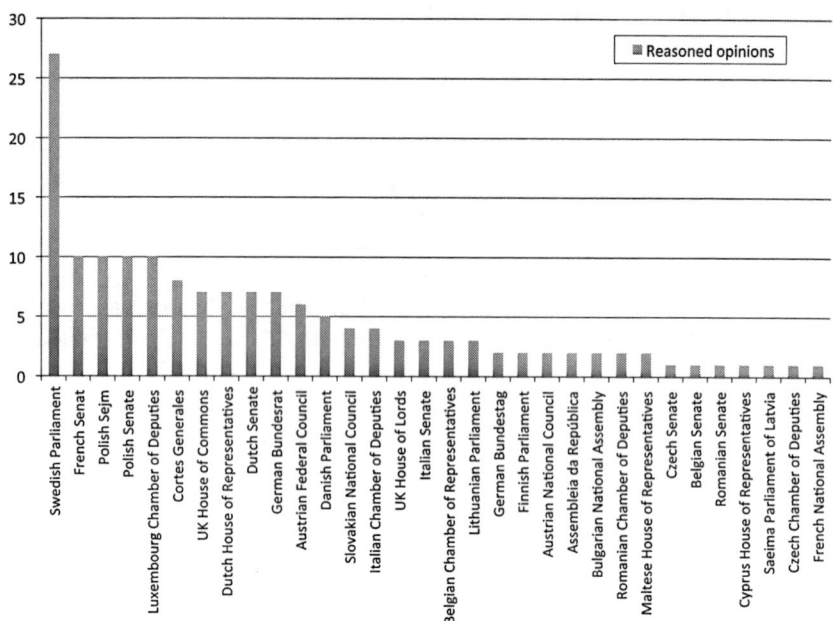

Source: Data presented on the IPEX platform. http://www.ipex.eu/IPEXL-WEB/home/home.do (3.10.2012)

The parliaments/chambers also express doubts regarding the adherence with the subsidiarity and proportionality principles apart from the form of justified opinion. This is a part of informal political dialogue initiated in 2006 in order to encourage the national parliaments to express their opinions on the European Commissions initiatives.[52] Such information takes various forms and names, from opinions through positions and resolutions. To the end of September 2012 the parliaments/chambers formulated 1420 important information containing 365 doubts pertaining to subsidiarity principle.[53]

Apart from the above listed forms of presenting objections concerning draft legislative acts' adherence to the subsidiarity principle, the parliaments/

---

52 Sixteenth Bi-annual Report..., p. 52. On the informal dialogue see D. Jančić, The Barroso Initiative: Window Dressing or Democracy Boost? Utrecht Law Review, Volume 8, Issue 1 (January) 2012, pp. 78-91.

53 Data based on the IPEX platform, http://www.ipex.eu/IPEXL-WEB/search.do (30.09.2012)

chambers pass so-called relevant information. This category is very broad and includes all kinds of information on parliaments/chambers positions on draft legislative acts, opinions on positions of their governments regarding particular draft legislative acts. Some parliaments/chambers such as the Portuguese and Bulgarian Assemblies formulate opinions and positions also on draft legislative acts towards which they do not have any objections in regards to compliance with the subsidiarity principle. Similar documents are passed by the French Senate (resolutions) and German Bundesrat (positions). Whereas the Polish Sejm presents in form of an opinion its lack of consent (not connected to the adherence with the subsidiarity principle) to proceed with a given draft legislative act. In these documents the parliaments present various remarks, objections and doubts concerning a draft legislative act.

Chart 2.   *Important information and relevant information on doubts in regards to respect of the subsidiarity principle sent by the parliaments to the EC by the end of September 2012.*

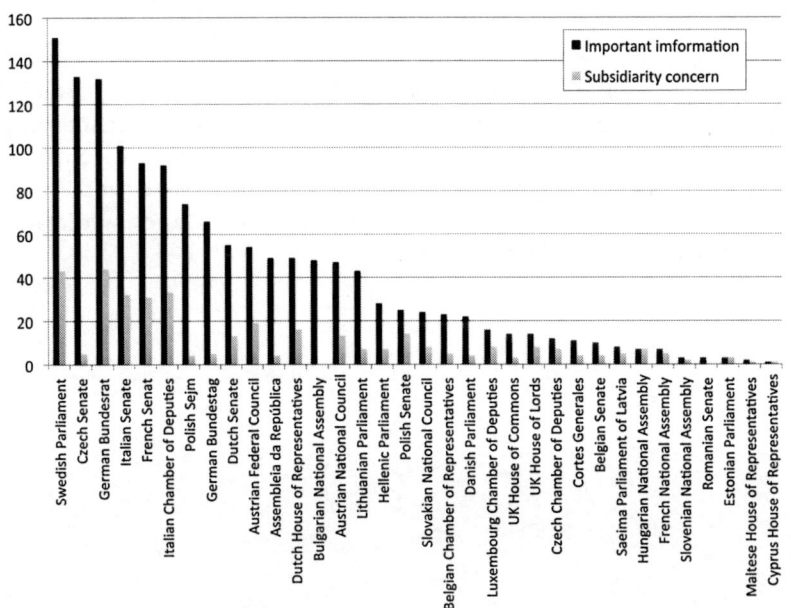

Source: Data available on the IPEX platform. http://www.ipex.eu/IPEXL-WEB/home/home.do (3.10.2012)

There are different reasons for this varied and constantly increasing[54] parliamentary activity. It seems that a lot depends on the topic of a draft legislative act and an answer to the question whether it is important from the point of view of state's interests. The position of a government is also important. In most of the EU countries rule the coalitions based on majority support in parliaments. The Commissions in these parliaments are built proportionally to party structure in a parliament, or a chamber in a two-chamber parliament. Thus majority belongs to ruling coalitions and their opinions, like in the Polish Sejm, are often convergent with government's stance.[55] More independent, as it seems, are opinions of other chambers, although there also a lot depends on party structure, which also means electoral system.

From the moment of the Lisbon Treaty entering into force till February 2012 the European Commission sent 442 responses to doubts expressed by parliaments/chambers in regards to adherence with the subsidiarity principle.[56] Unquestionable majority was an element of informal dialogue during the control procedure in the parliaments/chambers that presented their doubts in this dialogue. Often upon receiving the EC's reply parliaments/chambers would withdraw their doubts and did not formulate any reasoned opinions. The biggest number of EC's responses was directed to Swedish Riksdag (75), Czech Senate (41), Italian Senate (41), Romanian Chamber of Deputies (39), German Bundesrat (29) and Italian Chamber of Deputies (25). With these parliaments/chambers the EC conducted the most intense dialogue on the matter of adherence to the principles of subsidiarity and proportionality. (see Chart 3)

---

54 Sixteen Bi annual Report..., p. 52.
55 http://www.ipex.eu/IPEXL-WEB/search.do (30.09.2012)
56 Source: Data available on the IPEX platform. http://www.ipex.eu/IPEXL-WEB/search.do (10.10.2012)

Chart 3.   *Total numbers of responses to parliaments'/chambers' doubts containing subsidiarity concern sent by the EC till the end of September 2012*

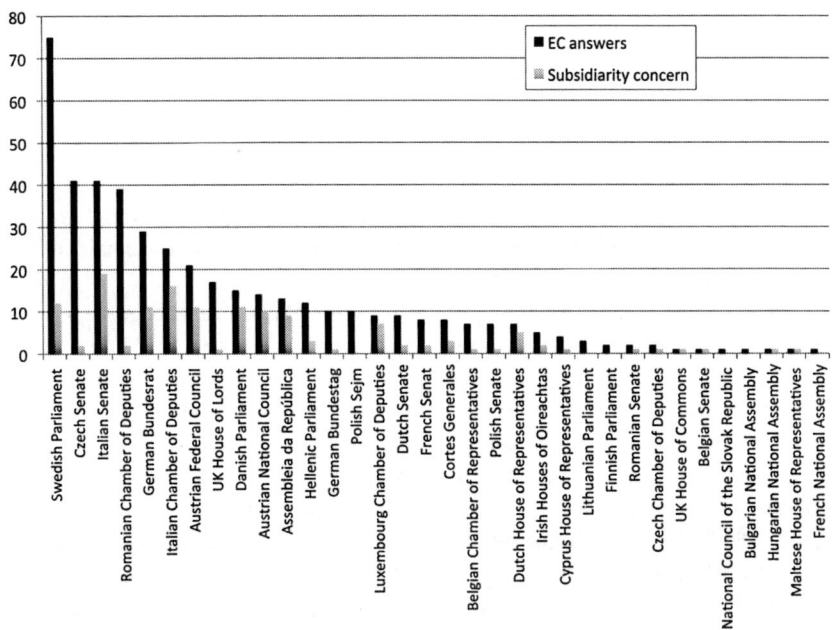

Source: Data available on the IPEX platform. http://www.ipex.eu/IPEXL-WEB/home/home.do (10.10.2012)

A novelty in the EU parliamentary scrutiny procedure is a treaty-based guarantee of equal rights in matters concerning parliamentary subsidiarity control for both chambers in two-chamber parliaments.[57] Both chambers have identical subsidiarity and proportionality control instruments and means of action. This fact is important not only in respect of strengthening second parliamentary chambers, but also in regards to the results of conducting parliamentary control. The above presented data show that more intense dialogue with the EC within the early warning system procedure is conducted by second chambers of two-chamber parliaments than by the first ones or by one-chamber parliaments. Second chambers are nearly one-third (32.5%) of parliaments/chambers participating in the procedure. During the period under consideration they have sent to the EC nearly 32% of all reasoned opinions, 47% of all important information, 44% of all relevant information expressing doubts

---

57   Protocol (No 2), articles 7. See P. M. Kaczyński, Paper tigers..., pp. 5-6.

concerning subsidiarity principle and received 43% of all the responses sent by the EC to the parliaments/chambers[58]. Among the reasons behind greater involvement of second chambers in the mechanism of early warning system one can probably mention the asymmetry of two-chamber parliaments (except for Italian and Romanian Senates) as well as more limited rights, and what results from it, less functions to exhibit in the country as well as connection with legislative bodies and regional governments in federal states. More involvement of second chambers can be observed in an informal political dialogue since 2006.[59] Presently second chambers benefit from these experiences and worked out solutions that had been employed in the early warning mechanism. The matter requires though a separate analysis.

On the basis of data pertaining to parliament's/chamber's engagement in the early warning system there are other tendencies to be observed. With a lesser intensity the dialogue with the European Commission, which includes also contacts within the early warning procedure, is conducted by parliaments/ chambers of post-communist states. Worthy of attention is above all the Czech Senate, which keeps up particularly active correspondence with the European Commission. Apart from that, two chambers of the Polish Parliament, Sejm and Senate, lead the way as far as the number of passed reasoned opinions is concerned (having been outscored only by the Swedish Riksdag). Many other post-communist states' parliaments/chambers (among others Slovenian, Latvian, Bulgarian, Lithuanian) do not show any extensive activity. Among one-chamber Scandinavian states it is the Swedish Riksdag which undoubtedly leads the way in this respect, whereas regarded to be strong in government control aspect Danish Folketing and Finnish Eduskunta do not show any special activity in the early warning system's area. In the other hand great involvement is seen on the side of the four biggest EU states. But still there are visible big disproportions between the involvement shown by German Bundesrat, French Senate and British House of Lords, and fairly small Bundestag, National Assembly and the House of Commons. Equilibrium is present though as far as involvement of both chambers of Italian parliament is concerned. It is worth to note here that the above-presented data do not always express the real work done in the parliaments as for the adherence to the subsidiarity principle. A clear example is the Portuguese Assembly of the Republic, which passes and sends to the EU institutions opinions on every evaluated project and because it always gives positive assessments there is no need to pass a reasoned opinion or additional sending doubts concerning subsidiarity principle.

---

58   The calculations are based on the data contained in Charts 1, 2 and 3.
59   See Jančić, op.cit., p. 84.

It seems that some parliaments/chambers remaining in minority have been more intensely engaged in implementing the early warning mechanism and to a great extend these are the same parliaments/chambers which are the most actively involved in an informal political dialogue with the European Commission.

Problems with implementing the early warning mechanism

The early warning mechanism, accept for the pilot programmes carried out by the COSAC, became an official procedure since the Lisbon Treaty entering into force. In the first stage of its implementation there have occurred many problems that national parliaments must address. In this part of the article I will try to look into chosen problems emphasised by the parliaments in their answers given in the survey which was the basis for The COSAC Secretariat to produce the above quoted Sixteenth Bi-annual Report: Developments in European Union Procedures and Practices Relevant to Parliamentary Scrutiny.

Responses of the European Commission

The European Commission is a party in a political dialogue with the national parliaments and therefore it actively participates in it, among others responding to the parliaments' remarks. It also committed itself to respond to reasoned opinions and it seems it does comply with the commitment. The quality of the responses to the reasoned opinions sent by the parliaments still varies. Some parliaments/chambers are satisfied with the Commission's replies, but other file all kinds of complaints and remarks concerning their quality. The explanations of the Commission are often short and general, and at times do not contain Commissions' stance regarding the objections pertaining to compliance with the subsidiarity principle presented in reasoned opinions. Sometimes they give an impression of being based on one scheme and therefore unable to relate to particular and varied remarks presented in reasoned opinions.[60]

The content of the response is usually discussed at the European Union affairs committees and other competent committees. Sometimes the content is presented to a broader circle of people, e.g. European Parliament deputies or political parties' representatives. It should be noted though that not in all parliaments/chambers the Commission's replies are discussed. Most of the parliaments stated also that the Commission did not keep set by itself three-

---

60   Sixteenth Bi-annual Report..., p. 33.

month term to respond. Some parliaments/chambers state that they have received responses after for or even six months.

The exchange of correspondence with the Commission ends after receiving a reply. So far the parliaments have not continued the dialogue with the Commission after having received and discussed the replies to reasoned opinions.[61]

Deadline for scrutiny of drafts compliance with the subsidiarity principle

An important issue in the context of conducting research and assessment of draft acts in regards to compliance with the subsidiarity principle is the time given to parliaments/chambers' disposal. Above half of them considers the eight-week deadline for assessing draft legislative acts compliance with the subsidiarity principle to be sufficient, although most of this half expresses all kinds of objections. Nine parliaments/chambers considers this deadline to be too short, and a dozen or so among those considering the eight-week deadline to be sufficient file many remarks as for the circumstances of keeping to the deadlines.[62]

The opinion on the deadline depends on few basic factors. First of all efficient time management depends on adopted scrutiny procedures and mechanisms, as well as organisational skills. Some parliaments, like for e.g. the Portuguese Assembly of the Republic or Danish Folketing have skilfully dealt with organisational problems setting for the specialised committees concrete time for working on the draft (for the Assembly 6 weeks, for the Folketing 5 weeks). This is the time meant to assess a draft not only in regards to subsidiarity principle but also its other very specialised aspects. After working in the committees a draft comes back to European Union affairs committees which taking under consideration specialised committees report passes an opinion or reasoned opinion. (see Table) In other cases, especially where control procedure requires a plenary meeting debate (House of Lords), or if memorandum from a government is required (House of Commons), this deadline may prove insufficient.[63]

Complexity and specialisation of a draft are also important for keeping to eight-week deadline. Many parliaments have problems with keeping to this deadline when the drafts are more complex and require specialised knowledge.[64]

---

61   Sixteenth Bi-annual Report..., pp. 33-34.
62   Sixteenth Bi-annual Report..., pp. 36-37.
63   Sixteenth Bi-annual Report..., p. 37.
64   Sixteenth Bi-annual Report..., p. 36.

It should be also remembered that forming a "coalition" of parliaments/ chambers for efficient scrutiny, which means the procedure of yellow or orange card, is time-consuming.[65] Another important aspect seems to be the requirement of parliaments'/chambers' taking advice from local and regional legislative bodies. Such consultations are usually time-consuming and as a result of it assessment of adherence to subsidiarity principle will be conducted under time-pressure.[66]

From many parliaments' point of view extending this period would facilitate more thorough project assessment. Nevertheless one should remember that such a change would stretch on already long legislative procedures.

Absence of a legal basis and incorrect justification

The parliaments while assessing adherence of a draft legislative act to the subsidiarity principle must relate to it as a whole. But in practice in order to assess the whole draft they must refer to its specific elements.[67] The subsidiarity principle has not been precisely defined in treaties which gives national parliaments a greater manoeuver room during assessment of compliance with this principle.[68] According to the COSAC report the parliaments that have passed reasoned opinions took under consideration different aspects of a draft legislative act.

Apart from assessing a draft's compliance with the subsidiarity principle they often shown a lack of a legal basis and a lack of or not sufficient justification in relation to subsidiarity principle.[69] The commission was obliged to present the Treaty a legal basis of a draft as well as stated in Article 5 of Protocol 2 necessity of justification. The parliaments often considered these deficiencies as the basis to pass a reasoned opinion.[70]

---

65 This fact was noted by the second chamber of the Dutch parliament. See Annex to the Sixteenth Bi-annual Report, p. 36. See also D. Král, V. Bartovic, The Czech and Slovak Parliaments..., p. 38; G. A. Bermann, The Lisbon Treaty: The Irish 'No'. National Parliaments and Subsidiarity: An Outsider's View, European Constitutional Law Review (EuConst), Volume 4, Issue 03, October 2008, p. 458.

66 Compare P. M. Kaczyński, Paper tigers..., p. 5.

67 See B. Pawłowski, Kontrola przestrzegania zasady pomocniczości..., p. 50.

68 See P. M. Kaczyński, Paper tigers..., p. 4.

69 This fact was noted by David Král. See D. Král, V. Bartovic, The Czech and Slovak parliaments after the Lisbon Treaty, Europeum Institute for European Policy, Praha 2010, p. 31.

70 Examples in Sixteenth Bi-annual Report..., pp. 37-41.

Impact assessment

Equally important issue, not only from the EU institutions' but also national parliaments' point of view, is an assessment of economic, social and environmental impact done by an institution authorised by the president of the Commission: Impact Assessment Council for more important political initiatives and legislative proposals under the Commission's agenda.[71] The national parliaments consider impact assessment to be important for good draft scrutiny as for the subsidiarity principle, but only few of them consider the assessments quality sufficient or satisfactory. Most of the parliaments note a poor quality of the assessments. Objections concern mainly routineness, randomness of remarks and generality, lack of information required as "detailed statement" mentioned in Article 5 of Protocol 2, based on too limited data base. They also note a lack of independence in impact assessments, considering them to present the Commission's point of view. According to some of the parliaments every proposal, and not only those considered important by the Commission, should include an impact assessment.[72] Big number of parliaments/chambers demand also translating all the impact assessments into all the EU official languages.[73] These objections, with a special emphasis on independent character of the impact assessment as well as transparency and openness of the Impact Assessment Council's and its experts' works, confirms the European Parliament.[74] Parliaments' negative opinions on the impact assessment shed some light on the European Commission's problems with the early warning system. The Commission is an institution that does the biggest work in the context of assessing the adherence to the subsidiarity principle. The EC has for years given great attention to the quality of impact assessment,[75] and it still fails on this level.

Interpretation of the subsidiarity principle

Among very important problems varied interpretations of the subsidiarity principle should be listed. The European Commission noted that the parliaments' interpretations of drafts vary, and often even while sending a

---

71   Sixteenth Bi-annual Report..., pp. 41-42.
72   Sixteenth Bi-annual Report..., pp. 42-44.
73   Sixteenth Bi-annual Report..., pp. 44-46.
74   Sixteenth Bi-annual Report..., p. 44.
75   Report from the Commission on Subsidiarity and Proportionality (18th report on Better Lawmaking covering the year 2010). COM (2011) 344, pp. 2-3.

reasoned opinion they refer to different violations of the subsidiarity principle.[76] The source of problems is also the parliaments' varied interpretation of what is a reasoned opinion, which obstructs inter-parliamentary cooperation.[77] A big problem is also a lack of parliaments'/chambers' activity coordination during an assessment of adherence to the subsidiarity principle. The COSAC does not fulfil in this regard the hopes that have been placed in it, and the IPEX platform still has some data gaps.[78]

The above review of the problems arising in the process of applying the early warning mechanism is in many ways convergent with the problems reported during conducting pilot programmes by the COSAC.[79] Thus it seems that the awareness of these problems has not brought forth their thorough elimination, which does not predict any major changes in this regard.

Conclusions

Analyzing the practice of applying the early warning mechanism shows that so far the parliaments were not able to take a full advantage of it, that is to activate the yellow (one case during three years) and orange card procedures, and therefore the strengthening of parliaments in decision making processes is rather unrealistic.

The parliaments/chambers try to monitor the content of chosen draft legislative acts and report objections to the Commission and other EU institutions. The parliaments'/chambers' interest in control of adherence to the subsidiarity and proportionality principles is very much varied. Besides the parliaments/chambers, which very conscientiously execute their duties, there is quite a big group of those which exhibit this control only to a minute extend.

The possibility of presenting reasoned opinions and objections concerning the subsidiarity and proportionality enables the parliaments/chambers, at least those that are active on this level, to strive for institutions' adherence to these principles. Yet they cannot gain a sense of any significant influence on the EU legislation. Data on the European Commission's having taken into consideration in draft legislative acts the objections presented in reasoned opinions are

---

76   Report from the Commission on Subsidiarity and Proportionality (17th report on Better Lawmaking covering the year 2009). COM (2010) 547, p. 12. See P. Kiiver, The Conduct of Subsidiarity…, pp. 541-545.

77   425th Resolution of the Senate of the Czech Republic on the Annual report 2010 on relations between the European Commission and national parliaments, 7 December 2011, Senate Press no. K 068/08.

78   Ibidem.

79   See COSAC Reports. http://www.cosac.eu/en/info/earlywarning/.

fragmentary and insufficient to form any conclusions.[80] None of the draft legislative acts has acquired a sufficient number of reasoned opinions in order to make the Commission and other legislative institutions review them. It should be noted though that there are drafts for which objections expressed by sending reasoned opinions has been filed by a few parliaments/chambers.

The problem is a lack of precise subsidiarity principle scrutiny criteria. While assessing the same draft legislative act some parliaments file for violation of the subsidiarity principle, whereas others do not see such a violation. Moreover, the parliaments that report non-compliance with the subsidiarity principle refer to different unrelated parts of an assessed draft. But this problem is hard to overcome because adherence to the subsidiarity principle varies according to economical, social and political priorities and it depends on the internal specificity of a country.

It seems that the parliaments should work on strengthening their positions by making small steps, that means first of all they should strive that the Commission takes into account reasoned opinions even if a one-third or one-forth level of votes has not been reached. In order to start the yellow or orange card procedure, better inter-parliamentary scrutiny cooperation or coordination is needed. The parliaments must improve the communication concerning draft legislative acts in such a way that a greater number of the parliaments chooses the same draft legislative acts to be reviewed as questionable in regards to adherence to the subsidiarity principle[81].

Issuance of reasoned opinions is often related to government's position towards a matter brought up in a draft legislative act. That means that when a government was negatively disposed towards a draft, its parliament or one of the chambers would send a reasoned opinion to the Commission. Thus for some parliaments/chambers the cooperation with government in EU related matters that has been developed over the years plays an important role in case of subsidiarity principle scrutiny.

Among positive aspects of the way the parliamentary scrutiny over the subsidiarity and proportionality principles that has been outlined in the Treaty of Lisbon and Protocols 1 and 2 functions, one must mention a dialogue conducted between the parliaments and the Commission, EU Parliament, as well as the dialogue between the parliaments themselves. One may argue that this dialogue is not sufficient, that the scrutiny is limited because of many parliaments low activity in this regard. Nevertheless what seems positive is big activity and serious approach to their rights on the part of some parliaments. Owing to that

---

80   Sixteenth Bi-annual Report..., pp. 34-35.
81   See. A. Cygan, National parliaments..., p. 524.

they are better informed and their doubts are cleared by the Commission, although the quality of their opinions is not always satisfactory. The parliamentary dialogue with the EU institutions undoubtedly contributes to decreasing democracy deficit in the European Union, although the level of the decrease is still unsatisfactory.

Some parliaments have prepared for active participation in the early warning mechanism through entering appropriate changes in constitutions, regulations of the chambers or procedures being applied. The data concerning activity of the parliaments/chambers shows that these parliaments, which have prepared, are more active.

The subsidiarity scrutiny procedures encourage information exchange between the parliaments (for which the IPEX platform and COSAC are used) as well as cooperation, and these are essential elements allowing parliaments future taking advantage of the rights granted by the "yellow card" and "orange card".

From the point of view of the national parliaments and advocates of decreasing of the EU democracy deficit, the information, although fragmentary, about Commission's including in the legislative draft proposals remarks present in the reasoned opinions, is encouraging. Often the parliaments, along with the remarks concerning the subsidiarity principle, point also to other aspects of draft legislative acts. Presently it is still hard to establish how many of such remarks are taken into account by the Commission during the review of the proposals, but the very fact of their being included might be the source of parliaments' hope for exhibiting greater influence on the content of legislative acts in the future.

Translated by Iwona Szuwalska

"Communication gap."
The European Union's Internet contacts with its citizens

Monika Łukasik-Duszyńska

In the modern world democratic states' societies on the one hand want the politicians to efficiently solve problems that bother them. But on the other hand they blame them for all hardships and crises. Presently one can note a drop in trust towards institutions and politicians or even complete lack of interest in them. In case of the European Union (EU) itself the citizens are focused on their own problems and do not have even basic information about its mechanisms. Although they are acquainted with the names of the EU institutions they neither have any idea what are the tasks of those institutions nor do they know what falls under their jurisdiction. As far as the decision making process is concerned, they are either totally uninformed or they rely on incorrect information, broadcast by the media or publicised by the politicians. That is very often why they do not identify themselves with the EU or plainly see it as the cause of all problems.

Practically since the European Economic Community (EEC) was created, and then the EU, the citizens perceived this organisation as something remote and hard to conceive. The politicians and officials who worked on the development of the Community initially did not even bother to change this way of perceiving things. Delay in the ratification process of the Maastricht Treaty (1992) drew attention to that issue. But only after the problems with passing the Treaty of Nice (2001) had occurred and the citizens of the Netherlands and France had rejected in a referendum the establishing of a Constitution for Europe (TCE) (signed in 2004), the need to take up active information and communication policy by EU institution officials, addressed to the citizens of the member states was noticed.

In the main documents signed after 2000 the emphasis has been put on the fact that the EU policy needs to be more open, easier to follow, and understand.[1] As far as the Union itself is concerned the demand "to become more democratic, more transparent and more efficient"[2] has been stressed. Additionally it has been stated that the vision of the future of Europe must be built on a clear

---

1   European Commission, European Governance, A White Paper. COM (2001) 428 final, p. 4; see also 3 and 7.

2   European Council Meeting in Laeken, 14-15 December 2001. Presidency Conclusions. Annex I – Laeken Declaration on the future of the European Union. http://ec.europa.eu/ governance/impact/background/docs/laeken_concl_en.pdf, access: 2 November 2011, p. 21.

understanding of citizen's needs and expectations. In order to help meet those ends the Commission must stimulate a wider public debate on the role and the functioning of the EU.[3] Efforts had been made to listen to the citizens so that the European Union could respond to the concerns expressed by them. It has been stressed that the EU citizens are entitled to having their voices heard.[4]

Apart from that in 2005 the European Commission accepted the *Action plan to improve communicating Europe by the Commission.*[5] The three main slogans of the plan were: careful "listening", better "communicating" and connecting with citizens by "going local" (p. 4). In the plan the emphasis has been made on communication that it is more than just information, as it helps to establish relationships and initiates a dialogue with EU citizens. It also assures that people are heard and helps connecting with them. It is not a worthless practice but rather an essential aspect of the political process (p. 3). It has been noted that "communication is a dialogue, not a one-way street." It had been stressed that that the EU institutions are expected not only to inform EU citizens but citizens should also have the possibility to express their opinions in such a way that the Commission could understand their points of view and concerns (p. 4).

At the same time one year later the White Paper on a European Communication Policy[6] stated that over the last two decades the EU had been transformed, but still the issue of the EU communication with its citizens had not been put into practice. It had confirmed the fact that there is a communication gap between the EU and its citizens. At the same time it has been additionally stated that communication is essential to a healthy functioning of democracy and the vice versa. "Democracy can flourish only if citizens know what is going on, and are able to participate fully" (p. 2). The emphasis has been made that over the past few years all the EU institutions have been giving special attention to communication work. It has been admitted though that the focus goes largely to informing people about the EU's activities, whereas listening to the people's views has not been given that much attention. "Though consultation mechanisms have become standard practice, these are limited to specific policy initiatives and citizens often have the impression that the channels through which they can take part in the debate are limited or

---

3   Communication from the Commission to the Council, the European Parliament, the European Economic and Social Committee and the Committee of the Regions – The Commission's contribution to the period of reflection and beyond: Plan-D for Democracy, Dialogue and Debate. COM (2005) 494 final, p.2.

4   *Ibidem.* p. 4.

5   Communication to the Commission: Action Plan to Improve Communicating Europe. Brussels: European Union. European Commission, Brussels 2005. SEC (2005) 985 final.

6   White Paper on a European Communication Policy COM (2006) 35 final.

inaccessible" (p. 4). Therefore it has been decided that some further steps must be taken to seal the communication gap. The European Commission has proposed a completely new approach – "a decisive move away from one-way communication" towards more emphasis and a dialogue; from institution-focused communication towards a citizen-focused one; from "a Brussels-based to a more decentralised approach." Since then the communication was to become "an EU policy in its own right, at the service of the citizens" and to be based on "genuine [whatever is that supposed to mean – author's note] dialogue" between the policymakers and the people, as well as lively political discussion among the latter (p. 4). Efforts have been made to find ways to seal the gap. A special website has been created[7] for exchange of views and comments on communication improvement (p. 3).

In the following documents the priorities were set and amongst them the citizens right to participate in the public debate on EU issues, express their views and have access to fair and diverse information.[8] The necessity of the EU institutions' and member states' greater involvement in informing the societies on the issues pertaining to the EU's functioning has been also brought up in a joint declaration of the European Commission, the European Parliament and the Council of 2008 titled *Communicating Europe in Partnership*. It stresses that the most important aim is to ensure the European citizens could exercise their right to take part in the "democratic life" of the Union, "in which decisions are taken as openly as possible and as closely as possible to citizens, observing the principles of pluralism, participation, openness and transparency."[9] The Treaty of Lisbon, which came into force in December 2009,[10] included the resolutions from the previous EU documents on giving citizens and representative associations the opportunity to publicly exchange and express their opinions in all Union areas of activity. The emphasis was put on the institutions' open, transparent and regular dialogue with the society (article 8b).

How then does this explaining, listening and maintaining contact with the citizens through the Internet look like? Is it an open regular dialogue? Does the European Union implement new technologies to develop the dialogue with its citizens? Or maybe Internet is just a means to transfer information? I would like

---

7   http:/Europa.eu.int/comm/communication_white_paper

8   Commission Working Document. Proposal for an Inter-Institutional Agreement on Communicating Europe in Partnership. COM (2007) 569 final, p. 3.

9   Joint Declaration of the European Parliament, the Council and the Commission. Communicating Europe in Partnership. http://ec.europa.eu/dgs/communication/pdf/political_ declaration_081022.pdf (28.10.2011).

10   Treaty of Lisbon amending the Treaty on European Union and the Treaty establishing the European Community, signed at Lisbon, 13 December 2007. O.J. UE 2007/C 306/01.

to emphasise that the problem outlined in this article could be the basis for further research on the matter.

As after 2000 the role of the Internet substantially increased in the lives of the societies, it has also acquired an important function in informing and contacting citizens. In 2001 the European Commission's admitted in the *White Paper on European Governance*[11] that in order to assure understanding, "information on the decision-making processes should be published on the websites available to an average user" (p.4). Apart from that on-line consultation should be developed as one of the ways of the interactive policy-making initiative (p.15). The important role of information and communication technologies has been also acknowledged. It has been confirmed that the EU's EUROPA website has been set to evolve into an interactive platform for information, feedback and debate in the Europe area (p. 11). The necessity of creating trans-national platform for the citizens from different countries to discuss important – from their perspectives – EU problems, has been noted. Such arrangement has been considered a helpful tool for the policy makers to maintain proper contact with the EU public opinion and to identify Union projects supported by general public (p. 11-12). Simultaneously the importance for all Union institutions to jointly develop the Internet EU documents' database EUR-LEX has been stressed. Additionally it has been decided that the documents should be translated into all the union languages so that the citizens could follow the decision-making process (p. 12). In the *White Paper* the European Commission has also recognised the important role of civil society in mobilising people to engage or to increase interest in EU activities. It has been stressed that the civil society's voice can also constitute a sort of early warning system, important for functioning of democracy and therefore should be heard by the EU institutions. With better management comes more efficient functioning, and the bigger is people's involvement the greater is the responsibility. Thus the European Commission decided to create, still before the 2001, a comprehensive on-line database with details pertaining to civil society organisations operating in Europe that could be sort of catalyst for their international activity (pp. 14-15).

In 2005 in *Plan-D for Democracy, Dialogue and Debate*,[12] the Internet has been acknowledged as one of the prime tools in stimulating the public debate (p.

11 European Commission, European Governance, A White Paper. COM (2001) 428 final.

12 Communication from the Commission to the Council, the European Parliament, the European Economic and Social Committee and the Committee of the Regions – The Commission's contribution to the period of reflection and beyond: Plan-D for Democracy, Dialogue and Debate. COM (2005) 494 final. p. 2.

4). The Commission has come to a conclusion that in order to play an active role in moderating the debate on the future of Europe it is necessary for it to explore any interactive communication medium that could be useful in that regard. Additionally, the Commission recognised the need to employ the newest Internet technology in presenting and advocating its policies. Cyberspace was thus acknowledged to be an important opinion-forming forum of debate. (p. 10) In *Action Plan to Improve Communicating Europe by the Commission*[13] the Internet, audio-visual programmes as well as printed media have been listed as essential tools for strategy implementation. The European Commission has confirmed the opinion that Internet and audio-visual services should be used in a more coordinated and cost-effective way across the Commission. Apart from that they should be handled in a way that secures the possible greatest impact (p. 11). The emphasis has been made that EUROPA beeing the largest public website worldwide and simultaneously "a rich source of information has a key role to play in the Commission's communication efforts." It has been decided to put greater emphasis on making its resources more accessible by facilitating navigation, implementing the newest technologies and ensuring proper standard multilingual presentation of the EUROPA pages. At the same time the necessity of focusing on editing news sites, specialist pages (to be managed by the DGs) as well as sites for young people and presenting information in local languages had been stressed (pp. 4, 12).[14]

In the *White Paper on a European Communication Policy*[15] of 2006 the importance of exploration of the Internet as one of the means to reach a citizen has been noted. Possibility of complementing EU websites with online forums – "virtual meeting places" – and with links to external information sources has been taken under consideration (p. 8). It has been mentioned that some considerable efforts was already made in order to improve the communication. The intention of the European Parliament to open itself up to the public through web TV has been also noted. Besides that, it has been emphasised that EUROPA "is the largest website in the world." Despite all those efforts the access to the information on functioning of the EU is still limited (p. 8). The information revolution has essentially increased the access to information and opened up the world of "interactive" media. Nowadays unprecedented numbers of people can easily connect with one another and take part in all kinds of networks.

---

13 Communication to the Commission: Action Plan to Improve Communicating Europe. Brussels: European Union. European Commission, Brussels 2005. SEC (2005) 985 final.

14 Strategy pertaining to improvement of the EUROPA portal has been presented in a document: Communication to the Commission. Communicating about Europe via the Internet. Engaging the citizens. SEC (2007) 1742. Brussels.

15 White Paper on a European Communication Policy COM (2006) 35 final.

Nevertheless it seems that a lot of work is required to fully take advantage of the potential that the information technology offers so that the communication gap with the public could be closed (p. 9). What is important, digital technologies such as the Internet can make some other channels available for the communication on EU matters such as new public debate forums and new tools for cross-border democracy. However political leadership is needed for Europe to fully take advantage of the Internet's potential and to ensure it does not create any further divisions in society. The aim of the *i2010 Initiative*[16] is to close the gap between those members of the information society who have access to the Internet and those who have none by addressing such issues as "equal opportunities, ICT skills and the inequalities between Europe's regions in terms of Internet access" (p. 9). In the *White Paper on a European Communication Policy* it has been noted and strongly emphasised that "citizens have a right to information about Europe and its concrete projects, a right to express their views about Europe and to be heard. This is the challenge of communication – to facilitate this exchange, the learning process, the dialogue" (p. 13). Was then the effort to use the internet for improving communication successful?

In Brussels in June 2006 the European Council expressed appreciation for the Commissions contribution to the reflection period with its *Plan D*. The European Council confirmed also its commitment to assuring more democratic approach, transparency and effectiveness of its structure (section 4). It also welcomed the intention to carry on further activities aimed at involving citizens in the debate on European issues.[17] Simultaneously it stresses that reinforced dialogue with the citizens requires adequate means and commitment (section 3) although no instructions were presented.

In the Communication of 2007 *European i2010 initiative on e-Inclusion. "To be part of the information society,"*[18] the Commission noticed that "despite all these valuable initiatives" even the aims of widespread Internet access and

---

16 The initiative supports an open and competitive digital economy, research in tele-information technology as well as their implementation in improving social integration, public services and the quality of life. (European i2010 initiative on e-Inclusion "To be part of the information society". Communication from the Commission to the European Parliament, The Council, The European Economic and Social Committee and the Committee of the Regions. COM (2007) 694 final).

17 Council of the European Union. Presidency Conclusions. Brussels, 17 July 2006. 10633/1/06 REV 1, section 2.

18 European i2010 initiative on e-Inclusion. "To be part of the information society." Communication from the Commission to the European Parliament, the Council, the European Economic and Social Committee ant the Committee of the Regions. COM (2007) 694 final.

using its potentials may not be achieved because of lack of progress. The actions taken towards development of information and communication technologies still remain on the level of fragmentation and lack of cooperation is evident. "Persistent digital divides affect cohesion and prosperity" (p. 2). Social differences in information and communication technologies usage are still present and in some cases they even tend to widen (p. 3). The emphasis has been made on the necessity of "enabling the conditions for everyone to take part in the information society by bridging the broadband, accessibility and tackling competences gaps" (p. 3). The ministers on the 2006 Riga Ministerial Conference set targets to be achieved by 2010. One of the plans was to reduce "gaps between average EU population and older people, people with disabilities, women, lower education groups, unemployed and 'less-developed' regions." At the same time it was taken into account that achieving most of these targets at overall EU level would be very difficult. Especially that at the end of 2006 there were still substantial gaps present between the EU-27 average population (45% are regular Internet users) and some groups, notably people older than 65 (10% Internet users), economically inactive (17% Internet users), with low education (25% Internet users)" (p. 3). On the basis of these projections the conclusion has been made that these disparities would still not be halved by 2010. Simultaneously accessibility of public websites and their compliance with the Web Content Accessibility Guidelines 1.0 was pointed to. Here a special attention has been given to issues important for disabled people. As it has been observed at the end of 2006 the aim was "still far from target at the end of 2006" (p. 4). It has been noted though that ICT use, and in particular that of mobile telephones and Internet services, have "rapidly spread across many segments of the population." Digital gap has lessened for example between women and men, age groups, unemployed versus working force. But many challenges have still remained (p. 4). Another barrier mentioned in the document is a "lack of available content in languages understandable to potential users" (p. 4). Simultaneously it has been noticed that "even though Internet penetration continues to increase, about 50% of the European population does not use the Internet regularly." Besides that the users voices are still "fragmented and relatively weak in Europe compared to e.g. the USA" (p. 5).

In the following communication (Communicating Europe in Partnership) of 2007[19] the Commission assures about its labours to "reinforce its communication activities by providing information and engaging in debate and

---

19 Communicating Europe in Partnership. Communication from the commission to the European Parliament, the Council, The European Economic and social Committee and the Committee of the Regions. COM (2007) 568 final.

discussion with citizens..." (p. 4). The Internet has been listed next to audio-visual media, the written press and publications as one of the main means of engaging in a dialogue with the citizens and increasing transparency (p. 4). But they have been considered the preferred and main source of information on European affaires." And to them most attention has been devoted. Nevertheless in the further part of the Communication it has been admitted that the Internet is the main medium that allows "combining text, sound and vision" and enables "feedback from and discussion among seers." The emphasis has been made that EUROPA website needs redevelopment" so that it could become more accessible and more user-friendly. Increasing interactivity has been planned along with implementing more image, video and audio material (p. 11). Apart from that it has been concluded that

> the EU needs to strengthen its presence on the web beyond EUROPA. The Commission wishes to encourage the development of a network of civil society and private or public sector websites which promote contact with or between European citizens by supporting websites that devote particular attention to European affaires and stimulate debate on EU policy issues. The Commission itself should also be more involved in interviews and participation in discussions in other sites. (COM (2007) 568 final, p. 11-12)

One year later, in a document titled *Debate Europe*[20] former decisions and activities has been summarised along with those directed towards promoting two-way dialogue between the EU institutions and the citizens of the Union. It has been recognized that the afore mentioned Plan D for Democracy, Dialogue and Debate of 2005

> has played a key role in testing innovative ways in which civil society organisations could involve citizens from all walks of life in debates on the future of Europe, combining virtual and face to face communication.... (COM (2008) 158 final, p. 4)

The projects executed within Plan D have showed that „participatory democracy can usefully supplement representative democracy" (p. 5). Simultaneously the results of the studies indicate "there was sometimes a gap between citizens' expectations and the actual domains of EU competence." Therefore it has been decided that the realisation of Plan D initiatives should be carried on. In the Conclusion the emphasis has been made that the EU's activities should be, amongst other things, centred around increasing the involvement of the citizens

---

20 Debate Europe – building on the experience of Plan D for Democracy, Dialogue and Debate. Communication from the Commission to the European Parliament, the Council, The European Economic and Social Committee and the Committee of the Regions. COM (2008) 158 final.

because "the EU needs more political debate and awareness if it is to achieve its objectives and deliver the right policies" (p.11).

At the same time in 2010 *Draft Report on journalism and new media*[21] by the Committee on Culture and Education of the European Parliament the debate was considered to be the basis of democratic governance, whereas citizen's access to information and communication between policy-makers and voters were recognised as the central elements of societies based on representative democracy. It has been stressed that in order for the debate to take place the participation of committed and well-informed citizens is essential. Because, according to the *Draft Report*, public authority should be guided by means of informed and critical discourse by the people and the media. While, it has been noted, that presently there does not exist any overarching European public sphere, and there is still clear evidence that the citizens are under-informed on European issues (p. 4). The emphasis has been put on the fact that „the lack of online news and information on the EU and its institutions is not the problem," because although all of these institutions launched their own news platforms they sill failed to captivate the public (p. 5). The problem is the very fact no single and easy solution can be offered in this case and moreover the EU is a complex entity, for which simple explanations will never be sufficient (p. 8). The dialogue has been said to be one of the effective means of engaging citizens. The importance of the online social media such as Twitter and Facebook has been acknowledged owing to its ability to reach new audiences who have no interest in conventional media channels. In order to reach them it is necessary to be present where the dialogue takes place, which means taking part in online social networks. It has been noted that "social media has tremendous potential to communicate with young people, an age group that the EU has traditionally found particularly hard to reach" (p. 11). Danish deputy, Morten Løkkegaard, confirmed this observation on the European Parliament forum on 27 April 2010. He stated that "there is a wealth of information in the EU but no communication. We need to approach this on the citizen's level, a bottom-up approach, not from the top down". He also emphasised that "new social media on the internet is where the conversation takes among young people who are used not only to having access to the media but to responding to it, sharing and using information". In his opinion "new European story" could be best told

---

21   Draft Report on journalism and new media – creating a public sphere in Europe. PE - Committee on Culture and Education, rapporteur: Morten Lokkegaard. 26.03.2010. (2010/2015 (INI)). PE439.380v01-00. (http://www.europarl.europa.eu/sides/getDoc.do? pubRef=-//EP//NONSGML+COMPARL+PE-439.380+01+DOC+PDF+V0//en&language=en (14.09.2011).

through this mean of communication. He stressed that these audiences could be reached only "where the conversation takes place," i.e. Facebook, Twitter or other online social networks. Furthermore, one of the PE deputies representing centre-right party, Jean Marie Cavada, has expressed his regrets that the EU institutions due to their arrogance are not willing to "explain things clearly."[22] At the same time just a few days later (on 23 June) on the European Parliament forum the Committee on Culture and Education called for increased online activity: "The role of the interactive Internet in generating European conversations and explaining the European Union should be cautiously expanded". While the Committee warned that "although social networks are a relatively good way of disseminating information rapidly, their reliability as sources cannot always be sufficiently guaranteed and they cannot be considered to be professional media" and therefore "the Parliament and the European Union should tread delicately in this area."[23] It should be noted though that the usage of these media by societies is growing rapidly along with interest and participation of all kinds of institutions and organisations: "It took television 13 years to reach 50 million viewers.... Facebook reached 100 million users in just a few months."[24] Therefore in this context the opinion that one must be there "where the conversation takes place" seems to be even more validated.

Meanwhile the EU institutions are really cautious as far as the communication with citizens through the social media is concerned. Although the European Parliament had opened its accounts on Twitter,[25] Facebook[26] and Flicker[27] before the elections in June 2009, it turned out that the Parliament's expectations were not met as that did not bring the expected higher turn out. One of the reasons was the fact that these portals were used as means to send out information rather than to initiate any dialogue. Moreover, even if on Twitter the communications are made in the Polish language (and other European Union

---

22 New media, new conversations, a new look UE? Information, 04.05.2010. European Parliament.
    http://www.europarl.europa.eu/sides/getDoc.do?pubRef=-//EP//NONSGML+IM-PRESS+
    20100430STO73839+0+DOC+PDF+V0//EN&language=EN (14.09.2011).
23 Culture MEP's call on EU for more European online conversation, Information – 29.06.2010
    – 13:15. European Parliament. http://www.europarl.europa.eu/sides/getDoc.do?pubRef=-//
    EP//TEXT+IM-PRESS+20100625STO76792+0+DOC+XML+V0//EN (14.09.2011).
24 Culture MEP's call on EU for more European online conversation, Information – 29.06.2010
    – 13:15. European Parliament. http://www.europarl.europa.eu/sides/getDoc.do?pubRef=-//
    EP//TEXT+IM-PRESS+20100625STO76792+0+DOC+XML+V0//EN (14.09.2011).
25 http://twitter.com/Europarl_PL (15.09.2011).
26 http://www.facebook.com/europeanparliament (15.09.2011).
27 http://www.flickr.com/photos/european_parliament/ (15.09.2011).

languages), the European Parliament's Flicker and Facebook pages are presented in English. The only webpage in the Polish is the one of the PE Information Office in Warsaw. The information presented on this webpage is mainly centred around Polish issues, and the visits of Polish politicians in to Brussels and Brussels politicians in Poland, whereas the EU or other states issues are hardly ever brought up.

The EU still cannot efficiently present a uniform stance to the public opinion. Actually the institution responsible for supplying information on functioning of the EU is the European Commission. It provides materials for the reporters as well as prepares information campaigns and publications for the Europeans. Additionally, the Inter-institutional Group on Information (IGI) has been operating since 2007 and one of its main tasks is coordinating communication on the EU issues between three institutions (European Parliament, European Committee, European Council).[28] But up till now they have no common press centre. Each of the EU institutions passes information on its activity and takes separate measures to inform the citizens on its ways of functioning. There is any cooperation between them on the Internet sites.

It is worth to note that EU information is presently available on many different Internet portals. For example, since 1995 there have been functioning an Internet website of a satellite television, *Europe by Satellite* (EbS).[29] It broadcasts events related to EU activities. But the EbS portal is available only in English and French. The Internet provides also the access to a radio stations consortium EURANET[30] (available in 18 languages including Polish) as well as a trans-European television channel EuroNews.[31] The latter is directed to viewers living in Europe and abroad. It is not translated into most of the European languages including Polish.[32] The Presseurop portal has also an informative character[33] just like the EuTube[34] video services activated in 2007. The former is translated into 10 languages and the latter functions only in English, German and French. Apart from that since 2008 the European

---

28 Communicating Europe in Partnership. Communication from the commission to the European Parliament, the Council, the European Economic and social Committee and the Committee of the Regions. COM (2007) 568 final., s.5

29 http://ec.europa.eu/avservices/ebs/welcome_en.cfm (15.09.2011).

30 http://www.euranet.eu/ (15.09.2011).

31 Founded in1993. http://www.euronews.net/ (15.09.2011).

32 Other languages are: English, German, French, Italian, Spanish, Turkish, Russian, Ukrainian, Portuguese, Arabic and Persian. And from 2012: Polish.

33 Presents information and articles on European issues available in European journals http://www.presseurop.eu/pl (15.09.2011).

34 http://www.youtube.com/user/eutube (15.09.2011).

Parliament has its own Internet television EuroparlTV.[35] It has mainly an informative character. In the Young Parliament section there is an interesting tab "Let's Talk – Talking Europe."[36] It includes short, of a dozen minutes or so long video clips (translated to EU languages) of Euro deputies' debates with the students from different countries including Poland. Its major function is an informative one. It deals with topics ranging from European Parliament elections to matters such as immigration, EU armed forced or Turkey's EU membership. They can be used as initial material for other groups of citizens interested in organizing similar debates on issues that are important to them. The question remains, who knows about the existence of this page or other Internet portals? As for my knowledge, there are no campaigns being run for advertising the websites directed to an average Internet user.

EUROPA is certainly an important portal to be used by the member states' societies dealing the EU matters, which is administered by the European Commission[37]. It contains basic information about EU member states, institutions, topics, activities, and conditions of life. It also provides access to the most important – from clerks' point of view – documents and union publications. Apart from that it presents contacts through which one can regularly receive bulletins on activities of individual EU institutions or electronic versions of documents. In this regard though one must contact respective Commission or Parliament offices. But all these elements still have just an informative character. The attempt to go beyond this function seems to be the "Take part!" tab. And indeed after clicking the "More about taking part" link, one can find a message: "Have your say! Join an online debate, take part in a public consultation or check out and comment on blogs and video clips."[38] It clearly shows that the purpose behind it is to inspire the people who use the portal to actively participate in the "Union's life." Blogs run by commissioners or other member states' officials allow to look at the EU matters from the point of view of the people directly involved with decision-making processes and might stimulate a debate. But their character is chiefly informative. Moreover the access to these blogs is limited because they are written in English, or sometimes in a native language of a person in charge a blog. Thus, although there is possibility to write comments on the contributions there are not many of them. Some of the contributions have no comments or at the most two or three. I

---

35 http://www.europarltv.europa.eu/ (16.09.2011).
36 http://www.europarltv.europa.eu/pl/young-parliament/let%27s-talk.aspx. (16.09.2011).
37 Information on institutions, history, decision-making process, access to documents issued by the EU institutions, etc. - http://europa.eu/ (16.09.2011).
38 http://europa.eu/take-part/index_en.htm (16.09.2011).

am not sure if numbers such as 6 to 7 thousand people who saw a contribution (but not necessarily read it) should be the reason for delight.[39] Another tab on the website features the information on the visits' schedule, that means it includes information about visiting Brussels and has no influence on dialogue development.

In the above mentioned "Take part!" tab there is a link to the *Prizes & Competitions* section. In this section the EU announces competitions for academics, journalists, students and pupils. In fact only special achievements in different fields are taken into consideration, although very often they focus around the European issues. Their purpose is to promote and publicise information about the EU, e.g. competitions for the EU logo or poster for the European Union days. The EU clerks rather check in this way how these institutions are being perceived by the citizens or what they are associated with. This initiates certain relations, but does it bring about any regular dialogue?

Some elements of communication can be certainly observed on some social networking services. They are connected with another Internet tab called: "Connect with EU on social networks." As I have already mentioned herein, some institutions, agencies or EU offices have created their official profiles on networks the aim of which is information exchange. Nevertheless they focus on passing information on themselves. For example, the sentence that is shown on the Twitter EP PressService: "President Jerzy Buzek on massacres in Norway,"[40] can hardly be seen as something more than just a short notice. It is true that these short sentences are linked to Internet sites. But there one can only find some additional information. Most of these are presented only in English, which definitely limits the number of receivers. What is interesting, next to the Twitter run by the EP PressService, there exists also the European Parliament's Twitter. This one is already available in different national languages. Nevertheless the communications given are not identical. While on the Polish website there is an entry: "Obejrzyjcie zaproszenie na wystawę 'Zaprojektowane dla prezydencji' przygotowane przez samych twórców," (which literally means: "See the invitation to the exhibition 'Designed for Presidency' prepared by artists themselves,"[41] the English language website entry is: "Return of the mythbuster: 'The EU budget is decided by Eurocrats without democratic procedures!' Wrong!... http://bit.ly/EUmyth5 #ep."[42] It is true they are still just

---

39   Blogs. Commissioners: Maria Damanaki – Commissioner for Maritime Affairs and Fisheries http://blogs.ec.europa.eu/damanaki/ (16.09.2011).
40   http://twitter.com/#!/EuroParlPress (16.09.2011).
41   http://twitter.com/Europarl_PL (16.09.2011).
42   http://twitter.com/#!/Europarl_EN (16.09.2011).

information, but they deal with completely different matters. So it seems that the communication between EU institutions and citizens takes place on Facebook. Under each communication released by the European Parliament there appear comments by different people. The number of these comments ranges from just a few to a few hundreds. But commonly there are from a dozen or so comments to about sixty. Sometimes[43] there are live chats organised with the participation of Euro-parliamentarians. There is also a discussion forum on which the users can express their opinions on different topics. The question is though to what extend the opinions appearing on Facebook are being heard and taken into consideration by the PE deputies while they make decisions. Apart from that, one may wonder whether the "I like it!" tab may be considered a reliable tool in the assessment of the European Parliament's activity? Besides that the problem is the fact that the EP's Facebook page is run in the English language. The information on the EP's Warsaw Office page is centred around national events and competitions. There are some single comments on different entries. There is even place for a discussion, but one can also observe the lack of those. Two entries (one from a year ago, another from 7 months ago) have not initiated any discussion. Similar is the situation on page of the European Parliament Office in Ireland. The entries are not long, just some single comments or "I like it!" clicks.[44] But the EP Information Office in the United Kingdom has not got any page on Facebook (as per 19 September 2011).

Meanwhile the English language page of the European Commission is totally desolate in comparison with the PE's page. No discussion is held there, and there are at maximum few comments on an entry.[45] Not much better looks the page of the European Commission Representation Office in Poland.[46] But while on this page one can still find a few comments, on the UK European Commission's page there are evidently none. The entries themselves are very

---

43 In fact there are no hard and fast rules in this regard. The last life chat has been organized on 15 September 2011 with Diogo Feio and Sylvie Goulard on economic governance. The previous ones were the 19 July 2011 chat on refugees and migrations flows in North Africa with Parliament's member Judith Sargentini, from the Greens/EFA, 12 July 2011 with Parliament's Liberal leader, Guy Verhofstadt, and 27 June 2011 with Jerzy Buzek, EP president.
    (http://www.facebook.com/europeanparliament?sk=app_188929731130869#!/europeanp arliament?sk=wall, [16.09.2011]).
44 http://www.facebook.com/pages/European-Parliament-Office-in-Ireland/374974667323. (19.09.2011).
45 http://www.facebook.com/europeanparliament?sk=app_188929731130869#!/ EuropeanCommission (16.09.2011).
46 http://www.facebook.com/europeanparliament?sk=app_188929731130869#!/ komisjaeuropejska (16.09.2011).

poor.[47] I must admit that the Facebook page of the European Commission in Ireland[48] looks much better. This can be seen not only by the number of "I like it!" clicks: 2 857 as per 16 September 2011. There are over half a thousand of them more than on the British page (1 011) not only under the entries but also under the comments that appear there. It is important to add that on the Polish page there are 4 235 "I like it!" clicks, whereas on the main European Commission site there are 15 716 of them.

The official Internet website of the European Parliament Information Office in Poland is – as the name speaks for itself – typically an informative one. One can find there EP Information Office's bulletins, publications on the EP, information about trainings and bids. The only opportunity for a visiting persons to express themselves is to write an email or make a phone call.[49] Similar situation is on the official webpage of the EP Information Office in Ireland[50] and EP Information Office in the United Kingdom.[51] These are pages of typically informative character with a possibility of enquiry. In cases of Polish and Irish pages both have the same graphic design and similar content. Whereas the British page differs in the colours used and it emphasises the information given. For example it has a column dedicated only to the PE elections, addressed to the media and the EuroAcademy for the teachers and students. The European Commission Representation offices web pages in Poland,[52] Ireland[53] or Great Britain[54] are informative.

However, an important section on the EUROPA portal seems to be the link to "Have your say on policies" webpage. At the very beginning appears the information: "Interested in getting involved in European policy making? You can take part in public consultations, petition the European Parliament or participate in surveys and debates. In the near future, you will also be able to launch a European Citizens' Initiative".[55] We can see here not only the realisation of the approach "explain better" but also signs of listening to the voices of the citizens, as well as starting and stimulating broader debate. The

---

47   http://www.facebook.com/europeanparliament?sk=app_188929731130869#!/ECinUK (16.09.2011).
48   http://www.facebook.com/europeanparliament?sk=app_188929731130869#!/EUIreland (16.09.2011).
49   http://www.europarl.pl/view/pl/index.html (19.09.2011).
50   http://www.europarl.ie/view/en/Homepage.html (19.09.2011).
51   http://www.europarl.org.uk/section/infocentre/infocentre (19.09.2011).
52   http://ec.europa.eu/polska/index_pl.htm (19.09.2011).
53   http://ec.europa.eu/ireland/press_office/index_en.htm (19.09.2011).
54   http://ec.europa.eu/unitedkingdom/ (19.09.2011).
55   http://europa.eu/take-part/consultations/index_en.htm (16.09.2011).

best example of that are public consultations. When starting the work on a new political initiative or reviewing the already existing legislation, the European Commission opens consultation on a particular topic. What does that mean? Individual persons, enterprises or organisations interested in a particular topic may express their opinion. But it is important to be up to date with *Your Voice in Europe* portal,[56] where appear the information on further open consultations in any particular field. As the creators of the afore mentioned portal assure, one can also take part in active policy-making through participation in on-line forums available for those interested, discussions on the officials' blogs as well as through advisory and informative services or direct contact with PE deputies, Committee of the Regions representatives or members of the European Economic and Social Committee. Unfortunately citizens' activity and participation in "Interactive Policy Making" is limited by the fact that most information which is supposed to stimulate a debate – that includes a set of Minimum Standards on Consultation[57] – is not being translated to all the European Union languages, Polish among other. Additionally the research conducted on the topic shows that the *Your Voice in Europe* website is known only to a small percentage of the citizens.[58]

The new form of activating the EU public, which is addressed in "Have your say on policies" column on EUROPA portal, is the European Citizens Initiative.[59] One million citizens representing a significant number (minimum 7) of the EU member states, due to the regulations of the Treaty of Lisbon (2009), may directly turn to the European Commission to take up a legislative initiative on matters falling under the EU's competence. But they have no guarantee, that their point of view will be heard or will there be created a legal act meeting their expectations. Moreover, every citizen – acting individually or in collaboration

---

56 http://ec.europa.eu/yourvoice/index_pl.htm (16.09.2011).

57 European Commission (2005) Towards a reinforced culture of consultation and dialogue - General principles and minimum standards for consultation of interested parties by the Commission, COM(202) 704 final.

58 http://ec.europa.eu/yourvoice/results/4/index_en.htm, accessed 16 September 2011. For example the survey conducted by the Polish Public Opinion Research Centre (Centrum Badania Opinii Społecznej, CBOS) has shown that the Internet page *Your Voice in Europe* is known only to 10.1% of all the surveyed Polish firms. http://webcache.googleusercontent.com/search?q=cache:4fNWh0AY5ucJ:www.mg.gov. pl/NR/rdonlyres/58E62D7C-07CC-4DF68C57D2FBDBFD125F/31682/konsultacje.doc+ Zestaw+minimalnych+standard%C3%B3w+konsultacji+wg+Komisji+Europejskiej&cd= 1&hl=pl&ct=clnk&gl=pl&client=firefox-a, p. 10 (26.10.2011).

59 http://ec.europa.eu/dgs/secretariat_general/citizens_initiative/index_pl.htm (26.10.2011).

with other people – may at any point file a petition to the EP.[60] "Such petitions – as it has been assured – give the European Parliament the opportunity of calling attention to any infringement of a European citizen's rights by a Member State or local authorities or other institution."[61] It must be noted though that the Parliament looks into the petitions concerning only particular matters. Such petitions may contain an individual request, a complaint or observation connected to the application of EU law or they may include an appeal to the European Parliament to take a stance on a specific issue. One must be conscious though, that the European Parliament does not issue any binding decisions on matters presented in the petitions. It may or may not issue a resolution on a particular matter or take it into consideration in its legislative work.

In section *Have your say on policies* one may also find online debates and surveys organised by The European Commission on particular issues. The surveys are limited though to some basic questions and simplified responses. They do not give any possibility to express detailed opinion on very often complex issues. It is hard to call it a dialogue. Surely along with the legislative initiative and petitions that can be filed by the citizens the EU institutions receive a feedback on their activities. Once more the problem is translation, as this section is available only in English, German and French.

Indeed the EUROPA portal itself, as well as other websites mentioned before, contains great deal of information on the EU's functioning and institutions. The problem with the EU's communication with the citizens through the Internet is not a result of a lack of information on the EU, but rather of a fact that most of these webpages have a one-way character, whereas a communication is a two-way process involving dialogue.[62] These webpages do not guarantee that the citizens will be heard. Additional problem is a fact that not all the parties, and at the same time not all the information, are translated to all the official EU languages which to a great extend limits the circle of potential recipients. At the same time it is hard to speak about stimulating any kind of

---

60   Annually there are about 1500 of such petitions filed with the PE (Petitions Committee: listening to the EU's citizens, 23-09-2008 - 13:00; http://www.europarl.europa.eu/ sides/getDoc.do?type=IM-PRESS&reference=20080922IPR37788&language=EN [26.10.2011]).

61   http://www.europarl.europa.eu/parliament/public/staticDisplay.do?language=EN&id=49 (19.09.2011).

62   Draft Report on journalism and new media – creating a public sphere in Europe. PE - Committee on Culture and Education, rapporteur: Morten Lokkegaard. 26.03.2010. (2010/2015 (INI)). PE439.380v01-00, s. 5, 9. http://www.europarl.europa.eu/sides/ getDoc.do?pubRef=-//EP//NONSGML+COMPARL+PE-439.380+01+DOC+PDF+V0// en&language=en (14.09.2011).

debate amongst all the citizens of the EU member states, not to speak of a regular debate. Another problem is the fact that the citizens did not like the EU institutions' information platforms as they are not clear enough and are hard to understand. The reason is not only the terminology used in the documents, but also lack of translations. Apart from that Internet websites are "no guarantee of creating interest among citizens in Member States."[63] And still a question arises what percentage of the citizens has any idea that such websites do exist. Discussions with the students conducted during classes on the European Union show that they do not know any EU Internet portals and so far they have not felt any need to get to know them. Meanwhile, in the days of information technology – when the Internet is indeed an important means allowing to establish contacts and relations giving a chance to engage the largest possible number of people in political life – the EU institutions use this means only to a limited extend. It is simply one of the sources of information and nothing more than that.

Translated by Iwona Szuwalska

---

63 Ibidem.

The Taiwan's intelligence services in cross-strait intelligence war

Sebastian Michalak

This article is an effort to characterise the Taiwanese intelligence services. At the beginning the genesis and the most important periods in the process of institutionalisation of those intelligence agencies have been described. Further the main methods of intelligence activity towards China have been presented. Then those episodes from the history of the services that appeared the most important from the evolution of methods and means of work perspective have been analysed as well as the current state of intelligence struggle across the Taiwan Strait have been assessed. The main sources drawn upon for the purpose of this discussion are the English language Taiwanese press and the source literature.

In the 1949-1986 period the political system of the Republic of China (ROC) was based on one-party rule with a strong executive, pervasive police control and frequent use of military courts (Copper, 2009, 107). The military and other parts of a security apparatus were the foundation of the authoritarian regime and played a significant political role in Taiwan. By the late 1980s the control over the ruling nationalist party Kuomintang (KMT) began changing from the cadres consisting mostly of the Mainland Chinese to local Taiwanese politicians. The KMT abolished martial law in 1987 and legalised the formation of new political parties. In 1988 the president Chiang Ching-kuo was succeeded by Lee Teng-hui whose presidency symbolised the end of the Mainland Chinese minority's hold on political authority (Copper, 2009, 53). With the presidential and parliamentary elections of 2000 and 2001 the Democratic Progressive Party (DPP) became the first party to oust the KMT from the government.

Until 1986 the most important political decisions in the ROC were made by and within the KTM. That party to a large extent controlled or manipulated the government (Copper, 2009, 133). The KMT took its organisational structure from the Communist Party of the Soviet Union. The party's activities were broad and involved guiding or dictating government policies (Copper, 2009, 132-133). The KMT had also intelligence organs that executed intelligence functions independent of the government's intelligence services while receiving full state financial support. Two KMT's intelligence agencies, the Mainland Working Commission (MWC) and Overseas Working Commission (OWC), participated in the monthly intelligence meetings convened by the ROC defence minister. Both agencies were recognised as formal members of the Taiwan's intelligence community (Tzeng, 2009, 72). Taiwan's secret services were developed from the intelligence branches of the KMT. The Intelligence Bureau grew out of the KMT's Military Statistics Bureau (MSB). The Investigation Bureau acting as domestic security intelligence began as the KMT's Central Statistics Bureau (Tzeng, 2009, 51). Although the director of the MWC was also the director of the Intelligence Bureau, the MWC recruited, trained and dispatched its own agents and informants to gather intelligence and perform clandestine activities in the mainland China (Tzeng, 2009, 72-73). The MWC targeted the mainland China and – in tandem with the Intelligence Bureau – used the state budget to deploy agents inside the mainland China to perform intelligence operations. The OWC worked on collecting intelligence from overseas Chinese communities and its offices were often located inside the official embassies (Tzeng, 2009, 52). The OWC agents usually had their overseas liaison offices inside embassy buildings and worked without hiding their identities (Tzeng, 2009, 73).

In 1957 the National Security Bureau (NSB) was founded "to coordinate international and mainland China intelligence activities and to supervise internal security intelligence and domestic public security" (Tzeng, 2009, 57). Whereas "in matters of domestic public security, the NSB became involved only in significant issues and events" (Tzeng, 2009, 59). During 1960-1975 the NSB cooperated with the US intelligence services in realisation of operational activities in the area of signals and human intelligence in and around the mainland China. Taipei from its own side would perform the tasks mainly through human intelligence assets controlled by the military intelligence (Tzeng, 2009, 57). The NSB was blocking overseas political dissidents. They were considered potential collaborators with the Chinese Communist regime and foreign conspiracy powers (Tzeng, 2009, 66). Taiwan's military intelligence services focussed on collecting intelligence, organising and conducting covert actions – that included subversive actions against the PRC – as well as fighting political opposition in Taiwan (Philips, 2009, 173-174). Till the end of the 1960s the military intelligence would conduct covert actions aiming at destabilising the PRC's authorities (Philips, 2009, 178). Taiwan's agents had been moving into and out of the mainland China from the offshore islands. The military intelligence conducted intelligence gathering operations in the mainland China acting for example under cover of a fishing company set up in Keelung in 1964. The company's fishermen had not been informed of the nature of their work. In July 1964 China intercepted two of the company's fishing boats and their crews' members were detained and tortured (Taipei Times, Aug 10, 2002). Most American officials dismissed human intelligence on the PRC produced during the 1950s and 1960s by Taiwan's intelligence services as essentially unreliable.

In the late 1960s, the CIA in Hong Kong learned that Beijing had compromised Taiwan's intelligence operations against the mainland. Taiwan's intelligence operations against the mainland China involved fast attacks such as blowing up a bridge, obtaining local documents or kidnaping local Communist cadre. They neither did any significant damage to the mainland China's economy nor impaired its military preparedness. Apart from that these operations did not provide any important information (Taylor, 2009, 454-455). The quality of information obtained from the military intelligence agents decreased after the first-generation of agents who had been left behind after 1949 withered (Tzeng, 2009, 167).

Taiwan's isolation from the international community – which was a result of its loss of recognition in the mid- and late 1970s – made its overseas intelligence operations and cooperation very difficult. The attention of the intelligence services gradually turned inward to internal security as well as overseas Chinese society (Tzeng, 2009, 84). The Intelligence Bureau started to recruit intelligence operatives from amongst Chinese emigrants (Philips, 2009, 61). In 1984 gangsters acting on the order of the military intelligence, assassinated in San Francisco an American citizen, Henry Liu, who was a triple agent working for the American, Chinese and Taiwanese secret services. The operation conducted on the US territory brought about crisis in relations between Taipei and Washington. The intelligence officers responsible for the assassination were expelled from the service and sentenced to imprisonment. The government of the ROC changed the lines of the military intelligence's activities. They were forbidden to interfere with the internal policy, business relationships and conducting covert intelligence operations, which the US government considered illegal. It pertained to actions on the US territory as well as in Thailand and Laos. In 1985 as a result of joining the Intelligence Bureau with the MND's Special Intelligence Office, the Military Intelligence Bureau (MIB) was founded and its tasks were the collection, processing, analysis and dissemination of military intelligence on the mainland China. Thus the Intelligence Bureau lost its institutional autonomy and the character of the strategic intelligence agency. The reform empowered the MND's chief of the general staff to supervise the MIB (Tzeng, 2009, 86). The MIB's mission was to obtain intelligence that is important for Taiwan's defence system (Philips, 2009, 176). In the mid 1980s there was control conducted in the MWC, which exposed inefficiency of this agency's actions. The government withheld subventions for this institution as a result of which its intelligence operations were terminated. In this way the KMT lost the possibility to independently procure intelligence (Tzeng, 2009, 87). However, the KMT's intelligence branches were the medium between Taiwan's intelligence services and overseas Chinese dissidents (Tzeng, 2009, 138).

Despite of reform that was enacted at the end of 1980s, the intelligence services were still deeply involved in domestic politics. Political surveillance against the opposition in the country was still very severe and overseas dissidents were not allowed to return home (Tzeng, 2009, 95-96). In the second half of 1992, right after the abolishment of the Garrison Command, the MIB took over its espionage personnel and equipment. The arrangement of absorbing the apparatus that was in charge of domestic espionage into the MIB structures allowed to make the public think the target was the mainland China and not the local politicians (Tzeng, 2009, 147). Presently, the MIB's Office for Electronic and Information Development is able to tap into phone lines, cell phones, and electronic signals deep into the Chinese mainland. There is an important signal intelligence facility in Linkou in northern Taiwan. Another facility is Linyuan Base, constructed in 2000, where imagery and signal intelligence are collected from China and from the sea region started operating in 2003 (Taipei Times, 26, 2010).

Taiwan's strategic thinking has always been dominated by the threat of the PRC's use of force (Copper, 2009, 197). During 1949–1990 the ROC government continued to claim jurisdiction over the mainland China. During the 1950's and early 1960s most of the government's officials believed they were soon to come back from Taiwan to the mainland and take over the power. Thus Taipei continued its "three no policy" – no compromise, no contact and no negotiation with the PRC – waiting for reunification. Eventually, in the late 1980's the ROC government began permitting Taiwan's citizens to visit the mainland China. Taipei began also stabilising relations with the PRC. It established some organs responsible for economic and social relations as well as institutions that were to negotiate the reunification. In 1991 the Taiwan's government gave up its claim to represent the whole China and announced the end of the Chinese civil war. Taiwan's economic ties with the mainland China strengthened significantly after 1990, both in terms of the amount of investment money flowing from Taiwan to the mainland and in overall cross-straits trade. By 2005 the PRC had become Taiwan's most important trading partner. During 2000-2008 period president Chen Shui-bai followed the policy of Taiwan's independence. The dialogue with the PRC was disrupted. In 2005 Beijing adopted an anti-secession law codifying the use of force to take back the island to the Chinese fold if independence was declared. After years of tension, relations between Taiwan and the mainland China warmed up after president Ma Ying-jeou had taken the office in May 2008. In July 2008 first direct passenger flights between Taiwan and the mainland China took place. Postal and shipping services were established between the two sides improving thus their economic exchange.

In 1990 the MIB recruited Chang Chih-peng, a Taiwanese businessman operating in the mainland China. During 1990-1996 the agent Chang procured two valuable human intelligence assets who were two high rank PLA officers. The recruitment most probably took place in 1992 (Tzeng, 2009, 124). Few days before the first direct presidential elections on Taiwan were called on March 1996, the PRC conducted military manoeuvres and the series of rocket missile tests in the waters around the island. This was the second faze of the military exercises initiated in the summer 1995. Chang claimed to have passed to the Taiwan's military intelligence the information coming form the agent working with the armaments section of the PLA's General Logistics Department that the rocket missiles were not fitted with warheads (Taipei Times, Mar 04, 2000). In 1996 the president of the ROC, Lee Teng-hui, disclosed this fact to the public opinion, which from Chang's point of view was an act of illegal disclosure of classified information. In August 1999 in the PRC two PLA officers were executed for espionage on behalf of Taiwan. Chang maintained that they were his agents. Business manager of Chang's Hong Kong office was also taken to prison to serve a sentence of 20 years (Taipei Times, Jun 27, 2001). Chang claimed that Beijing took over his business and blocked his assets deposited in Chinese banks. He himself was able to escape to Taiwan where he approached the MIB with a request to pay him compensation for material damage incurred as a result of exposing his activity and to grant help to his imprisoned collaborator. The amount of compensation offered by the MIB was not satisfying for the former agent. In March 2000, during a press conference organised especially for that purpose, Chang told the reporters about his espionage past and publicly accused Lee of unlawful disclosure of classified information, which in the former agent's opinion helped the Chinese security organs expose his spy ring. During the press conference Chang appealed to Taiwan's authorities to organise a funeral for the executed officers and to grant help to those who had been arrested. President Lee denied Chang's accusations and the ROC's Ministry of National Defence refused to comment on this matter (Taipei Times, Mar 04, 2000). In May 2000 the press reported that Chang decided to go to Beijing and surrender himself to the authorities there in exchange for freeing the employee of his company. The former agent was also planning to take legal action in order to gain compensation for the damage he had incurred (Taipei Times, May 06, 2000). In June 2000 he approached the MIB and NSB directors with an appeal to pay compensation to the families of the executed Chinese officers and to bring to Taiwan other exposed agents (Taipei Times, Jun 09, 2000). In December 2000 the former agent lodged a complained against the president of ROC. Half a year later, because of the hazard of revealing the state secret the ROC's authorities did not permit Chang to leave and they detained him at the international Taipei airport. In the interview given the same month for *Taipei Times* Chang held the MIB chief directly responsible for exposing the personal intelligence sources. According to Chang's statement of president Lee directed the suspicions of the PRC's security organs, but did not provide evidence necessary to charge and sentence the suspected spies. Chang said that the MIB director had sent to the PRC an agent named Yang, who was to run intelligence activity while Chang was away. The fact that this agent went to Beijing and was in possession of the voice recording of one of the agents cooperating with Chang provided, according to Chang, the Chinese security services the evidence that the person was guilty of the espionage crime (Taipei Times, Jun 29, 2001). It is hard to assess to what extent were the allegations presented by Chang real. There is a great possibility that the PRC did not want to waste warheads and following the example of other countries used for the manoeuvres the unfitted missiles. President Lee did not need § in order to present such thesis. Apart from that the ROC's military intelligence could attain such knowledge simply by taking over one of such missiles discharged in the first series of the tests (Taipei Times, Jun 30, 2001). His own view on the matter expresses Lai Changxing, the author of the book titled *The Dark Secrets Behind the Yuanhua Case*, who maintains that the person responsible for the death of the ROC agents was Yeh Ping-nan, the chief of the MIB's residence in Hong Kong, who shortly before his retirement decided to turn to the PRC's side. For the sake of encouragement, he presented to the security organs the list including names of few agents operating on the PRC's territory. Soon after that he retired from his duties. Beijing took up the game and invited Yeh for a meeting with the agents from the Ministry of State Security. At the beginning of 1999 Yeh went for a business trip to Fujian Province where he was detained (Taipei Times, Aug 21, 2001). After his release from the prison Yeh returned to Taiwan in May 2003. The MIB refused to comment on the alleged relation between Yeh and the collapse of Taiwan's intelligence network in Hong Kong and China (Taipei Times, Jun 26, 2003).

Today it is known that in January 1996 the Taiwan's intelligence was aware of the fact that the PLA was planning to conduct in March the military exercises with rocket missiles. Taipei knew also that the missiles would not be fitted with the warheads. The PRC was not intending to attack the island. The manoeuvres were an element of the psychological war. Beijing was hoping to frighten the voters and thwart president Lee's plans of re-election. Lee knew the intelligence reports and used this knowledge for his electoral campaign, which brought adverse results for MIB's intelligence operating inside the PLA. Out of fear of the exposure of the intelligence sources human intelligence assets were disconnected en masse. The MIB and NSB were forced to take up alternative measures by collecting intelligence from Taiwanese businessmen and Chinese dissidents in exile, which significantly impaired the quality of intelligence (Tzeng, 2009, 126). The loss of agents was undoubtedly the failure of the military intelligence. In December 2001 the MIB informed the press that it suspended the operations conducted in the mainland China. One of the reasons was the loss of connection with some of the agents who during 1999-2001 broke contacts with case officers (Taipei Time, Dec 11, 2001). Until 2008 there were no direct airline connections between the island and the mainland China. Therefore the meetings of the agents with the case officers took place in Hong Kong (Taipei Times, Nov 14, 2010). Until 1997 the MIB was controlling the activity of the agents operating in the mainland China from Hong Kong. The MIB's station in Hong Kong had a limited number of staff and it were in fact the KTM's local workers who were gathering most of the intelligence. The KMT for many years maintained quite an extensive intelligence network in Hong Kong (Taipei Times, Jun 26, 2003). After 1997 the Taiwan's military intelligence developed its intelligence stations in the Southeast Asia (Taipei Times, Jul 19, 2006). Some meetings with the Chinese agents took place in Vietnam (Taipei Times, Jul 21, 2006). Another failure on the part of the MIB came in June 2006 when its agent residing on the PRC's territory, colonel Chu Kung-hsun, who was in charge of the MIB's Southeast Asian intelligence network, was arrested (Taipei Times, Jul 19, 2006).

The Chang's issue put into question the ROC government's ability to protect the safety of its agents but it first of all brought up the problem of the intelligence officer's loyalty (Taipei Times, Jun 30, 2001). Until the 1980s the basic Taiwan's secret services' cadre comprised mostly of people coming from the mainland China who supported the KMT's views on the reunification of China. This cadre was quite a hermetic circle. Most of the intelligence personnel have come from the military background (Taipei Times, Sep 29, 2000). The Investigation Bureau transformed later into the Ministry of Justice Investigation Bureau (MJIB) – that is the civil counterintelligence and internal security service – was exceptional in this regard as it employed mainly civilians. Nevertheless until 1994 the service's directors were exclusively military officers. Usually the mission of managing the services was entrusted to graduates of the KMT's Huang Pu Military Academy. The training camps for the services' recruits were also militarised. (Tzeng, 2009, 67). The NSB tended to employ some experienced officers of the military secret services, policemen and some recruits straight from the training camps that were organised jointly by the Investigation Bureau and Police Academy. Many of the intelligence officers would follow their family role models, taking example of their parents working in the security structures of the KMT. They were thought that the biggest enemies of the ROC are the Chinese Communist Party and the independence movements in Taiwan. The intelligence officers were expected to exhibit absolute loyalty not only towards their country but also towards their superiors. The political officers had cultivated in the uniformed services the ideal of identifying the national interests with the KMT's policy. In 1980s Mainland Chinese from the military, security and intelligence services were gradually replaced by Taiwanese who were less committed to the KMT's cause of unification of China (Philips, 2009, 170). In the 1990s the intelligence community was already internally divided. The higher rank intelligence officers were convinced that the process of personnel replacement was threatening the efforts of unifying China. They themselves were trying to stay true to their ideas. This was not easy due to the changes in the party's courses as well as the growing distance between the KTM organs and the state institutions. The process of normalisation of the relations with the PRC that had been started by KMT and after that taking over the power by the DPP caused for some of the intelligence officers a serious identity and loyalty crisis. The officers observed how so-far hard-line anti-Communists from the KMT supported better relations with the PRC (Copper, 2009, 136). And thus the ideal of being true to the ROC in Taiwan was questioned. Some of the younger officers would even look into the vision of an independent Taiwan propagated by the supporters of the opposing DDP. The victory of this fraction's candidates in the presidential elections of 2000 seemed to make the realisation of this postulate closer. Native Taiwanese leaders promoted a stronger Taiwanese identity. Therefore many of the Mainland Chinese suspected that they favoured the ideal of Taiwan's independence from the PRC. In fact many DPP members supported independence or permanent separation of both states (Copper, 2009, 135). As a result of the independence aspirations of the DDP government, some mainland intelligence agents lost their spirits and were no longer eager to risk their lives (Taipei Times, Oct 28, 2001). Thus many the Mainland Chinese living in Taiwan started to develop private contacts with the PRC. Some intelligence officers decided to resign from their service and retire in order to start doing business in the mainland China (Taipei Times, Dec 27, 2001). For example, in November 2003 two employees of the military intelligence who were friends to each other were detained in Taiwan on the charges of espionage on behalf of the PRC (Taipei Times, Nov 15, 2003). One of them, who had been already retired, had been recruited during one of his stays in mainland China. The other one had remained in active service and was passing his friend intelligence that was later being faxed to Beijing (Taipei Times, Nov 14, 2003). This example shows that the former officer's mainland visits always posed a serious risk of unlawful disclosure of classified information (Philips, 2009, 183).

At the beginning of June 2000 the press in Taiwan informed that Pan Hsi-hsien, a former head of the NSB's Personnel and General Affairs Department, broke the binding emigration laws and flew to Shenzhen in the PRC. The NSB management baffled by the report, maintained that the Ministry of the Interior had not informed the service on time about the change of laws concerning traveling of the retired agents (Taipei Times, Jun 26, 2000). The wife of the retired officer said that he had not been aware that the amended regulations had come into force (Taipei Times, Jul 02, 2000). The NSB's general director admitted during a press conference that the service knew nothing about the travelling plans of its former officer (Taipei Times, Jul 01, 2000). The NBP's internal investigation disclosed that he had spoken about his travelling plans to his colleagues during the farewell party organised to celebrate the end of his service. This information clearly did not reach the NBP's director (Taipei Times, Jul 24, 2000). The emigration authorities did not stop the former officer from leaving the island since they did not receive from the NBP the information about his retirement. The emigration laws amended in March 2000 obliged the service to inform about such matters within 14 days. Since the purpose of Pan's trip was not known there was a suspicion that he might pose danger to Taiwan's security. The DPP members of the Parliament called the government to launch a preliminary investigation in this regard (Taipei Times, Jun 28, 2000). At the end of June 2000 the NSB informed the media that the investigation did not show any disclosure of classified information concerning Taiwan's intelligence operating in the PRC (Taipei Times, Jun 29, 2000). At the beginning of July the press informed that on the 30th of June Pan had been arrested by the mainland China's security services. Then the Taiwan's authorities appealed to the mainland China's authorities to free their former intelligence officer (Taipei Times, Jul 02, 2000). The Straits Exchange Foundation sent a message in this regard to its mainland counterpart, the Association for Relations Across the Taiwan Strait (Taipei Times, Jul 04, 2000). It was still not known whether Pan turned to the PRC's side and what could be the potential results of such treachery. The NSB's general director was trying to pacify the public opinion and said at the press conference that Pan had only had some knowledge on personnel and the NBS operational activities on the island and thus could not pass to the PRC services about any crucial information jeopardising safety of Taiwan's intelligence agents operating on the PRC's territory. At the same time, he admitted that the NSB has committed a serious mistake failing to stop Pan from breaking the law (Taipei Times, Jul 02, 2000). According to NSB, the immediate purpose of Pan's trip was a business meeting. Pan's wife said he travelled to Shenzhen to meet the representatives of subsidiary company of a Taiwan-based firm that had reportedly offered him a position as a deputy

general manager (Taipei Times, Jul 01, 2000). She meant a branch of the
Taiwan-based Tiwen electronics company in Shenzhen (Taipei Times, Jul 04,
2000). The governmental investigation showed that the NSB had discipline
problems amongst its staff but Pan's motives remained unrevealed (Taipei
Times, Jul 21, 2000). In September 2000 the press reported that they had been
informed by some anonymous intelligence members about Pan's having left the
PRC and flown to the United States. According to the informants the services of
the PRC had arrested the former officer in order to convince Taipei that Pan had
testified under pressure. Opposing the NSB's statement the anonymous
informants maintained that the intelligence archives contained evidence Pan had
been responsible for training agents for operating in the mainland as well as had
been involved with passing intelligence between Taiwan and the USA. Apart
from that Pan was allegedly also responsible for employment, assessment and
training of the intelligence officers (Taipei Times, Sep 14, 2000). As per the
informants opinion the PRC authorities had freed the former officer simply
because he had not been needed any longer. His arrival to the USA had been
probably arranged by the American authorities, which wanted to cover the
details of their intelligence cooperation with Taiwan. As opposed to those
reports the NSB maintained that Pan was still held in the PRC's jail (Taipei
Times, Sep 29, 2000). In March 2001 the NSB's spokeswoman told the
reporters that the former officer resided in one of the mainland China regions
and could freely move around that zone. She also added that at that time he did
not contact the Taiwanese-owned company he allegedly worked for (Taipei
Times, Mar 20, 2001). Pan came back to Taiwan in April 2004. During an
organised press conference the former officer stated that while going to the
mainland China he had no knowledge of legal consequences of his actions. He
said that while being held by the PRC authorities he had not been forced to
testify. He stated that he had not revealed to the PRC any information or secret
documents (Taipei Times, Apr 14, 2004).

The issue of Pan has few threads, which are worth having a closer look at.
Firstly, it is obvious that the rules of law have failed. In March 2000 Taiwan
sharpened the regulations concerning permissions for the mainland travels of the
people who had access to classified information while performing their service.
The rules of examining the application by the committee called on for that
purpose, in which amongst others sat some NSB members, and granting
permissions were specified in regulations of the Ministry of the Interior Affairs.
The people engaged in active service who broke the regulations risked a loss of
their positions. Whereas the retired officers were prone to a 100 thousand
Taiwanese dollars fine. According to the rules of law the services were obliged
to inform the emigration authorities about the retirement of their employees

within two weeks. Those who had access to classified information were forbidden to freely travel to the mainland China throughout the period of three years after having retired. The regulations allowed such trips before this period with the permission of the authorities. The NSB was participating in the regulations amendment works (Taipei Times, Jun 26, 2000). Therefore it is hard to accept that Pan really did not know his legal situation before the trip (Taipei Times, Jul 07, 2000). It cannot be ruled out that he consciously took advantage of the legal loophole (Taipei Times, Jun 27, 2000). He had left the island before the time by which the NSB was obliged to inform the emigration authorities about his retirement. Yet the very application of these regulations was problematic. Taiwan had no means to assess whether the law was infringed in case when the PRC border had been crossed from the territory of the third country (Taipei Times, Jul 07, 2000). In 2001 the governmental control revealed that from January 1999 to July 2001 nearly half of 414 retired militaries and secret service officers travelled to Hong Kong transgressing the emigration laws. It was also confirmed that 11 of higher rank officers had then also crossed the PRC's border (Taipei Times, Dec 25, 2001). In December a National Police Administration spokesman stated there had been noted 144 cases of policemen who had repeatedly visited Hong Kong and Macau without having acquired any permission (Taipiei Times, Dec 25, 2001).

Pan could have been motivated by ambition and desire to gain financial profits. It is known that at the end of his NSB service he underwent a rode control, which revealed he had driven his vehicle under the influence of alcohol. The matter was presented to the NSB's general director who demanded strict discipline from his subordinates. It cannot be ruled out that Pan was forced to retire six months earlier than he had planned. He thus lost his three-month salary and the possibility to receive higher pension (Taipei Times, Jul 03, 2000). The press reported that the NSB was trying to persuade Pan to come back to the island. He was allegedly promised to get back his pension that had been held upon his having left Taiwan (Taipei Times, Sep 14, 2000). Pan's case reminds in this regard a situation from the summer 2000 involving the pilot of the Taiwan's air forces who was suspected of unlawful revealing to the PRC some classified information on the air combat strategies. The pilot had been forced to retire in the course of redundancy programme. This was not an isolated case as the programme encompassed mainly some middle rank young-aged officers who due to the lack of required years of service were not entitled to earlier retirement. The investigation conducted in that regard showed that many of them were later leaving to China in search of some business opportunities. It was not ascertained though how many of them had passed the information to the PRC services (Taipei Times, Tue, Jul 11, 2000).

In case of Pan, just like in Chang's one, the press was in possession of some information passed on most probably by people from the intelligence community. Leaking of information to the media made it harder to protect the methods and means of the intelligence services. It also compromised Taiwan's credibility as an intelligence cooperation partner (Taipei Times, Mar 25, 2002). Substantial amount of information leakages occurred after the DPP's having taken over the power which proved the existence of strong opposition within the intelligence circles against this political group. In the other hand the journalists in Taiwan thought that they had to report what was necessary (Taipei Times, Oct 03, 2000). In October 2000 the press received some information concerning the investigation run by the military prosecutor's office on money embezzlement by Liu Kuan-chun, former chief accountant and former chief cashier of the NSB. It concerned the appropriation of some of the funds that had been deposited on secret NSB accounts during 1988-2000 (Taipei Times, Jan 11, 2004). Within the "dollar diplomacy" programme Taipei paid some countries for maintaining diplomatic relations. For that purpose economic support was granted and overseas think-tanks were also rewarded. In 1994 the NSB on behalf of Taiwan's Ministry of the Foreign Affairs paid over 10 million US dollars to the government of the Republic of South Africa in exchange for maintaining diplomatic relations with Taiwan. In 1999 this amount along with the interest was returned to the NSB by Taiwan's ministry (Taipei Times, Nov 18, 2003). During 1988-2000 the NSB was working to establish some unofficial bilateral cooperation channels between Taiwan and the United States and Japan. A yearly budget of a Taiwanese operator in Tokyo was 2.7 million Taiwanese dollars. That money was coming from a special state affairs fund used for financing secret diplomacy undertakings (Taipei Times, Aug 29, 2011). With the NSB president-only secret account lobbyists and paid US think-tanks had also been financed in hope of influencing the US's Taiwan policy. This measures had been prone to a limited NSB's internal control (Tzeng, 2009, 138).

Beginning with the 1990s Taiwan's intelligence services were often criticised for the quality of intelligence products they disseminated. The release of intelligence about the PRC's missile exercise in 1996, which led to the exposure of information sources, also resulted in a wave of disconnections. Given the circumstances, military intelligence officers had doubts about the effectiveness of human intelligence on the mainland China territory, since many of agents left during the Chen Shui-bian administration (Tzeng, 2009, 167). The loss of many agents held by the PRC's services in the mainland China decreased also the quantity and the quality of information procured by the intelligence services. One of the methods of agent recruitment used by the MIB in the mainland China involved developing in the candidates the conviction that the information they were to provide would serve the purpose of uniting the two sides of the Taiwan Strait. The independence aspirations of the DDP government resulted in some mainland intelligence agents' becoming reluctant to risk their lives (Taipei Times, Oct 28, 2001). Those agents did not trust president Chen Shui-bian's pro-independence slogans and no longer believed in what they had been fighting for (Tzeng, 2009, 167). The MIB was forced to recruit Taiwanese business people to collect information in the mainland China. It was a risky and costly operation that did not bring the expected effects (Taipei Times, Jan 17, 2004). Taiwanese businessmen had been lacking professional training. For example, in 2003 the MIB recruited a China-based Taiwanese businessman Lo Pin to collect military intelligence for Taiwan. In the period from February 2004 to October 2005 Lo Pin had visited the mainland China ten times. In 2005 the MIB ended the cooperation with Lo Pin, suspecting that he had been exposed by the PRC's services. They detained Lo Pin during his stay in the mainland China in July 2006. In return for his being freed the businessman took up the cooperation with the PRC's intelligence services as a double agent. After coming back to Taiwan Lo Pin recruited a high rank military intelligence officer Lo Chi-cheng. Beginning with 2007 the intelligence officer passed on to the businessman information which were further transferred to the PRC's intelligence in Hong Kong. Lo Pin had also passed some false intelligence to Lo Chi-cheng and then used it to obtain monetary rewards from Taiwanese authorities. In November 2010 both the spies had been detained (Taipei Times, Apr 29, 2011).

In order to find solutions to solve the problems troubling the Taiwanese services the revisions of legal acts pertaining to intelligence activity were reached for as well as some efforts were made to improve discipline and professional conduct amongst the intelligence services employees. The governmental draft act increasing the amount of the fine for an unauthorised traveling to the PRC's territory from 100 thousand to 1 million Taiwanese dollars and allowing to take away the pensions from the people who break the law was presented to the parliament at the end of 2001 (Taipei Times, Dec 25, 2001). Stricter background checks for determining whether persons undergoing them could obtain a security clearance were introduced. In June 2002 a legislative draft on this matter was presented in the parliament. Persons who were suspected on some solid ground of having relatives in the mainland China, maintaining connections with foreign secret services, whose standard of living was higher than their regular income, who were addicted to alcohol or other abusive substances or psychotropic drugs, or were actively involved with subversive organisations were to be expelled from their service or not to be recruited (Taipei Times, Jun 15, 2002). In August 2002, new regulations were brought into effect. They restricted the government personnel's ability to travel to the PRC as for that purpose the NSB employees and retirees were from that time on required to obtain permission from the Interior Ministry's Immigration and Emigration Management Bureau (Philips, 2009, 185). The families of the high rank NSB officers were obliged to report to the ROC authorities about their plans of travelling to the mainland China and had to be prepared to undergo a security check (Taipei Times, Jan 27, 2006). According to president Chen it was important to introduce changes to the services work culture that would make them apolitical and loyal to the country rather than to a political fraction. In 2000 a group of the Ministry of Justice Investigation Bureau (MJIB) officials demanded reforms that would separate police functions from the intelligence ones as well as depoliticising the MJIB which was often publicly accused of keeping people under surveillance due to its political partiality. In a special declaration announced in October 2000 that the then MJIB director had stated the service was to stop political surveillance activities. In 2001 president Chen called off the MJIB chief entrusting this position to his collaborator. The opposition regarded that to be an act of politicising the services by the DPP (Philips, 2009, 180-183). During the electoral campaign the chiefs of the services would not conceal their sympathy for their political opponent Chen. The president assumed that maintaining ethnical balance on the managerial level would make it easier for him to keep the security and intelligence services under control. According to the presidential administration those actions were also supposed to make the situation in the services – which had a hard time to get used to the DPP rule – healthier. For the above given reasons some personnel changes were made in the managerial positions of other security and intelligence services. During the KMT rule for the chief positions in the services would mostly be appointed Mainland Chinese. W 2001 the position of the NSB general director was given to a native Taiwanese and the afore mentioned chief of the MJIB of Hakka tribe descent. It seems that the reform did not encompass the intelligence services as the presidential administration had entrusted the mission of directing the MIB to a Mainlander (Taipei Times, Aug 10, 2001).

The sanctions imposed for trespassing the regulations concerning trips to the mainland China were not a sufficiently discouraging means. In November 2003 two military intelligence employees were held in Taiwan on the grounds of suspected espionage on behalf of China (Taipei Times, Nov 15, 2003). One of them, who while being arrested was already a retiree, had been recruited during one of his stays in the mainland China. Another one was still in active service and passed to his colleague the intelligence which was then faxed to Beijing (Taipei Times, Nov 14, 2003). According to the commentators, the efforts such as stricter surveillance checks or the idea of taking away the pensions from the people breaking the laws had rather been something like a symptomatic treatment (Taipei Times, Dec 27, 2001) as these were the actions meant to pacify the public opinion. The assumption was that as a skilled liar, a good spy was able to cheat a lie detector and undergo the surveillance procedure (Taipei Times, Apr 10, 2002).

In the 2000s, during the legislature's annual budget review, the quality of intelligence provided by the intelligence agencies was criticised and the NSB decided to offer awards as an incentive to groups and individuals involved in intelligence gathering. This effort was made in order to improve the state of affairs and raise the morale in the services. It is not clear how this incentive scheme influenced the atmosphere in the intelligence services and the efficiency of their performance. The MIB was gradually taking more relaxed stance in the war with the PRC and, following a spate of arrests of Taiwanese intelligence agents conducting their activity in the mainland China, was forced to introduce some changes to its operational procedures. That had a negative impact on intelligence gathering in that country. Taiwan's government was criticised for its disregardful attitude towards the MIB (Taipei Times, Nov 01, 2010).

People opposed to president Ma's policy state that the closer cross-strait relations become and the more economically reliant Taiwan becomes on the mainland China, the more the Presidential Office and corporations will exert pressure on the intelligence agencies to moderate their opinions on threats from the PRC intelligence services (Taipei Times, Mar 29, 2011). In 2010 the NSB would worn retired intelligence officers against visiting the mainland China where they were at risk of being held and interviewed. The NSB director Tsai Der-sheng who repeated that, on several occasions was accused of "playing up" and "politicising" the intelligence services (Taipei Times, Aug 09, 2011). Meanwhile an increased movement of people across the Taiwan Strait and increased opportunities for bilateral contacts give the intelligence services better opportunities to recruit agents and conduct gathering of human intelligence on the PRC territory. Despite of warming up the relations, the cross-strait intelligence war is still going on. In February 2011 Major General Lo Hsien-che, the head of communications and electronic information at the Army Command Headquarters, was arrested on suspicion of espionage. The Taiwan's Ministry of National Defence called it the worst espionage case within the last 50 years (Taipei Times, Feb 10, 2011). Lo had apparently been recruited by Chinese agents in 2004 while operating in Thailand. He is known to have leaked information about the Po Sheng (Broad Victory) digital multi-service integrated command, control and intelligence system and is also suspected of passing on highly confidential documents and files about the army's strategic areas communication system, the procurement of Apache helicopters and the layout of the nation's underground fibre optic communication network (Taipei Times, Feb 13, 2011). Lo reportedly started to work for the Chinese intelligence in 2004 in return for a reward of about 1 million US dollars he had received from Beijing. Despite of his on-going espionage activity he repeatedly managed to pass loyalty checks and was promoted to a major-general position in 2008 (Taipei Times, Jun 08, 2011). In July 2011 the military court sentenced Lo to life imprisonment for spying on behalf of the PRC (Taipei Times, Jul 26, 2011). Then, in June 2011 Taiwan's legislature reacted to this case and passed an amendment to the regulations granting lenient treatment or even pardons to double agents who turn themselves in. Under the above mentioned regulations, Taiwanese agents who spy for the PRC or another foreign country would have to face a life imprisonment sentence even if they surrendered to the authorities, which was a major disincentive to those who regretted their betrayal and wanted to change they ways. The amendment said that the agents recruited by other countries and "the enemy" would have their sentence reduced or be pardoned if their reporting to the authorities prevented damage to Taiwan's security or interests (Taipei Times, Jun 08, 2011).

Conclusion

Until 1986 Taiwan's intelligence services were part of the security system that protected the authoritarian regime. Their tasks were correlated with the aims of the ROC government's foreign policy, which evolved from a military confrontation with the PCR for the purpose of regaining control over the mainland China and defending Taiwan's territory to normalisation of the relations and tightening economical cooperation ties across the Taiwan Strait. In the regime's service the intelligence agencies would fight the political opposition and their involvement with internal matters increased due to Taiwan's diplomatic isolation on the international arena. Taiwan's democratisation process that began in 1987 brought about personnel changes and re-evaluation of aims and directions in the intelligence services' activities. The political system transformation strengthened the internal divisions within intelligence officers' circles and for many of them it brought about identity and loyalty crisis. Till the end of 1960s Taiwan's military intelligence had been running covert operations aiming at gathering intelligence and destabilising the PRC's authorities. The PRC's counterintelligence had compromised Taiwan's intelligence operations against the mainland. The quality of information being obtained from the military intelligence agents decreased as the first-generation agents who remained in service after 1949 gradually withdrew. Better results were recorded in the area of signals intelligence which infrastructure had been developed with the technical and financial help of the United States. The loss of the military intelligence agents in 2000 was a bitter failure for Taiwan's military intelligence, which overshadowed its earlier achievements. Taiwan's counterintelligence successes prove a high rate of espionage crime detection but simultaneously show a striking extent of the PRC's espionage (Taipei Times, Mar 02, 2012). In 2000 the MJIB stated that about 500 PRC nationals who visited Taiwan were suspected of espionage activities. They have come to the island under the cover of identities ranging from scholars and businessmen to relatives of Taiwan's citizens. During 1997-2000 as many as 376 PRC citizens were repatriated for having been engaged in activities not compatible with the purposes of (their) visits. (Taipei Times Feb 15, 2000). Statistics show that during 2002-2011 thirteen people – including senior military officers, a Presidential Office official, as well as serving and retired intelligence officers – have been arrested in Taiwan for spying on behalf of China (Taipei Times, Oct 15, 2011). In fact it is not known how many agents were able to get into the Taiwanese military and security apparatus, political parties and high-tech sector unexposed and pass information to their case officers in Beijing (Taipei Times, Oct 04, 2011). Identifying them is not an easy task because intelligence gathering against Taiwan is also conducted through academic exchange and commercial activities (Taipei Times, Jan 10, 2011). Nevertheless merely few of the exposed PRC spies had been able to operate for a longer time (Taipei Times Mar 18, 2012).

The relations between Taipei and Beijing have been improving since 2008. In December 2011 with the invitation of the Chinese Communist Party (CCP) former Taiwanese intelligence officials for the first time paid a formal visit to China (Taipei Times, Jan 10, 2011). Yet Beijing has not abandoned the military option and continues its impressive arms build-up and modernisation programme (Taipei Times Mar 02, 2012). Some commentators maintain that under Ma's presidency the Taiwanese intelligence agencies were ordered to reduce intelligence activity in the mainland China (Taipei Times, Feb 02, 2011). In the past, these agencies tended to focus on providing early-warning intelligence or long-term threat assessments. According to some opinions expressed in the media, in the current situation it is best for Taiwan to gather intelligence that would help improve trade and politics, develop the its ability to deal with the mainland China by using soft power and to strengthen Taipei's global strategic position (Taipei Times, Feb 08, 2010). Nevertheless the espionage cases such as the exposure of Lo Hsien-che show that the spy war never ends.

Translated by Iwona Szuwalska

Bibliography

Taylor, J. (2009). *The Generalissimo. Chiang Kai-shek and the Struggle for Modern China*, Harvard University Press.

Tzeng, Y. (2009). *Civil-Military Relations in Democratizing Taiwan, 1986-2007*, A Dissertation submitted to the Faculty of Columbian College of Arts and Sciences of the George Washington University.

Phillips, S. E. (2009). Taiwan's Intelligence Reform in an Age of Democratization in *Reforming intelligence. Obstacles to Democratic Control and Effectiveness*, eds. T. C. Bruneau and S. C. Boraz, University of Texas Press.

Copper, J. F. (2009). *Taiwan. Nation-State or Province?*, 5th ed., Westview Press.

One China policy impact
on Taiwan's political relations with the EU

Sebastian Michalak

This paper describes the findings of the research conducted during my trip to Taipei. I am grateful to the Ministry of Foreign Affairs of Republic of China who made me a recipient of the Taiwan Fellowship in 2011. I would like to express my thanks to the European Union Centre in Taiwan for welcoming me as a visiting scholar. The starting point of the analysis is specifying the European Union's, Taiwan's and China's interpretation of the one-China doctrine. Later certain EU's preferences and choices that have a direct impact on the nature of bilateral relations with Taiwan are described. Finally, the EU's limited support for Beijing one-China principle is elaborated. This report is based on reviewing the observations of the specialists in the field and interviews conducted with Taiwanese scholars.

The European Union (EU) does not have diplomatic or formal relations with Taiwan. It does not recognize the island as a sovereign state because of the EU's being in line with the one-China policy. For this reason the EU also does support Taiwan's taking part in activities of international organizations on the level that does not involve the statehood issue.[1] In fact Taiwan is a separately governed territory, which operates autonomously from the People's Republic of China (PRC). Taiwan has some aspects of sovereignty as democratically elected government and ability to maintain diplomatic relations with other countries but it lacks international recognition for not being externally recognized as a sovereign state[2]. Brussels respects Taiwan's economic and commercial independence.[3] Taiwan is one of the largest EU's trading partners in Asia. Brussels supports bilateral flow of trade and investment. According to the statistics in 2009 the EU was the biggest investor into Taiwan but its market potential have been not yet explored by European businesses.[4] The European Commission (EC) holds regular contacts with Taiwan authorities in order to maintain balanced and undisturbed cooperation. Annual consultations cover non-political areas of mutual interest such as trade and investment. In 2003 the

---

1   EU and Taiwan (Chinese Taipei), http://eeas.europa.eu/taiwan/index_en.htm

2   Winkler, S. (2008). Can trade make a sovereign? Taiwan–China–EU relations in the WTO, Asia Europe Journal, No. 6, 469-471.

3   Taiwan & the EU, http://eeas.europa.eu/delegations/taiwan/eu_taiwan/index_en.htm

4   EU-Taiwan trade and investment fact file 2010, http://eeas.europa.eu/delegations/taiwan/documents/more_info/2010_eutw_tandi_factfile.pdf.pdf

EC has established its permanent office in Taiwan in order to facilitate communications with the Taiwanese and to extend the range of cooperation. The EU supports a peaceful resolution of Taiwan's sovereignty issue through constructive cross-strait talks. Brussels insists that any agreement between Beijing and Taipei can only be achieved by rejecting any means the involve force, on acceptable basis for both sides and with adherence to the will of the Taiwan people. The EU encourages Beijing and Taipei to strengthen economic integration to secure a solid ground on which the issue of Taiwan could be ultimately resolved.[5]

All the issues involving Taiwan are dealt with caution in order not to disregard China's stance, which restricts Taiwan's independent cooperation on the international arena including the interactions with the EU countries.[6] Although Beijing and Taipei did commit to pursue the one-China policy their vision of what it actually should represent utterly differs on many grounds. For Beijing's its policy towards Taiwan is not a matter of looking for practical solutions but rather an issue of maintaining some kind of symbolic status. Yet the PRC leaders exhibit their power by emphasizing the issue of status as a matter of principle but simultaneously remain sensitive to political correctness on matters involving Taiwan.[7] On the other hand Taiwanese governments have been trying to develop Taiwan's independent international relations in order to prove the PRC's view of Taiwan as a province of China unfounded.[8] But there is another aspect of China's policy towards Taiwan that keeps the whole issue immune to any external involvement. Precisely, China maintains that the Taiwan issue is not to be interfered with by any external powers since it is a purely internal affair. Nevertheless China strives for international support for her position on the one-China principle.[9] According to Chinese authorities Taiwan is a part of Chinese territory and as such should not be considered an independent state.[10] This approach has gained a worldwide recognition. Since the early 1990s

---

5   EU and the Cross-Strait Relationship, http://eeas.europa.eu/delegations/taiwan/ eu_taiwan/eu_cross-strait_relation/index_en.htm

6   Winkler, S. (2008). Can trade make a sovereign? Taiwan–China–EU relations in the WTO, Asia Europe Journal, No. 6, 468.

7   Shirk, S. L. (2009) China's Domestic Insecurity and Its International Consequences, in Global Giant eds. E. Paus; P. Prime and others, Palgrave Macmillan, 215.

8   Guo, R. (2009). How the Chinese Economy Works, 3th edition, Palgrave Macmillan, 306.

9   Jakobson L., (2008). A 'Greater Chinese Union', Asia Europe Journal, No. 6, 50.

10 Pan, Ch. (2010). Westphalia and the Taiwan Conundrum: A Case against the Exclusionist Construction of Sovereignty and Identity, Journal of Chinese Political Science, No. 15, 376.

the one-China policy has been internationally accepted which results in Taiwan's political position considerably diminished.[11] The PRC took some steps towards developing stronger relations with the EU and strove to enter the WTO. When faced with the requirements put forward for her by the EU, and anxious of not being able to cope with them in order to acquire the WTO membership, China started to be more cautious in her attitude towards the Old Continent. In 2003 Beijing issued a policy paper in which the one-China policy was advocated in order to gain the EU's support for it.[12] Beijing puts an emphasis on presenting one-China as a generally accepted policy both by the People's Republic of China and Taiwan, expressing the ideal of the island being unified with its motherland by peaceful agreement rather than any forced actions. Beijing does not accept Taiwan's independence and does not refer to it as a state but merely as a political entity. Mutual verbal consent has been achieved regarding the acceptance of the one-China policy but there is no say as far as the understanding of how it should be implemented. Therefore the very question of what it practically means remains open and both sides involved are free to hold on to their own different concepts.[13] Edward Friedman perceives the one-China policy as Taiwan's opportunity to gain some democratic autonomy as it offers the island the right to maintain informal political and business relations around the globe.[14]

The one-China policy has a direct impact on the nature of bilateral relations and the means at the EU's disposal to develop its policy.[15] According to Francoise Mengin's estimations of 2002 the EU in a long run would not be able to resist the one-China policy. The reason behind it was to be the need to take advantage of Taiwan's economic potential on the one hand and no precise idea as how the island's political future should unfold on the other hand.[16] For the EU has not been able to present anything like a fully-fledged support on the political

11   Rozman, G. (2010). Chinese Strategic Thought toward Asia, Palgrave Macmillan, 216.

12   Curran, L. (2009). Chasing the Dragon: The Emerging EU–China Relationship and Its Impact on Business, in China Rules, eds. I. Alon, J. Chang and others, Palgrave Macmillan, 207-208.

13   Cabestan J-P. (2009). Taiwan: An Internal Affair! How China's Domestic Politics and Foreign Policy Interact on the Taiwan Issue?, East Asia, No. 26, 3.

14   Friedman, E. (2008). An End To Europe's "One China" Policy?, The "One China" Dilemma, eds. P. Chow, Palgrave Macmillan, 151.

15   Coppieter, B. (2006). The European Strategic Culture on Secession an the Cross-Strait Relations,International Conference on the EU Relations with Taiwan and China, 01-02 December 2006, Institute of European and American Studies, Academia Sinica, Taiwan, 5.

16   Tubilewicz, C. (2008). Taiwan and Europe in Europe-Asia Relations, eds. R. Balme; B. Bridges, Palgrave Macmillan, 172.

ground despite of Taiwan being its fourth largest trading partner. Taiwan did not take part in the Asia-Europe Meeting (AEM), which could be perceived as an outcome of the EU's siding with the one-China policy, although the AEM have been regularly attended by the European Commission (EC), all the EU member states representatives, as well as the leaders of 13 Asian states. Another example of excluding Taipei from the similar international undertaking was the EU's Generalized System of Preferences. The issue of arranging for a free trade area between Taiwan and the EU has been being repeatedly brought up by the former since 2002 but the latter does not seem to respond with any noticeable interest.[17] The European Economic and Trade Office is not supposed to be involved in any political activity. This was emphasized in an article published by the EC's press. The release stated that the office would not be involved in any diplomatic or political relations in order to adhere to the one-China policy. In order to avoid any possible discontent on the part of China, the EC restricts its contacts with the Taiwan authorities. Although it specifically restrains from informal contacts, there are no restrictions involved as far as the issues pertaining to some practical co-operation between the EU and Taiwan are concerned.[18] The one-China policy issue makes the relations between Taiwan and the EU somewhat clandestine. The Old Continent is rather reserved in its dealings with Taipei, avoiding excessive publicity during meetings with the Taipei's representatives in Brussels.[19] Taiwan's interests were usually on a lost position when confronted with the EU's need to maintain good relations with Beijing. The European state's leaders have been always ready to sacrifice Taiwan's interests for the sake of securing their good relations with the PRC. In this regard one-China policy seems to be an ever resorted to trial ground whenever the loyalty towards China must be accentuated for the sake of the EU's improving its relations with her. When that is put on stake any requests from Taiwan are disregarded and even an open critique against Taiwan's pursuit of independence from China is often being launched.[20]

In 2002 the European Parliament (EP) commended the Council and the Member States "to issue visas to the President and all high-ranking officials of

---

17 Geldenhuys, D. (2009). Contested States in World Politics, Palgrave Macmillan, 223.
18 Winkler, S. (2008). Can trade make a sovereign? Taiwan–China–EU relations in the WTO, Asia Europe Journal, No. 6, 468.
19 Tang, S. (2003) EU's Taiwan policy in the light of its China policy, Asia Europe Journal, No. 1, 524.
20 Su, H. (2010). The EU's Taiwan Policy in a New Context, Issues & Studies, 46(1), Institute of International Relations National Chengchi University, Taipei, Taiwan (ROC), 23-24.

Taiwan for private visits to the European Union"[21]. China set as one of the aims of her policy towards the EU regarding the Taiwan issue to prevent the important political personalities of Taiwan from visiting the EU.[22] As a result of some steps taken in that regard the EU states indeed did not promote any official visits by Taiwan's political representatives. Nevertheless there was neither legal act passed as for refusing visas to such persons nor there was any joint position expressed on that issue.[23]

Another thing pertaining to the PRC's policy towards Taiwan that is worth of mentioning is the "anti-secession law" adopted in 2005. This law has plainly put forward the means to be adopted in the PRC's dealing with Taiwan's issue. There were some legal statements made regarding the policy towards Taiwan and the unification ideal was presented as the higher objective worth of resorting even to "non-peaceful means" if required. This was though utterly contradictory to the EU's efforts to maintain peace and stability in the East Asia. Despite of that the Council remained quite subdued in its response to the matter, declaring barely that it "has taken note" of an "anti-secession law" adoption. The most daring expression of discontent was referring to its previously articulated "opposition to any use of force." The EP also expressed its doubts as for the anti-secession law because it "does not comply with international law and is a tool that undermines the fragile security balance in the Far East"[24]. The role of the EP in in the area of the Common Foreign and Security Policy is quite restricted as it is limited to advice and counseling. Despite of that, the issues dealt with by the EU have been in great deal influenced by the resolutions passed by the EP.[25] These were not the only institutions that uttered some unfavorable opinions on the matter. The EC expressed its "strong opposition to the use of force."[26] So generally speaking the EU seemed to express a pro-Taiwan line of thinking validated in the form of "protests" on the part of EC or

---

21 European Parliament resolution on the Commission Communication on Europe and Asia: A Strategic Framework for Enhanced Partnerships, P5_TA(2002)0408

22 Snyder, F. (2009) China and International Economic Law Series : European Union and China, 1949-2006: Basic Documents and Commentary, Oxford, GBR: Hart Publishing Ltd., 492.

23 Tang, S. (2003) EU's Taiwan policy in the light of its China policy, Asia Europe Journal, No. 1, 523-524.

24 European Parliament resolution on relations between the EU, China and Taiwan and security in the Far East, P6_TA(2005)0297.

25 Su, H. (2010). The EU's Taiwan Policy in a New Context, Issues & Studies, 46(1), Institute of International Relations National Chengchi University, Taipei, Taiwan (ROC), 22.

26 Communication from the Commission to the Council and the European Parliament – EU – China: Closer partners, growing responsibilities, COM (2006) 632 final, 11.

even the EP resolutions. Nevertheless such voices of sympathy for Taiwan were not in any way formally demonstrated in the Councils stance as it expressed an open support for the one-China policy. Such was a situation in 2007 when the Council decisively stood on the PRC's side.[27] Despite of this clear support Beijing remained cautious and conscious that not all of the EU's institutions were satisfied with the anti-secession law. Tang Shaocheng maintains that the PRC's employed some measures in order to avoid dealing with the EU's protests against the proclamation. It was as early as 2003 that the PRC has already sought support from the US and the EU in order to prevent Taiwan from taking any steps towards the independence. The policy seems to have proven successful as in the following years brought about the EU's growing support for Beijing regarding the Taiwan's issue.[28] This situation proves very unfavorable for Taiwan. The closer are the relations between the EU and the PRC the more marginalized are the matters related to Taiwan .[29] Therefore, as a result of the above-described dynamics, although the EU sees Taiwan as an important trade partner, still its position as such is greatly diminished when the relations and cooperation with Beijing were to be jeopardized.[30]

The period of 1996–2009 was for the EU marked with intensified concerns as for the issues pertaining to the Taiwan Strait. The only way to secure the EU's trade relations and investments in the in the East Asia is to preserve peace and stability in this area. For that reason the EU is very much concerned not to envenom the already sensitive situation that has transpired between Taipei and Beijing. Hence the EU's main objective is to maintain peace in the area.[31] Therefore in order to release the tension built up in the Taiwan Strait, the Old Continent accepts more restrained position and tries to act rather as a mediator than an advocate of either party to the conflict. This is to simply encourage

---

27 Su, H. (2010). The EU's Taiwan Policy in a New Context, Issues & Studies, 46(1), Institute of International Relations National Chengchi University, Taipei, Taiwan (ROC), 20.

28 Tang S., (2009). The European Union and the Taiwan Strait Relations (1996-2009): A Content Analysis.

29 Su, H. (2010). The EU's Taiwan Policy in a New Context, Issues & Studies, 46(1), Institute of International Relations National Chengchi University, Taipei, Taiwan (ROC), 24.

30 Zanon, F., (2005). The European Parliament: An autonomous foreign policy identity? in The role of Parliaments in European foreign policy, eds. E. Barbé, A. Herranz, Office of the European Parliament in Barcelona (Barcelona), http://www.iuee.eu/pdf-publicacio/20/Eb2V9FwpCaNXbHibFVLF.PDF

31 Tang, S. (2009). The European Union and the Taiwan Strait Relations (1996-2009): A Content Analysis, 8-9.

peaceful solutions and secure its interests with both the PRC and Taiwan.[32] Thus the EU resists any moves that could possibly increase the conflict. As it was mentioned above the EU's main objective is to maintain peace and stability in the area and therefore if necessary it expresses disapproval towards any steps on the PRC's or Taiwan's parts that could interfere with that aim. The EU policy is to rather maintain the present status quo than to search for some radical changes. Any alterations in that regard are not to be enforced by some third party powers.[33] At the present the EU consequently strives to soften the views of China and Taiwan on the cross-Strait conflict.[34] But that line of policy was taken already in 2006 when the delegation of European experts took some diplomatic steps in order to start a track-two dialogue between the PRC and Taiwan. This effort was one of the first EU's practical steps taken towards securing and encouraging peaceful resolution of the sensitive issue of Taiwan status in relation to China.[35]

Nevertheless until 2007 the EU did not come forward with any kind of uniform one-China policy approach. In fact even between the EU institutions, what to speak of the member states, there was no common policy adopted in that regard. On the one hand the EP resolutions present its clear pro-Taiwan position, but on the other hand we the Council of European Union and the European Commission present quite a different stance expressing disapproval for Taiwan's pursuit of independence.[36] In that line in 2002 the EP presented the EU's support for the one-China policy as a positive reaction to the PRC's willingness to peacefully resolve the issue of Taiwan's claims. Moreover considering the EP's pro-Taiwan stance being utterly different from the Council's and the EC's positions one may put into question whether the EU as such had really supported the one-China policy.[37]

---

32 Tang, S. (2009). The European Union and the Taiwan Strait Relations (1996-2009): A Content Analysis, 6.

33 Laursen, F. (2008). EU-Taiwan Political and Economic Relations: Background and Recent Developments, International Conference on the EU-Asian Relations in 21st Century, 04-05 December 2008, Institute of European and American Studies, Academia Sinica, Taiwan, 10.

34 Winkler, S. (2008). Can trade make a sovereign? Taiwan–China–EU relations in the WTO, Asia Europe Journal, No. 6, 468.

35 Tang, S. (2009). The European Union and the Taiwan Strait Relations (1996-2009): A Content Analysis, 16.

36 Su, H. (2010). The EU's Taiwan Policy in a New Context, Issues & Studies, 46(1), Institute of International Relations National Chengchi University, Taipei, Taiwan (ROC), 17-18.

37 Zanon, F., (2005). The European Parliament: An autonomous foreign policy identity?, The role of Parliaments in European foreign policy, eds. E. Barbé, A. Herranz, Office of

The one-China policy leaves a little possibility to move towards any satisfactory solution. The EU became very cautious as not to upset China that owing to her stunning development became the economical power not to be taken for granted.[38] However the issue of Taiwan's claims is a matter on which China and Europe cannot reach full agreement. Although the EU's position on the one-China policy did not change so far there are no solid grounds to consider Brussels a supporter of the PRC's policy towards Taiwan. The EU did not consent to the Beijing's idea of resolving the Taiwan issue by "peaceful reunification, one country two systems." During 2004–2007 this particular phrase was removed from the EU's and the PRC's joint statements published after each of the annual China-EU Summits.[39] The EU also did not accept the stance that Taiwan is a part of China or a part of the PRC.

The PRC considers proper dealing with the Taiwan problem to be very important for China-EU future relations. Therefore it strongly discourages the EU from allowing Taiwan political personalities to visit the EU member countries. Apart from that Beijing advises not to maintain any official contacts with Taiwan authorities, which includes restricting Taiwan's accession to or even participation in any international organization that involves statehood. The EU's relations with Taiwan are expected to be strictly unofficial and should not be governmental in nature, which means e.g. that no arms, equipment, goods, materials, or technological inventions, which could possibly be used for military purposes, shall be sold to Taiwan.[40] The European states adhered to China's expectations on the issue of Taiwan. For instance in 1994 France promised the PRC to no longer sell weapons to Taiwan. Beijing offered her in exchange some business cooperation.[41] Nevertheless the EU tends to follow the American strategic policy line regarding the Taiwan question since it basically perceives it as a US security concern. While the EU accepts the policy of resisting Taiwan's quest for independence it condemns the use of force on the part of China. Still

the European Parliament in Barcelona (Barcelona), http://www.iuee.eu/pdf-publicacio/20/Eb2V9FwpCaNXbHibFVLF.PDF

38 Laursen, F. (2008). EU-Taiwan Political and Economic Relations: Background and Recent Developments, International Conference on the EU-Asian Relations in 21st Century, 04-05 December 2008, Institute of European and American Studies, Academia Sinica, Taiwan, 24.

39 Tang, S. (2009). The European Union and the Taiwan Strait Relations (1996-2009): A Content Analysis, 7.

40 Snyder, F. (2009). China and International Economic Law Series: European Union and China, 1949-2006 : Basic Documents and Commentary. Oxford, 490.

41 Friedman, E. (2008). An End To Europe's "One China" Policy?, The "One China" Dilemma, eds. P. Chow, Palgrave Macmillan, 150.

this is all far away from being actively involved in the cross-straits relations as any practical steps would require the EU to interfere with the problem to a degree that even the US would not consider welcome.[42] The PRC strongly defends her authority position over Taiwan and is dissatisfied over her inability to gain the support of the EU on the matter. Additionally the EU has not revoked its arms embargo, which was imposed on China in 1989. The reason for not ending this embargo was that after 2005 the PRC proclaimed its right to use force against Taiwan.[43] This decision was the first explicit expression of the EU's concern about the military balance across the Strait.[44] The reasons given for restraining from revoking the embargo were Taiwanese security and human rights concerns. On the other hand the role of America's position in that regard should not be underestimated. On the other hand according to China's perspective the EU tends to be too stubborn and lacks flexibility to rise beyond the human rights perspective in her approach to issues centered around China.[45]

Conclusion

Taiwan obviously suffers from a lack of formal diplomatic relations with global players, which has a direct impact on its status as a nation state. Taipei's contacts with the EU are primarily commercial. The economic and trade ties with Taiwan are solid and healthy. The EU is Taiwan's fourth largest market. The research and technology, education and culture, fisheries, environment and intellectual property rights sectors are objects of mutual talks held in order to increase activities coordination and coherence. In line with the one-China policy the EU maintains only unofficial diplomatic relations with Taipei. This policy has had its direct effects on development of relations between the EU and Taiwan.

The latest common policy of the European Union towards Taiwan has been described in the "Guidelines on the EU's Foreign and Security Policy in East Asia" issued by the Council of the European Union in 2007. According to Gudrun Wacker all the measures the EU would take to support peace and

42 Fox, J., Godement, F. (2009). Policy Report: A Power Audit Of Eu-China Relations, European Council on Foreign Relations, 61, http://ecfr.3cdn.net/532cd91d0b5c9699ad_ozm6b9bz4.pdf

43 Friedman, E. (2008). An End To Europe's "One China" Policy?, The "One China" Dilemma, eds. P. Chow, Palgrave Macmillan, 151.

44 Tang, S. (2009). The European Union and the Taiwan Strait Relations (1996-2009): A Content Analysis, 16.

45 Pan, Z. (2010). Managing the conceptual gap on sovereignty in China–EU relations, Asia Europe Journal, No. 8, 239.

stability in cross-Strait relations "are on the level of welcoming positive developments and expressing concern over negative ones. The Guidelines do not address the question what the EU would do if such preventive measures failed."[46] From Taipei's perspective stabilization of the cross-Strait relations in political terms can be better secured if Beijing would renounce the use of force against Taiwan. Therefore Taipei would opt for drafting an agreement with the PRC. Taiwan would welcome the EU's support in this regard. Mainland China perceives Taiwan issue as its internal affair and opposes third part interference. The new era of Taiwan reconciliation with Beijing which begun in 2009 brings a need for the EU to rethink and reformulate its current strategy on China and its policy toward Taiwan.

What impact does the EU foreign policy have on the cross-Strait relations? Taiwan approves EU's positive role on developing trade and economy relations with East Asia. Meanwhile, Taiwan is looking forward to negotiate the FTA with the EU, no matter under what name it is. Also, the EU could play an important role in promoting human rights in the East Asia, which is also an aim shared by Taiwan. The recent improvement in cross-Strait relations is centered on mutual economic benefit. Similar to the process of EU integration, it demonstrated how important the economic benefits were. But the most important aspect of the EU integration was that the member nations held a positive thinking and believed that further integration was brought about shared benefits. Taiwan and the mainland China should push forward further integration in order to create larger market and develop closer cooperation. Experiences of the EU integration showed that the smaller countries could gain stronger positions in the process. The EU set a good example for both parties across Taiwan Strait to learn from it about the ways of solving the conflicts between them. What Taiwan can expect from the EU? Firstly, the Taiwan-EU Free Trade Agreement could be signed under a de-politicized name like "economic cooperation agreement." Secondly, it could gain support for participation in international organizations, particularly the International Civil Aviation Organization and the United Nations Framework Convention on Climate Change.[47]

The EU tries to maintain the status quo in the cross-Strait relations. Brussels has less strategic interests in the East Asia region than the US. Trade and economic cooperation with the PRC and Taiwan are high on the EU's external

---

46   Wacker, G (2010). The European Union and East Asian security: Prepared for the future?, in China, Europe and International Security, eds. F. P. van der Putten, Chu S., Routledge, 127.

47   Interview, Taipei, 19 August 2011.

relations agenda. The most important condition for strengthening the cooperation between all these partners is a safe environment in order to secure their interest. Therefore the EU has tried to play a role of the mediator engaged in easing tensions between Taipei and Beijing. During 1996-2008 the EU's institutions issued many declarations and statements appealing to both sides to stay calm, keep the status quo, not to overreact and make peace with one another. The EU does not have any significant leverage over the Taiwan Strait. The distance factor and limited capacity makes the EU's proactive policy restricted to verbal expressions of its position. Brussels also tries to link it to some other policies, for example the visa liberalization. The EU urges Taiwan to put in place a moratorium on executions. Geographical location of Taiwan is suitable not only for establishing the representative offices for testing the marketing strategies before going to the PRC. Since 2008 Taiwan served as a kind of springboard for the EU's Member States for doing business with China.[48] The current détente in cross-Strait relations serves the best to the European interests in the East Asia region.

---

48   Interview, Taipei, 5 August 2011.

William G. Max-Müller.
British diplomat in Poland (1921-1927)

Monika Łukasik-Duszyńska

Sir William Max-Müller came to the capital of Poland on 27 January 1921 as Envoy Extraordinary and Minister Plenipotentiary of HM. During his seven year work in Poland as the head of the British Legation in Warsaw he was trying his best to release the tension that was at that time present in Polish-British relations, and with time became a friend of Poland, which is confirmed by his maintaining contact with this country even long after his retirement.

The activities of this British diplomat at the post in Warsaw, as well as those of other Great Britain's Envoys Extraordinary and Ministers Plenipotentiary in Baltic States (Lithuania, Latvia and Estonia), George Kidston, Ernest Renny and Tudor Vaughan, were described in the book published in the Polish language *H.M.'s Ministers Inform... Relations Between Poland and Baltic States (1920-1926)* (*Brytyjskie poselstwo donosi...Posłowie brytyjscy wobec stosunków Polski z państwami bałtyckimi w latach 1920-1926*) (Academica 2008). But William Max-Müller's personality has not been yet elaborated in any extensive publication in the English language. Therefore I have decided to write this article. I present herein chosen – in my opinion important and interesting – facts about his life, as well as events connected to the II Republic of Poland that are not necessarily known to an English language reader.

HM's Minister started his diplomatic career in 1892 (Liński, 1926, p. 2). He was born in Oxford on 9 June 1867 in the house of the great philologist and world-renowned professor Friedrich Max-Müller and Georgina Adelaide, who were of German origin. William Max-Müller after having completed his education at Eton and Oxford, where he studied administrative law, worked at the diplomatic posts in Constantinople (1892-1897), The Haag (1898), Washington (1899-1900), Madrid (1901), Mexico (1905-1906), Oslo (1907-1908),[1] Beijing (1909-1910) and as the consul general in Budapest (1 June 1913 – 13 August 1914) (Sierpowski, 1994, p. 80; FOL for 1928, p. 332-333). At the outbreak of World War I he was transferred to work at the Foreign Office[2] in London. He was drawing up reports on the economic condition of the Central Powers. It is most probably because of his knowledge that Max-Müller was

---

1   There he also met his future wife Wanda Maria, the daughter of professor Jacob Heiberg, and he had two sons with her.

2   What was specific about that name was that the clerks of the Foreign Office (FO) and diplomats addressed it also with the terms 'Whitehall' or 'Headquarters'.

assigned to the post in Warsaw after his predecessor Horacy Rumbold's resignation.[3]

On the day of the presentation of his Letter of Credence in Warsaw on the last day of January 1921 William Max-Müller gave a short speech full of friendly words. He expressed his pride and satisfaction at acting as a British Minister in the Second Republic of Poland, and the hope for a successful conclusion of the ongoing negotiations and making peace with Russia, as well as establishing relations with other neighbouring states on more secure and permanent footing. In his speech he mentioned the patriotism of the Polish people which allowed them to surmount safely a crisis and dangers of the greatest magnitude, he referred to "the cordial and friendly relations" between Poland and Great Britain hoping for the cooperation with the Marshal Józef Piłsudski. He did not forget to mention the British Government's sincere desire to develop and cultivate the economic relations. He promised to spare no effort to contribute towards the maintenance and lightening of the bond uniting "our two peoples". In his accreditation speech he also mentioned that his "countrymen have followed these events [taking place in Poland] with the closest interest," not only because of their very sincere feeling of friendship for the Polish people, but also because they were convinced that the successful outcome of these negotiations would to a great extent deepen the restoration of stable political and economic conditions throughout Europe.[4] Was this statement the expression of knowledge or just plain courtesy words? It was many years later in 1944 that Max-Müller admitted "there are few countries in Europe about which the average Englishman knows so little as about Poland. This ignorance I believe to be due, in part, to the fact that we are prone to look at Poland, her people and her politics through the eyes of the hard-working German propaganda machine which exercised during the period between the two wars, and still exercises, I regret to say, a powerful and most pernicious influence among certain circles in this country [Great Britain]...." It had been so until Poles' patriotism and struggle against the Nazis, their sacrifice, loyalty and belief in victory brought about, as Max-Müller maintained, a substantial change in public opinion in Great Britain, and "today none of the Allies are more popular or held in higher esteem in this country than the Poles." (Max-Müller, 1944, p. 4, 5). The very lack of precise knowledge about the current situation, what to speak of historical events, could have made him positively disposed towards the actions of the government of the Second Republic of Poland.

---

3   P. Leśniewski (from Edinburgh, specialising in Polish-British relations), letter of 3 and 13 March 2004.

4   Public Record Office (PRO), Foreign Office (FO) 371/6830, N 1721/1061/55, p. 70, 71.

William Max-Müller as an HM Envoy was obliged to explain to Polish government the ways of British politics as well as Polish politics to London authorities. Apart from that he himself, as well as those who worked under him, were supposed to influence the politics of the Second Republic of Poland in various ways, direct it in order to counteract the French power (Piszczkowski, 1975, p. 229, 249). Yet initially these tasks were not easy to be carried out. The atmosphere pervading in Poland in 1921 seemed to a new British Envoy Extraordinary and Minister Plenipotentiary very much alarming. For the first few months he was living in fear of Bolshevik's reoccurrence and was so much in anxiety about it that he would not allow to unpack his luggage. "The perspectives were promising," as he added after some years had passed (Liński, 1926, p. 2). One of his first assignments was to prepare the annual report on external and internal policy of the Second Republic of Poland for the previous year (1920, during which he was not yet present in Poland). On his shoulders rested also the matter of the renewal of the lease of Branicki Palace, where the British Legation had been established.[5] Apart from that he had to arrange for some necessary renovation works, painting the bedroom and the bathroom of his wife, Wanda, as well as her boudoir, in order to make they dwelling there comfortable. There were also other tenants living in the building, whom Max-Müller was trying to move out appealing to the Polish Ministry for Foreign Affairs.[6]

His hard first year at the post in Poland the diplomat summed up positively, concluding that at that time "the fate was completely unfavorable for Poland although the situation started changing and even before the first year of my stay in this city [Warsaw] had passed the difference was noticeable since the country was gradually moving from the period of war to more peaceful atmosphere" (Liński, 1926, p. 2). At the same time he noticed that before the close of the year the relations between Poland and Great Britain had become more satisfactory and "the position of this Legation (…) correspondingly easier" (Report 1921, Poland, p. 5, paragraph 19).

William Max-Müller as Envoy Extraordinary and Minister Plenipotentiary of HM was on the one hand gaining his knowledge about Poland from other employees working at the post, and on the other hand from his own observations and contacts with other diplomats accredited in Poland. The documents sent by him to London show that the main source of information were the meetings with the Ministers of Foreign Affairs. These would give him one perspective on the

---

5   PRO FO 371/6829, N 441/2944/2959/4205/441/55, p. 3-8, 14-15, 16-22, 35-38; PRO FO
     371/6833, N3614/1724/55, p. 95.
6   PRO FO 371/6829, N 4205/441/55, p. 35-38.

ongoing events, and allowed Warsaw authorities to influence the point of view of the British diplomats.

The study of the reports sent from Warsaw to London shows that William Max-Müller had been accepting the assurances of the Polish ministers without any critical analysis. The reports lack any deeper insight of the reasons behind the actions of the government and Józef Piłsudski. Neither are there any explanations why Polish politicians strived to incorporate the Vilnius Region. It is most probable that while residing in Poland he was not even aware of many of the Polish governments' actions. He, just like other representatives of western powers, simply was not informed about all the measures being taken by the Polish politicians. The point of view of the British Minister was also influenced by very good relations with the Polish Ministers of Foreign Affairs. In fact there is scarcely any data in the documents on the subsequent Polish Ministers: Eustachy Sapieha, Gabriel Narutowicz, Marian Seyda, Roman Dmowski, Maurycy Zamoyski or August Zaleski. But he kept particularly close relations with Konstanty Skirmunt and Aleksander Skrzyński, the Minister who stayed at their post the longest.[7] And to them Max-Müller paid the greatest attention in his reports.

The British diplomat was clearly influenced by Konstanty Skirmnut. He wrote about him in a very positive manner. From the beginning the relations between them were very good and lasted long after Max-Müller's retirement (Skirmunt, 1997, p. 7, 22, 113-114, 187). The Minister contributed to him a major role in developing the principles of the Warsaw's foreign policy and was particularly positive about his activities aiming at further consolidating the international position of Poland which rendered it "stronger and more assured," and she gained her stability in politics and trade in the Eastern Europe. And it was "the wise policy pursued by M. Skirmunt – according to the Envoy of HM – to which the country owed this happy development leading to the removal of the "chauvinism attaching to Poland's foreign policy" as well as abandoning "its policy of adventure and was determined henceforward to live in peace with its neighbours and to devote its energies to internal reconstruction" (Report 1922, Poland, p. 2, paragraph 1, 2; p. 6, paragraph 20; p. 33, paragraph 157). Because Max-Müller, just like Whitehall, defined the overall struggle of Poles in the

---

7   The periods of holding the office of the Polish Minister of Foreign Affairs: from 23 July 1920 to 25 May 1921 – Eustachy Sapieha; from 11 June 1921 to 6 June 1922 – Konstanty Skirmunt; till 9 December 1922 – Gabriel Narutowicz; till 25 May 1923 – Aleksander Skrzyński; till 27 October 1923 – Marian Seyda; till 19 December 1923 – Roman Dmowski; from 19 January to 27 July 1924 - Maurycy Zamoyski; from 27 July 1924 to 5 May 1926 again Aleksander Skrzyński; from 25 June 1926 – August Zaleski (Baumgart, Walczak, Wątora, 2001, p. 15-32).

period of 1919-1922 for restoration of a strong state with the secure borders in terms of adventurism. Konstanty Skirmunt, and after him Gabriel Narutowicz and Aleksander Skrzyński, made maximum efforts to convince Europe it was not so; that the Republic of Poland really wanted peace and the European governments do not had to worry about any unpleasant surprises on the part of Warsaw (Nowak-Kiełbikowa, 1994, p. 248-250; Wandycz, 1999, p. 149).

The analysis of the annual reports for 1921 and 1922 prepared by the employees of the Legation in Warsaw allows the conclusion that the opinion on the matter of joining the Vilnius Region to Poland was indeed influenced by the policy of Konstanty Skirmunt which had already before softened an anty-Polish attitude of Max-Müller. Because he stated in these reports that the Second Republic of Poland made some progress towards political stability. He was assuring of peaceful policy and the commencement of the era of consolidation. He mentioned the Second Republic of Poland as a strong factor in the cause of European peace. Simultaneously he pointed to its geopolitical position between Russia and Germany (Report 1921, Poland, p. 2, paragraph 3 and 4, p. 4, paragraph 13 i 14; p. 30, paragraph 161; Łukasik, 2005, p. 175). These words became the major points in his telegrams and subsequent reports. He was repeating them almost at any occasion and would not let the clerks of the Whitehall oversee them.

Max-Müller's positive opinion about Aleksander Skrzyński, as it was in case of Skirmunt, could have been the outcome of the count openly trying to develop closer relations with Great Britain since this country, as he would say, is awe-inspiring and admirable because of its "deep wisdom and unparalleled policy style" (Pajewski, 1992, p. 137). The Minister of Foreign Affairs emphasised by his activities that „our policy is the policy of peace, creative peace, peace based on cooperation, building and organizing the coexistence" (Skrzyński, 1925, p. 4). In his annual reports Max-Müller praised Skrzyński for him being an ardent supporter of closer relations with Great Britain (Report 1924, Poland, p. 29, paragraph 153; Report 1923, Poland, p. 8, paragraph. 34). He attributed to him a great role in improving the relations between London and Warsaw, as well as in convincing Europe that that Poland can be counted on as an factor of peace and stability (Report 1925, Poland, p. 11, paragraph 46; Report 1926, Poland, p. 9, paragraph 35; p. 6, paragraph 20; p. 7, paragraph 27).

And undeniably the influence of these two Polish Ministers' ideas is very prominent in the documents sent by the British Envoy to London. Already in one of his first letters (from 29 March 1921) from Warsaw to London William Max-Müller stressed that he was not yet utterly sure as for Poland being able to survive as an independent country when "once her two big neighbours have recovered." Yet he hoped that – "this recovery" – would take long years.[8] Some years later, in September 1939, the Second Republic of Poland ceased to exist. Max-Müller would come back to this issue every now and then in his correspondence. He would emphasise that Poland made a noticeable progress towards stability both at home and abroad, and the international position of that country was defined in the treaties signed. Nevertheless Poland must be particularly "...sensitive to the changing conditions in those two neighbouring States [Germany and Russia].... Nevertheless, she seems to have learnt that her wisest policy lies in keeping quiet and developing her vast economic resources.... The impartial observer may hesitate therefore to assert that Poland has once for all abandoned her policy of adventure and entered definitely on a course of internal consolidation.... It is not too much to say that the growing hope of Poland's stability became one of the bright spots in the general darkness of Europe politics. Poland at peace and free from alarms may well become an important factor in the restoration of Europe. (Report 1921, Poland, p. 4, paragraph 14; Report 1922, Poland, p. 6, paragraph 20). He has already mentioned in his telegrams the sincere desire for peace on the part of the Second Republic of Poland, that "the majority of the Polish nation had abandoned their earlier dreams of conquest" or that Poland should be regarded rather as a factor of peace.[9] As I have mentioned before, the British perceived the ways of Poles struggling for regaining a strong country with solid borders, as a policy of chauvinism and adventurism. Probably that was also why Max-Müller was constantly bringing up the role of the Republic of Poland on the geopolitical arena of Eastern Europe, speaking about her giving up the „policy of adventure" and assuring about the stable political situation and peaceful intentions.

He was also frequently reminding about the dangers lieing in the very position of the country by the Vistula River. In his view she was still endangered not only internally but also pertaining to future strength restoration of Germany and USSR (Report 1922, Poland, p. 6, paragraph 20). Although in his opinion the country by the Vistula River was nevertheless in the fortunate position of being aware of her two traditional enemies.[10] The expressions constantly repeated by Max-Müller found their response from London. In February 1925 James Headlam-Morley (1930, pp. 182-183), historical advisor at Whitehall, wrote: "It is the real interest of this country to prevent a new alliance between

---

8   PRO FO 371/6829, N 4205/441/55, p. 35.
9   *Documents on British Foreign Policy 1919-1939, First Series, Vol. XXV, Russia 1923-5, Poland and the Baltic States 1924-5*, ed. by W.N. Medlicott, D. Dakin, G. Bennett, London: HMSO, 1984 documents no. 412 and 373, p. 761, 813.
10   Ibidem, document no. 404, p. 801.

Germany and Russia, an alliance which would no doubt be cemented by an attack on Poland. We cannot now be indifferent...." But Great Britain still was showing a lack of appreciation for the important role of the Second Republic of Poland. She considered it to be a country of lesser importance. However Max-Müller had no doubts that „a strong, self-reliant and contented Poland means peace in the east of Europe" (Report 1926, Poland, p. 3, paragraph 8).

The information sent by William Max-Müller to Whitehall was prepared in the form of various notes, telegrams and other correspondence. Weekly and annual reports were issued on the policy of the country he was residing in. These were to help the Whitehall clerks in London prepare the surveys on Poland and lay out the direction for the foreign policy of Great Britain in this region of Europe. The annual reports on political events in Poland during 1920-1926 sent by William Max-Müller, the Envoy Extraordinary and Minister Plenipotentiary of HM from the Warsaw Legation were directed to North Department (dealing with the Polish issues) of the Foreign Office. It is though worth to mention that British diplomats had poorly developed independent sources of information. According to Edward H. Carr, a Whitehall clerk, neither William Max-Müller nor Tudor Vaughan (who was working at the post in Kaunas) had any means of checking the statements made by the Lithuanian and Polish governments. "This correspondence therefore tends to become a mere repetition of Lithuanian and Polish propaganda."[11] The telegram (of 20 May 1924) he received from Max-Müller regarding Lithuanian increased activity on the Polish frontier described as "5 proc. real anxiety" and "95 proc. propaganda."[12] Whereas the account dealing with the causes and subsequent course of events of the May Coup d'État in 1926 was drawn largely on the basis of information published in the newspapers. Nevertheless Max-Müller immediately pointed out that such sources of information could not be gullibly accepted as accurate and impartial.[13] Moreover the Foreign Office clerks during Max-Müller's service at the post in Poland were constantly complaining about the delays in sending his annual reports. According to the rules stated in the Foreign Office Circular of the 15th May 1909, the annual report should have been received at this office as soon as possible after the 1st January of each year.[14] However the his annual reports would usually reach London in the second half of the year. Every year the reminders were being sent from Whitehall to Poland. Yet the Legation would not respond very much to these. When the report for 1926 arrived on 10

---

11   PRO FO 371/10363, N3101/196/59, p. 51 - Max-Müller (Warsaw), 7 IV 1924, p. 51.
12   PRO FO 371/10364, N 4336/196/59, p. 56.
13   PRO FO 371/11762, N 2346/41/55 - Max-Müller (Warsaw), 19 V 1926, p. 182.
14   PRO FO 371/5474, W 812/812/50.

October 1927 it was taken as a scandal that the reports never reach the land by the Thames before the autumn of the next year. This initiated a discussion which the North Department clerks conducted in written on the jacket of the report. According to Laurence Collier the reason for the delay of the 1926 report was simply its inordinate length. He suggested that a private note should be written on that matter by then Head of North Department, George Mounsey. Collier's associate, Michael Palairet opted for sending Max-Müller an official request for the future annual reports to arrive Whitehall before the end of March. And this idea was supported by Duncan Gregory himself, who at that time was the Assistant Under-Secretary of State (Report 1926, Poland, p. 216). As a result of it on 11 November 1927 Palairet had sent to Max-Müller (on behalf of the Secretary of State for Foreign Affairs) a note, in which he courteously thanked the diplomat for the care and labour bestowed on his exhaustive report – read with interest. Simultaneously he requested him politely to send them in the future before the end of March. (Report 1926, Poland, p. 248). He did not mention anything about making these reports less extensive. No matter how great was the indignation in North Department caused by the delay of the annual reports, the note was written in a polite manner. That proved sufficient though. The report for 1927 was sent by the end of March 1928 and arrived London already on 10 April but it was 23 pages shorter than the previous one. It should be noted though that the report was prepared not by Max-Müller but Reginald Leeper, Legation's chargé d'affaires, by the time of arrival of a new Envoy Extraordinary and Minister Plenipotentiary William Erskin. It is hard to say without doubt if the report would have reached London faster if it was Max-Müller who had watched over its preparation as at that time he had retired.

By the end of January 1926, five years had passed since he took over the office of an Envoy Extraordinary and Minister Plenipotentiary in Poland. On this occasion he was requested by the *The Polish Courier* (*Kurier Polski*) to give an interview. And although the clerks of Whitehall were not very fond of such initiatives they ultimately had no objections.[15] In a short introduction the editorial staff positively summed up his previous achievements. "During his five fruitful years at the Warsaw post he has accomplished a lot in bringing Great Britain and Poland closer together and it is certainly chiefly due to Sir Max-Müller's reports that his motherland and his fellow countrymen have gradually gained a proper understanding of Poland and her importance. He and his wife lady Wanda Max-Müller won the greatest favour of the majority of the Polish society" (Liński, 1926, editorial note, p. 2). Indeed the British Envoy was very pleased with the kindness and esteem he had experienced not only from the

---

15   PRO FO 371/11760, N160/41/55, p. 28, 29, 31.

successive Polish governments, but also from all the clerks. He spoke very positively about his relations with the Polish: "During my nearly thirty years of work as a diplomat nowhere else have I encountered, not even in America, greater kindness and hospitality than in Poland, and I suppose I am not wrong thinking that when we are to leave, we will part not only with acquaintances but also with sincere friends, who will feel sad as we will that we leave them and Poland as it was for us and shall never cease to be." At the same time he mentioned that "maintaining peace is presently the main line in the policy of Poland – and expressed – great trust that she will keep her reputation as a bastion of peace in the middle and eastern Europe" (Liński, 1926, p. 2). During his five year stay in Poland he observed that everything changed for better, from the way Warsaw looked to the construction of roads and railways across the country. He promised that his government will be positively inclined towards all the requests for financial or economical help that was in the best interest of Poland. He was eager to do anything possible to develop trade between the Republic of Poland and Great Britain. He supported investing British capital in Polish enterprises in spite at times discouraging actions on the Polish side. He wanted Poland to be "rich and thriving" country (Liński, 1926, p. 2).

Meanwhile in Warsaw there were many rumours in the air concerning Marshal Piłsudski's political activities. "Though conscious of the recrudescence of the Marshal's influence during the past few weeks... I am still unwilling to believe – confined Max-Müller in his telegram (of 20 January 1926) to Whitehall – that his influence constitutes a danger to the State.... I make bold to assert that he has no idea of making himself military dictator and would never be a party to any revolutionary act against the interests of the State...."[16] But as the rumours of the Marshal's regaining the power spread some accusations started coming up which were very unpleasant for the diplomat and his family.[17] At the end of April Max-Müller informed Whitehall about the gossips against him. He reported that the Legation's Passport Control Officer, captain Derbyshire, was travelling by a train back from a suburban resort that was under his office to Warsaw when four young Poles entered his carriage and at once started to discuss politics. Perhaps they concluded that "such an obvious Englishman would not understand them." According to them Piłsudski was soon to come back to power again with a strong support of the British. "He then mentioned me by name as being the pay-master [of this venture]."[18] Max-Müller ignored the gossip. As he informed London about it he commented that it did not seem

---

16   PRO FO 371/11760, N 340/41/55.
17   PRO FO 371/11760, N 680/41/55.
18   PRO FO 371/11761, N 2049/41/55, 27 IV 1926, p. 25, 26.

worth while of taking any serious steps to root it up. He assumed it would just die out by itself with time.[19] Yet the rumour spread with an increased force after the May Coup. Why the HM Minister would not react? Maybe because the clerks of Northen Departament of the Foreign Office thought it was better to not to take up any steps in this matter. For how to understand otherwise Collier's comment (of 5 May) that he could not "see that any good would be done by denials... Moreover, it appears not unlikely that Piłsudski will return to power in the nearest future; and he would hardly be grateful to us for denying that we are his friends. ... it might not be a bad thing for our own prestige in Poland to have it believed that we stood well with those in power."[20] The Assistant Under Secretary, Duncan Gregory, advised to ignore the rumour.[21] The consequences of this decision personally touched Max-Müller.

The May Coup surprised the Legation employees. In their memorandum sent on 14 April Max-Müller and Military Attaché, colonel Emilius Clayton, were still convinced, that the Marshal would not take any active steps. "Dictatorship is discussed by everyone – wrote the envoy (on 14 April) – and even among the Rright it is recognised that Piłsudski is the only possible dictator, but he has never made the slightest step in that direction.[22] The unawareness of the British Legation in Warsaw, as Tomasz Duszyński asserted (2000, p. 76-77, 69, 90; see also: Nowak-Kiełbikowa, 1989, p. 149-155, 302-3), seemed peculiar, if you considered the fact that both, the British Envoy and the colonel Clayton, had often paid their visits in Sulejówek before the May Coup. And that set the basis for the rumours. If those meetings had not been taking place to support Piłsudski in his regaining the power, still surprising is the fact that nobody took under consideration that the Marshal might decide upon an independent action.

After the May Coup a new government was appointed with Kazimierz Bartel as a Prime Minister. Max-Müller, despite of the appointment of new government having been strictly constitutional, had some moral objections and therefore hesitated to recognise it. His concerns were not shared by London and he was advised to develop good relations with the new government.[23] During that period revived the "foolish tales" implying British involvement in supporting the Marshal with an emphasis on Max-Müller's role (Report 1926, Poland, p. 10, paragraph 38). This "fable," as the diplomat reported to Whitehall

---

19 PRO FO 371/11761, N 2049/41/55, 27 IV 1926, p. 27.
20 PRO FO 371/11761, N 2049/41/55, p. 24.
21 PRO FO 371/11761, N 2049/41/55, 27 IV 1926, p. 29.
22 PRO FO 371/11761, N 1753/41/55.
23 PRO FO 371/11761, N 2197/41/55, s. 76.

(23 May), had made progress, especially among the National Democrats and in certain circles of society where the love of discussing politics was only equalled by the lack of knowledge of the subject under discussion. The story was that the British Envoy had been informed about intending the coup d'etat and that was why he had asked his wife to leave the capital of Poland.[24] Yet he did not utterly disprove this information since his wife had indeed left Warsaw. He maintained that he had no idea about the coup and that he had not spoken to Piłsudski since he had he dined with him in May 1923.[25] But all these rumours were the result of his above mentioned baffling visits to Sulejówek. August Zaleski, Polish Minister of Foreign Affairs, advised the British diplomat to deny the rumours, but in his opinion the circumstances were not favourable. "I am too directly concerned and feel too indignant.... There is also another side to the question, and that is that with a nation containing such a large proportion of crazy people and political fanatics is always the possibility of some disagreeable incident arising which might really hale serious consequences. ...so perhaps it would be better to let the question stand over until we can discuss it... in London" – he wrote to Gregory. Max-Müller was planning a monthly visit to Great Britain around 10-12 June.[26] Issuing an official denial Whitehall deemed inadvisable. The diplomat was allowed to leave Warsaw and in the second half of June he arrived in London. But when ha came back to Poland in July the issue was still in the air. The newspapers published against him and his wife some "loathsome insults". The diplomat was irritated by this whole situation. He reacted fretfully. Chamberlain requested the envoy to restrain himself taking into account the imminent meeting of the League of Nations in Geneva.[27]

What was then the attitude of William Max-Müllera towards Piłsudski and his actions? The diplomat referring to the internal situation in Poland during the first years after the war emphasized twice that "the preponderant role and the arbitrary character of the present Chief of the State" complicated for the Polish government the task of administering the country (Report 1920, Poland, p. 32, paragraph 212). In his subsequent reports he stressed that Piłsudski wielded far greater political power than it should be held by the constitutional head of a democratic state. He did not express though his opinion whether that was for the good of the Republic of Poland or not. He just mentioned that the points of view in that regard might vary (Report 1921, Poland, p. 31, paragraph 165). On the other hand in the report for 1922 he referred to Piłsudski's dominating personality as well as policy

---

24   PRO FO 371/11763, N 2549/2704/41/55, p. 99-101, 157.
25   PRO FO 371/11763, N 2743/41/55, p. 190.
26   PRO FO 371/11763, N2549/41/55, p. 104-105.
27   PRO FO 371/11759, N 3428/24/55, p. 88-91, 97.

matters decided on his initiative and carried out by his personal entourage. In spite of the struggles of the Diet and the Government to assert their authority, he [the Marshal] had grown to regard himself as superior to any constitutional limitations." His will was a decisive factor in Polish policy. (Report 1922, Poland, p. 35, paragraph 166). Max-Müller was critical about the overwhelming selfconfidence of the Marshal and his pride in his achievements, the way he constantly spoke of the various benefits he had bestowed unaided upon his country, and his not always quite successful attempts to exercise a dictatorship.[28] The May Coup inspired another series of critical statements about Piłsudski's actions by the British Envoy. In one of his telegrams he wrote about the harm done by the Marshal to the good name of Poland. He questioned his sanity. He reminded that the Marshal was not a normal individual. The immense influence he exerted by his personal magnetism and esteem he was held in for the devotion to his country made him, according to Max-Müller, a source of grave danger. He was not consistent, as Max-Müller would append. He tried to give the impression of a hard, determined man, but in reality – as Max-Müller asserted – he had not got the strength of his convictions, or, at all events, he did not go through with his projects, but would stop them half way.[29] That was, according to him, the case when he ordered General Lucjan Żeligowski to capture Vilnius, enraging thus the Allied Governments, but after reaching that city he gave up proceeding to Kovno although it was easy to conduct and apart from that by seizing Kovno "he would have saved his country innumerable difficulties."[30] According to the HM Envoy, Piłsudski exhibited similar inconsistency when he had decided upon dictatorship, yet announced his will to act according to the Constitution and to preserve the forms of legality. "These words, in the mouth of a man who had just upset the Government by a military coup d'etat, are in themselves sufficient to raise doubts as to his sanity."[31] The diplomat wrote about Józef Piłsudski, that he was "a conspirator all his life, preferred to work behind the scenes and to enforce his decisions, not through the direct exercise of his personal authority, but under a fiction of constitutionality through his Ministers, who, in practice if not in theory, were responsible only to him." This – as he would append – "have differentiated the Marshal's from other dictatorships" (Report 1926, Poland, p. 30, paragraph 122). In July he sent to Whitehall the description of the most prominent members of the new government. He recalled his previous statements on Piłsudski. Simultaneously he added that the greatest defect of the Marshal's character was

---

28 PRO FO 371/8141, N 10905/1876/55 – Max-Müller, 8 XII 1922 r., p. 8, 10.
29 PRO FO 371/11762, N 2346/41/55 – Max-Müller (Warsaw), 19 V 1926, p. 182.
30 PRO FO 371/11762, N 2346/41/55, p. 182.
31 PRO FO 371/11762, N 2346/41/55, p. 182.

his impetuosity, both in word and deed as well as intolerance of resistance, almost insane suspicion of his equals, grossly exaggerated opinion of his own talents and powers, and inability to create any precise programme or to reach the aims he had set. He also mentioned abrupt manners of the Marshal and that he was a weak men who frequently changes which made him unaccountable and unreliable in action.[32] He stressed that the May Coup and creating a new government in 1926 were one of the veils covering a dictatorial power, although "Marshal Pilsudski did not, as was at first expected, take advantage of his victory to establish a dictatorship" (Report 1926, Poland, p. 38, paragraph 152).

Whereas at the end of 1927 he favourably assessed the events of may 1926. In his opinion the situation of the Republic of Poland on the international arena and its internal policy improved since the coup d'etat took place and Piłsudski seized the power. "As a result Poland finds herself more than ever in the limelight of international politics – he wrote after she had won a permanent seat on the Council of the League of Nations – and if not as yet accepted as a Great Power, at all events recognised as one of the most important factors in determining the question of peace or war in Europe (Report 1926, Poland, p. 2, paragraph 1, p. 30, paragraph 121). At the same time he stressed that "the Poles have recovered confidence in themselves. This tendency, of course, has its good side, but, if carried to far, has in it also the germs of future trouble." He expressed full agreement with the remarks of Mr Reginald Lepper, then the first secretary of the Legation, on the inevitability of other countries to regard the position and the attitude of the Second Republic of Poland.[33]

In December 1927 Max-Müller retired, and along with him was recalled the current Attaché colonel Clayton. The reason behind it was probably the fact that both of them were not in good relations with the new regime in Poland and their names were associated with the rumours about the British support for the May Coup (Piszczkowski, 1975, p. 323; Łaptos, 1993, p. 127). Nevertheless William Max-Müller left "the best memories" after his stay in Poland, "during which – as put it Ignacy Mościcki, the President of the Republic of Poland, welcoming Erskine (the successor of Max-Müllera) – we had an opportunity to see in various circumstances his exceptional virtues as a man and diplomat. In the period of years that were particularly hard for the consolidation of the Polish State we could find in him a faithful translator of many impediments that we had no choice but to overcome...."[34]

---

32   PRO FO 371/111763, N 2763/41/55 – Max-Müller (Warsaw), 12 VI 1926, p. 224.
33   PRO FO 371/12573, N 5469/23/55, p. 210, paragraph 2-5.
34   Archiwum Akt Nowych (Warsaw), Ministerstwo Spraw Zagranicznych, vol. 907, p. 52.

Although the diplomat had retired and since then had been living in London, he not only kept in touch with the Republic of Poland (he would visit the country for business purposes), but in difficult times was also her advocate. He was preparing memoranda and was sending letters to Whitehall about his travels[35]. One of the Whitehall employees, who had read them described the former Envoy as "an experienced observer who knows Poland well", and his correspondence found worth reading.[36] This assessment was confirmed by another employee, who said Max-Müller was "a good judge."[37] Also during World War II he stood in support of creating the independent Poland that would stretch from the Tatra Mountains to the Balic, and which in his view could not exist without free and open access to the sea (Max-Müller 1944, p. 2-5). He supported Poland in important moments and till the end of his life remained under the spell of her charm.

Translated by Iwona Szuwalska

Bibliography:

Annual Report on Poland for 1920 from Mr. Max-Müller, 18 III 1922, PRO FO 371/8143, N2900/2900/55.

Annual Report on Poland for 1921 from Mr. Max-Müller, 23 XII 1922, PRO, FO 371/9312, N 30/30/55.

Annual Report on Poland for 1922 from Mr. Max-Müller, 29 IX 1923, PRO, FO 371/9330, N8023/8023/55.

Annual Report on Poland for 1923 from Mr. Max-Müller, 1 VII 1924, PRO, FO 371/10461, N 5630/5630/55.

Annual Report on Poland for 1924 from Mr. Max-Müller, 16 X 1925, PRO, FO 371/ 11005, N 5966/5437/55.

Annual Report on Poland for 1925 from Mr. Max-Müller, 16 X 1926, PRO, FO 371/ 11774, N 4788/4788/55.

Annual Report on Poland for 1926 from Mr. Max-Müller, 3 X 1927, PRO, FO 371/ 12580, N 4749/4749/55.

Annual Report in Poland for 1927 from Mr. Leeper, 30 III 1928, PRO, FO 371/13308, N 2025/2025/55.

Baumgart, M.; Walczak, H.; Wątor A. (ed.) (2001). *Ministrowie Polski Niepodległej 1918-1945* (Minister of Independent Poland, 1918-1945), Szczecin.

---

35   One of them addressed directly to Orme Sargent, a Whitehall employee, together with a 19-page memorandum describing the experiences form his travel as well as the copy of the letters to Gauleiter Förster, his friend living in Gdańsk, and Alexander Cadogan, Permament Under-Secretary of State (PRO FO 371/23022, C 10009/54/18, p. 266-286).

36   Illegible signature under the comment (PRO FO 371/23022, C 10009/54/18, p. 266).

37   The initials were L.O. (PRO FO 371/23022, C 10009/54/18, p. 266).

Duszyński, T. (2000). *Przewrót majowy 1926 roku z perspektywy brytyjskiej* (Coup d'État in Poland 1926, from the British point of view), manuscript, Wrocław.

The Foreign Office List and Diplomatic and Consular Year Book, 1928, ed. by Godfrey E. P. Hertslet, Compiled from Official Records, by Permission of the Secretary of State for Foreign Affairs, London: Harrison and Sons.

Headlam-Morley, J. (1930). *Studies in Diplomacy*, London.

Liński, H. (1926). Pięć lat na Placówce (Rozmowa z P. Max-Müller) (Five years in Legation, Conversation with sir Max-Müller), *Kurier Polski*, 31 (XXIX), p. 2.

Łaptos, J. (1993). *Dyplomaci II RP w świetle raportów Quai D'Orsay* (Diplomats of the Polish Republic in the light of the reports *Quai D'Orsay*), Warsaw.

Łukasik, M. (2005). Polityka polska wobec Litwy w latach 1920-1922 w świetle raportów brytyjskiego dyplomaty Williama Max-Müllera (Polish policy towards Lithuania during the years 1920-1922 in the light of the reports, the British diplomat, William Max-Muller) [w:] T. Kulak (red.), *Studia z dziejów XIX i XX wieku*, Prace Historyczne XXXVII, Wrocław, p. 159-176.

Łukasik-Duszyńska, M. (2008). *Brytyjskie poselstwo donosi...Posłowie brytyjscy wobec stosunków Polski z państwami bałtyckimi w latach 1920-1926* (HM's Ministers Informs... Relations Between Poland and Baltic States (1920-1926)), Wydawnictwo SWPS Academica, Warsaw.

Nowak-Kiełbikowa, M. (1994). Konferencja genueńska 1922 r. w koncepcjach ministra spraw zagranicznych Konstantego Skirmunta (Genoa Conference, 1922, in conceptions of Polish Foreign Affairs Minister Konstantyn Skirmunt) [w:] *Z dziejów polityki i dyplomacji polskiej* (History of Polish politics and diplomacy), Studia poświęcone pamięci Edwarda hr. Raczyńskiego Prezydenta Rzeczypospolitej Polskiej na wychodźstwie, Warsaw, pp. 236-254.

Nowak-Kiełbikowa, M. (1989). *Polska – Wielka Brytania w dobie zabiegów o zbiorowe bezpieczeństwo w Europie 1923-1937* (Poland and Great Britain during the era of building collective security in Europe, 1923-1937), PWN, Warsaw.

Max-Müller, W. (1944). *Poland's Access to the Sea*, London.

Pajewski J. (ed.) (1992), *Ministrowie spraw zagranicznych II Rzeczypospolitej* (The Ministers of Foreign Affairs the Second Polish Republic), Szczecin.

Piszczkowski, T. (1975). Anglia a Polska 1914-1939, W świetle dokumentów brytyjskich (Britain and Poland 1914-1939, In light of the British documents), London.

Sierpowski, S. (1944). Polityka zagraniczna Polski międzywojennej (Polish Foreign Policy between two Wars) [w:] J. Buszko, A. Garlicki (ed.) *Dzieje narodu i państwa polskiego*, III (65), Warsaw 1994, pp. 80);

Skirmunt, K. (1997). Moje wspomnienia 1866-1945 (My memories 1866-1945), oprac. E. Orlof, A. Pasternak, Rzeszów .

Skrzyński A. (1925). Mowa Ministra Spraw Zagranicznych (The Speech of the Minister of Foreign Affaires), Warsaw.

Wandycz, P. (1999). Z Piłsudskim i Sikorskim, August Zaleski – minister spraw zagranicznych w latach 1926-1932 i 1939-1941 (With Piłsudski and Sikorski. August Zalewski – Minister of Foreign Afaires during 1926-1932 and 1939-1941), Warsaw.

Appealing to patriotic sentiments as the SB's secret collaborators recruitment method

Sebastian Michalak

In 1944-1954 the Polish communist public security apparatus was functioning under the Ministry of Public Security, the institution exhibiting enormous power. The most important organs of that resort were the Office of Security – political police units – known by their abbreviated form UB or as *bezpieka*. UB resorted to methods typical for secret police of totalitarian states. The first decade of post-war communist rule was marked with the symbols of terror and lawlessness, mass repressions, violent investigations, abductions and political murders. UB functionaries recruited people and kept personal information sources. They also resorted to setups, surveillance, and arrests. After taking over the cases of the operational division investigating officers investigated people and drew up indictments. The subjects of the security apparatus's operational activity were authentic or imaginary enemies of the communistic rule. Prosecution was directed against people dissatisfied with the political system imposed on them, those who criticized the authority's actions, as well as against those who were not able to cope with the standards enforced on the society by the communist party. In 1944–1956 the Polish underground independence movement was broken in cooperation with Soviet Union, the political opposition was crushed and Polish post-war social elites were destroyed. Polish Catholic Church and peasantry were attacked. In course of political turn that took place in October 1956 the public security apparatus fell under the supervision of the Ministry of Internal Affairs (MSW). On the basis of UB cadre and structure Security Service (Służba Bezpieczeństwa) further addressed as SB which had been formed. Until 1990 when it was dissolved UB had been playing a role of secret police.[1] Members of the communist party would call it the „security apparatus" and on informal ground they would speak about it as „the arm of the party."[2]

---

1   Aparat bezpieczeństwa w Polsce. Kadra kierownicza 1944-1956, red. K. Szwagrzyk, Warszawa: Instytut Pamięci Narodowej Komisja Ścigania Zbrodni przeciwko Narodowi Polskiemu, 2005, s. 19-25.

2   F. Musiał, Podręcznik bezpieki. Teoria pracy operacyjnej Służby Bezpieczeństwa w świetle wydawnictw resortowych Ministerstwa Spraw Wewnętrznych PRL (1970-1989), Kraków: Instytut Pamięci Narodowej Komisja Ścigania Zbrodni przeciwko Narodowi Polskiemu, 2007, s. 39.

Since 1956 the party held an actual and not just a statutory, as it used to be so far, supervision over the security apparatus.[3] SB was to implement directives passed by the party and further by the government.[4] Besides that the political police was responsible for personal protection of the highest representatives of the party and the government as well as for informing the heads of the party and the government authorities about internal situation of the country and external threats.[5]

The activities of the security apparatus were regulated by operational work directions from a supervising ministry. Such directives were normative in nature. They would specify the code of functionaries' conduct and issues pertaining to their day-to-day work. Such issues were not elaborated in details leaving some room for more specific training directions.[6] Norms included a general operational work theory and specified basic means and methods of operational activities. On the basis of such norms each operational division of the secret police developed its own theoretical interpretations and working methods. The directives often sanctioned changes in operational practices.[7]

The article focuses on explaining the procedures behind recruiting secret collaborators by the political police in 1953–1970 – which was one of the personal information sources – on the basis of appealing to their patriotic sentiments. The author mostly referred to publications by the historians from the Institute of National Remembrance including a source edition of security apparatus's operational directives by T. Ruzikowski,[8] a monograph and studies by F. Musiał,[9] work by R. Terlecki[10] and a study by ed. A. Fary et al.[11]

---

3   Aparat bezpieczeństwa w Polsce. Kadra kierownicza 1956-1975, red. P. Piotrowski, Warszawa: Instytut Pamięci Narodowej Komisja Ścigania Zbrodni przeciwko Narodowi Polskiemu, 2006, s. 10.

4   See Instrukcja o pracy operacyjnej Służby Bezpieczeństwa resortu spraw wewnętrznych, Załącznik do zarządzenia nr 006/70 Ministra Spraw Wewnętrznych z dnia 1 lutego 1970 r. w sprawie pracy operacyjnej Służby Bezpieczeństwa resortu spraw wewnętrznych [w:] T. Ruzikowski, Instrukcje pracy operacyjnej Aparatu Bezpieczeństwa (1945–1989), Warszawa: Materiały pomocnicze Biura Edukacji Publicznej IPN, T. 1, 2004, s. 126.

5   F. Musiał, Podręcznik bezpieki. Teoria pracy operacyjnej Służby Bezpieczeństwa w świetle wydawnictw resortowych Ministerstwa Spraw Wewnętrznych PRL (1970-1989), Kraków: Instytut Pamięci Narodowej Komisja Ścigania Zbrodni przeciwko Narodowi Polskiemu, 2007, s. 40-41.

6   T. Ruzikowski, Instrukcje pracy operacyjnej aparatu bezpieczeństwa (1945–1989), Warszawa: Materiały pomocnicze Biura Edukacji Publicznej IPN, T. 1, 2004, s. 4-5

7   F. Musiał, Podręcznik bezpieki, s. 275.

8   T. Ruzikowski, Instrukcje pracy operacyjnej aparatu bezpieczeństwa (1945–1989), Warszawa: Materiały pomocnicze Biura Edukacji Publicznej IPN, T. 1, 2004.

9   F. Musiał, Podręcznik bezpieki...

In 1953–1960 the secret police used the term „secret collaborator" as a general name for three categories of the personal information sources which were agents, informants, and residents.[12] An agent was a secret collaborator, who was responsible for exposing and dismantling anti-state activities of organizations, groups and individuals. That category of personal information sources was being recruited from the circles of people occupied with anti-state activities or predisposed by the secret police to be recruited and brought into an anti-state organization. An informant was a secret collaborator who associated with the circles of people potentially state-hostile and suspected by the secret police to be involved with anti-state activity. Informants were used for systematic informing about the circles and people who the political police was interested in. Such informants would observe and expose the signs of state-hostile activities, perform tasks necessary in order to gather information on particular persons. A resident was a reliable secret collaborator who would be in charge of a group of informants assigned by the political police.[13] Secret collaborators were the basic and the most effective means of operational work. In specific situations they were allowed to take initiative and have influence on the course of events. They could be used for offensive actions. They were not only a source of information but also a tool in operational activities which included surveillance of people and groups, misinforming activities meant for inspiring certain ways of actions, impeding and disorganizing plans. They also served the purpose of disintegrating and weakening the circles considered hostile.[14]

According to the directive about working with the agent network of 1953 collaborators recruitment process involved selecting a candidate to be recruited, collecting information on the selected person, choosing the method and technique of recruitment, and finally recruitment itself. Selecting a candidate for recruitment had a certain purpose and was a result of the plan realised by the political police, predispositions and potentials of the candidate, the chances for successful recruitment, the ability of the candidate to complete the task

10 R. Terlecki, Miecz i tarcza komunizmu. Historia aparatu bezpieczeństwa w Polsce 1944-1990, Wydawnictwo Literackie, s. 117-118.
11 Pozyskać „Dobrego" Wywiad PRL wobec Franciszka Chrapkiewicza i jego rodziny, pod red. A. Fary, P. Szopy, R. Witalca, Instytut Pamięci Narodowej Komisja Ścigania Zbrodni przeciwko Narodowi Polskiemu Oddział w Rzeszowie: Rzeszów 2008.
12 F. Musiał, Podręcznik bezpieki, s. 348.
13 See Instrukcja nr 012/53 o pracy aparatu bezpieczeństwa z siecią agenturalną [w:] T. Ruzikowski, Instrukcje pracy operacyjnej Aparatu Bezpieczeństwa (1945–1989), Warszawa: Materiały pomocnicze Biura Edukacji Publicznej IPN, T. 1, 2004, s. 31-32.
14 F. Musiał, Podręcznik bezpieki, s. 91.

Sebastian Michalak

entrusted, and the possibility of keeping such recruitment in secret.[15] The decisive role in choosing the candidate for recruitment from organisations showing a negative attitude towards the authorities played a careful assessment of the evidences of the candidate's being engaged in anti-government activities and possibility to reach such candidate. While choosing the candidates for penetrating the anti-state groups a special attention was given to people who according to information collected were to be recruited by foreign intelligence services or an anti-state organization for cooperation, those who volunteered, or were friends and relatives of the illegal groups' members. It was advised that the candidates for informants were recruited from hostile or suspected circles or from amongst the people who were close to them. As for the resident candidate the character of his current work had to facilitate him with wide contacts with people. Above that it had to be a person thoroughly tested who met nearly all the requirements that political police functionaries were to meet.

Vetting the candidates for recruitment involved collecting as much information on them as possible. The records of the political police were checked, official characteristics were studied, community interviews were conducted and the reports by the secret collaborators were drown upon. Candidate's political views, private life, professional career, character, habits and addictions were all taken into consideration. It was advised to conduct a meeting of an undercover political police functionary with the candidate in order to verify the information collected.[16] The above mentioned agent, informant and resident candidates vetting rules were confirmed in the directive on rules of working with the agent networks published in 1955. In the following years the candidates for secret collaborators were subjected to such vetting.[17]

The materials collected in the course of such vetting were to help choose the appropriate recruitment basis and the effective method. The chosen methods and the ways of recruitment were a direct consequences of implementing one of the three basis of recruitment: recruitment based on appealing to patriotic sentiments, ideology or loyalty; recruitment based on compromising materials; or recruitment based on proposing financial profits or some other material benefits. In the directive of 1953 there was a notice that recruitment based on proposing financial profits or some other material benefits was rarely resorted to which according to the heads of the Department of Public Security was a result of weak or completely neglected stage of vetting the candidates.[18] Moreover it

---

15   See Instrukcja nr 012/53 o pracy aparatu bezpieczeństwa z siecią agenturalną, s. 33.
16   Ibidem, s. 34-35.
17   F. Musiał, Podręcznik bezpieki, s. 284-285.
18   See Instrukcja nr 012/53 o pracy aparatu bezpieczeństwa z siecią agenturalną, s. 37-38.

was stated that that people who were open for cooperation on the basis of appealing to their patriotic sentiments were not to be offered money for their cooperation since that could have had a corrupting effect on them.[19] Compromising materials were understood as information to be used for moral embarrassment of the candidate in his closest environment, or information that would make him liable to prosecution. Secret collaborators recruitment from amongst the members of state-hostile organisations could be conducted only by presenting the candidate such compromising material or by offering material benefits. Such recruitment was possible only if the candidate admitted his anti-state and anti-nation activities. In 1950s the compromising materials in operational political police practice were understood as information which could be the basis for prosecution of the particular person. Such information would be known later on as aggravating materials. Morally discreditable materials were resorted to in 1950s e.g. in cases such as recruiting candidates from clergy. Clear distinction between compromising and aggravating materials was introduced in the operational work directive of 1960.[20]

The authors of the directive maintained that participation of the citizens in governing the state, educating the nation in patriotic attitude and attachment for the fatherland gave a wide spectrum of recruiting possibilities facilitating the secret police with people who were able to expose and defang the enemies of the state. For cooperation in scrutinizing the anti-state circles it was advised to recruit the people who had long ago changed their convictions and became loyal citizens of their country just by appealing to their loyalty. Before proceeding with the recruitment process based on appealing to patriotic sentiments an interview with the candidate was recommend during which the person was to be reassured about his or her patriotic attitude towards the country. The interrogation was to be conducted with caution as a recruitment supporting method since it could potentially dishearten the candidate. Appealing to hatred against the enemies of the state was justifying the necessity of taking up cooperation with secret police. The functionaries were warned against a common in their environment conviction that such recruitment is the most easy. It had been noticed that persuading the candidate to take up cooperation required from the recruiting functionary a certain level of sophistication and political awareness.[21] On the basis of appealing to patriotic sentiments the candidates for residents – the trusted secret collaborators, who supervised a certain number of other secret collaborators assigned by the secret police – would also be

---

19   Ibidem, s. 39.
20   F. Musiał, Podręcznik bezpieki, s. 286 i 289.
21   See Instrukcja nr 012/53 o pracy aparatu bezpieczeństwa z siecią agenturalną, s. 37.

recruited.[22] In order to understand what the recruitment on the basis of appealing to so called patriotic sentiments was all about it is crucial to look at the context within which the directive concerned had been issued. In 1940s any sign of patriotism or respect for ones country and its traditions or values such as honour and faithfulness was called nationalism. For communist authorities nationalism was a threat since the persons cultivating such values were immune to lies and propaganda. The censorship actively supported creating new language which was modelling the reality. New meanings of the words such as „nation" or „patriotism" were introduced. After 1947 the term "nation" started to lose its historical and cultural context starting to be equivalent of terms such as "society" or "people".[23] In those days a patriot was supposed to be positively disposed towards the Soviet Union.[24] In a norm of 1953 one can track a typical communist motif of people's fatherland and hatred for imperialism. Ministry of Public Security would draw on Stalinist theory of increasing intensity of class struggle. Secret collaborators and completely dedicated to the communist ideal functionaries of *bezpieka* were to defend the communist country against its internal enemies.[25] In Stalinist period the propaganda equally as terror was a tool in the hands of communist authorities. The idea was to tame the society into adoration of the communist power and hatred of anything that was not coming form it. By various means the stereotypes of "people's reign" or "imperialism" were created and saturated with emotional content that would invade the intuitive plain. Propaganda banners would also influence the will, discouraged any signs of rebellion or bring enthusiasm and encourage working for the authorities. All these methods were to a certain extend effective and the number of people influenced by the propaganda would steadily increase.[26] Patriotism of 1940s and 1950s would appeal to proletarian values which were associated with national sentiments. The whole nation under the guidance of the working class was to build its socialist fatherland and above that it was understood as people. Perceived in this light the idea of nationwide front line was to mobilize the society to be more alert and engage in an uncompromised struggle against the

---

22 Ibidem, s. 43.
23 M. Zaremba, Komunizm, legitymizacja, nacjonalizm. Nacjonalistyczna legitymacja władzy komunistycznej w Polsce, Warszawa: Wydawnictwo Trio, 2001, s. 175.
24 J. Hera, Narodziny cenzury, Biuletyn Instytutu Pamięci Narodowej, Nr 5-6, 2007, s. 111 i 119.
25 R. Terlecki, Miecz i tarcza komunizmu. Historia aparatu bezpieczeństwa w Polsce 1944-1990, Wydawnictwo Literackie, s. 110-111.
26 A. Albert, Najnowsza historia Polski 1914-1993, Warszawa: Świat Książki, 1995, s. 237-238.

class enemy – that would be those whom the party had pointed to.[27] According to Stalinist propaganda the mortal enemy of Poland was the American imperialism. Although the struggle against this threat was led in the name of peace and international friendship the hatred against imperialism was fuelled by nationalist jargon.[28] The secret police leadership had many times mentioned that the most welcome were the secret collaborators recruited on the basis of appealing to patriotic feelings. In 1950s reality there were not many such recruitments since at that time in general society persisted the idea that cooperating with UB is not to Poland's best interest. It is quite possible that persons recruited on this basis were actually informing on others out of fear pretending their patriotic ardour in front of UB.[29] During 1944-1956 about 70–80% of secret collaborators were the agents and informants recruited on the basis of compromising materials – that means under a strong pressure.[30] The directive of 1953 advised that the recruitment place had to guarantee secrecy and an ease of the recruitment process. For such reasons the recruitments would take place e.g. in conspirational premises, places of work, or candidates residence venue. Accept for the cases of recruitment on the basis of presenting compromising materials the candidate was supposed to be escorted to the recruitment place in a way that would not cause any negative feelings such as fear or mistrust. The former would be escorted after secret arrest. But in cases of the recruitment on the basis of appealing to patriotic sentiments or loyalty towards the state the possibility of setting an appointment with the candidate was permitted. In the course of recruitment an effort was made in order to overcome any inhibitions or hesitations about the cooperation proposed. Equally important was to bring the secret collaborator closer to the political police and make him feel connected to it. The results of secret collaborator's work were believed to depend a great deal on the candidate's developing friendship with the secret police and the relation of trust. The last stage of the recruitment process was to acquire from the recruited person a written commitment of cooperation, secrecy, and informing officially known as denunciation (*donos*).[31]

In March 1954 the UB functionaries started to hear more and more voices coming from the party members as well as from scrutinized circles criticising the

---

27 K. Tyszka, Nacjonalizm w komunizmie. Ideologia narodowa w Związku Radzieckim i Polsce Ludowej, Warszawa: Wydawnictwo IFiS PAN, 2004, s. 138-140.

28 M. Zaremba, Komunizm, legitymizacja, nacjonalizm, s. 205.

29 R. Terlecki, Miecz i tarcza komunizmu, s. 93.

30 H. Dominiczak, Organy bezpieczeństwa PRL 1944-1990, Warszawa: Dom Wydawniczy Bellona, 1997, s. 42-43.

31 See Instrukcja nr 012/53 o pracy aparatu bezpieczeństwa z siecią agenturalną, s. 36-39.

use violence and unjustified arrests.[32] Law and order was demanded. The Minister of Public Security complained about functionaries' lack of appreciation for the leading role of the communist party.[33] In September 1954 Józef Światło, a high rank functionary of the Ministry of Public Security who escaped to the West spoke for the Radio Free Europe about the methods of the party's power wielding, infringements of rights and crimes of the political police. Pressed by the public critique the leadership of the party introduced in December a security apparatus's reform. The public opinion was informed that the decisions taken were the result of e.g. cases of serious infringement of law and order by *bezpieka* having been discovered. There were also complains that the secret police functionaries would try to lord over the party.[34] The then head of Department of Public Security said that the secret police functionary is supposed to act according to the party's directives and lead the life pertaining to its ways.[35]

In March 1955 in a situation of clear demobilisation and disorganisation of *bezpieka* the directive about the rules of agent surveillance and operational archives was issued. The recommendation articulated in the directive of 1953 pertaining to strict following by the secret police functionaries revolutionary law and order was replaced by the twice stated command to follow PRL's legislation and observance of the people's law and order. Simultaneously the need of acting under the parties supervision was emphasised.[36] In the preamble there were also some other motifs different from the previous directive. Apart from commands pertaining to adhering to law, the tasks of security apparatus were expanded by fighting the Church and the enemies of the established party politics.[37]

According to another new provision pertaining to the rules of cooperating with the agent network which was introduced simultaneously with the above mentioned directive, the informant candidates were to be recruited from amongst the patriots and loyal citizens.[38] The residents were usually predestined

---

32 R. Terlecki, Miecz i tarcza komunizmu, s. 117-118.
33 H. Dominiczak, Organy bezpieczeństwa PRL 1944-1990, s. 28.
34 A. Albert, Najnowsza historia Polski 1914-1993, s. 290-291.
35 H. Dominiczak, Organy bezpieczeństwa PRL 1944-1990, s. 115.
36 See Instrukcja nr 03/55 o zasadach prowadzenia rozpracowania agenturalnego I ewidencji operacyjnej w organach bezpieczeństwa publicznego [w:] T. Ruzikowski, Instrukcje pracy operacyjnej Aparatu Bezpieczeństwa (1945–1989), Warszawa: Materiały pomocnicze Biura Edukacji Publicznej IPN, T. 1, 2004, s. 52.
37 R. Terlecki, Miecz i tarcza komunizmu, s. 128-129.
38 See Instrukcja nr 04/55 o zasadach pracy z agenturą w organach bezpieczeństwa publicznego PRL [w:] T. Ruzikowski, Instrukcje pracy operacyjnej Aparatu Bezpieczeństwa (1945–1989), Warszawa: Materiały pomocnicze Biura Edukacji Publicznej IPN, T. 1, 2004, s. 71.

to become the secret collaborators who were recruited from amongst the members and membership candidates of the communist party.[39] It was not allowed to recruit Polish citizens an the basis of material benefits. Recruiting on the basis of offering material benefits was resorted to in cases of gathering intelligence in the western countries. On this basis the representatives of the western countries, the employees of the western companies, foreign sailors, and people form emigrant circles.[40]

Analyzing the above mentioned directives one may conclude that in the mid 1950s the secret collaborators recruitment process based on appealing to the patriotic sentiments and loyalty involved three stages: the interview proceeding the recruitment, cooperation proposal and candidate's documented cooperation agreement. The talk was supposed to help collecting some additional data on private life and professional career of the candidate as well as his contacts. The opinion on behaviour and actions of persons known to the candidate were taken into consideration. A functionary was to assess the candidates possibilities as for exposing and vetting the persons targeted by the political police. In case the interview brought positive results a functionary was to assure the candidate that taking into consideration his so far patriotic activity on professional and social grounds the secret police proposed him help with tracing and exposing the enemies of the Polish nation. It was recommended that the candidate was personally describing the facts known to him or her which fell within the scope of the secret police's interest. Otherwise the interview on the above matters was advised. This procedure was believed to sometimes bring about a successful recruitment and specific engagement of the secret collaborator in the future.

In 1955 there were two recruitment methods implemented. Usually the whole procedure was completed within a single recruitment interview. In some cases though the gradual method was resorted to. It was advised not only in cases of persons negatively disposed towards the prevailing political system but also the patriots and loyal citizens – especially if there had been any chance that documenting the recruitment during one interview might have met the candidates disapproval. In order to avoid that the functionary would make a personal contact with the candidate and ordered him single, at first less important, and later more serious tasks. In this way the candidate was gradually recruited for the secret collaboration. A person recruited by such means was to immediately sign a written commitment to keep secret the fact of meeting the functionary and executing his or her orders. The functionaries were advised to take such written cooperation commitments from nearly all persons who had

---

39   Ibidem, s. 69.
40   Ibidem, s. 76-77.

been recruited on the basis of presenting them compromising materials. In cases of recruiting the secret collaborators from amongst patriots or loyal citizens the written commitment could be omitted if there were good chances for the person recruited to be faithfully performing the tasks entrusted to him or her just based on spoken promise of collaboration. Written commitment would have been also omitted if the very fact of proposing such a form of agreement had made a possibly negative impact on the candidate's attitude towards the authorities. Is those cases the only commitment made was the one of preserving the secret of the fact and the content of the recruitment interview. It was assumed that such a recruitment would anyway be consolidated by handwritten denouncements and informing about the compromising facts and state-hostile activities of the person known to the candidate.[41]

In 1956 the public opinion demanded punishing the persons responsible for Stalinist crimes in Poland. Some of the most corrupted functionaries held guilty for terror had to leave the ranks of the secret police. Security apparatus fell under the supervision of Ministry of Internal Affairs.[42] The fact of breaking the rules of law and order was also being criticized by some young functionaries of the department. Brutality, human resource policy and the methods of work were denounced. The authorities were afraid of excessive weakening of the political police and therefore did not allow punishing any bigger groups of UB employees.[43] Because of usefulness of the security apparatus the extend of cleansings in the department was quite limited.[44] Two years later the secret police started to grow again in order to protect the party's interests and power monopoly.[45]

In 1957 the Ministry of Internal Affairs decided that previously employed forms of agent operations were already greatly exposed and discredited by the public opinion. In 1960 the directive on general methods and means of operational work was issued, which although accepting the voluntariness as the basis of recruitment, after deeper analysis one could see it did not introduce any meaningful changes.[46] According to the directive the secret police's work including exposing and counteracting anti-state activity required introducing to secret collaboration the people who were trusted or those who had possibilities of reaching the persons, groups or circles targeted by the secret police, which would enable them to perform the operational tasks entrusted by the secret police. SB was also trying to make sure the information continues to come from

41 Ibidem, s. 75-78.
42 A. Albert, Najnowsza historia Polski 1914-1993, s. 314-314.
43 H. Dominiczak, Organy bezpieczeństwa PRL 1944-1990, s. 142
44 A. Albert, Najnowsza historia Polski 1914-1993, s. 362.
45 Ibidem, s. 374.
46 H. Dominiczak, Organy bezpieczeństwa PRL 1944-1990, s. 142

the participants of state-hostile activities recruited for collaboration as well as from introducing the recruited person to the hostile organisations or group. The range of assignments granted to secret collaborators would according to the needs include information gathering or certain ways of dealing with the enemy.[47] The category of secret collaborators included also the residents recruited from amongst the people fully devoted to the political ideal of the state, deeply connected to the political police, properly verified and operationally experienced. In some special cases it was permitted that the residents mediated cooperation with the secret collaborators.[48] The secret collaborators introduced into agents and informants positions were from then on the basic category of personal source of information.[49]

In 1960 there were two basis of recruitment mentioned. The first one described as a volunteering attitude was based on motivation which was political, material or psychological by nature and made the candidate voluntarily agree to collaborate with SB. It was advised to assess the candidate's character, way of life, desires and aspirations. The motives of taking up secret collaboration did not have to be political. The aversion to persons targeted by SB could also be a sufficient basis, as well as clash of interests and aspirations between the candidate and his or her environment, conflicts of ambitions. Sometimes certain material interests would make a fertile recruitment ground or constitute the exclusive recruitment basis. Compulsion method was based on compromising materials which allowed to put pressure on the candidate and force him or her into taking up cooperation. The aggravating materials would pertain to candidates' committing some offences or crimes which could spoil his or her career and reputation. It was cautioned though that there should not be used any materials that might split the family. The compulsion method was to be particularly applied in cases of secret collaborator candidates recruited from the circles engaged in anti-state activities. The possibility of recruiting such candidates on the basis of free will was not excluded though.[50]

The recruitment on the basis of voluntary commitment was considered the most beneficial for the future work with the secret collaborator. In the text of the directive the term „recruitment" (*werbunek*) was replaced with the term „enlist"

---

47 Instrukcja nr 03/60 z dnia 2 lipca 1960 r. o Podstawowych środkach i formach pracy operacyjnej Służby Bezpieczeństwa [w:] T. Ruzikowski, Instrukcje pracy operacyjnej Aparatu Bezpieczeństwa (1945–1989), Warszawa: Materiały pomocnicze Biura Edukacji Publicznej IPN, T. 1, 2004, s. 97.

48 Ibidem, s. 102.

49 F. Musiał, Podręcznik bezpieki, s. 279.

50 Instrukcja nr 03/60 z dnia 2 lipca 1960 r. o podstawowych środkach i formach pracy operacyjnej Służby Bezpieczeństwa, s. 98-100.

(*pozyskanie*), which suggested more voluntary means of cooperation.[51] The patriotic attitude expressed by concern with at least some of the state's interests or by negative opinion about some criminal activities that were not compatible with candidate's patriotic sentiments or moral values could in some cases turn to be favourable or sufficient element to gain candidate's voluntary consent of cooperation.[52] This bombastic wording rarely had anything in common with selfless desire to help SB being just a result of political attitude of the secret collaborator. More often the animosities, aversion or common human envy were skillfully fanned by SB functionaries. Different recruitment methods could be combined depending on the needs and conclusions that would come as a result of vetting the candidate.[53] In the process of enlisting the candidate on the basis of voluntary commitment the cooperation proposal was to be presented from the perspective of overall state protection needs and its interests instead of referring to narrow SB's departmental affairs.[54]

The so far accepted two recruitment methods of one interview versus gradual involvement in cooperation were supplemented by the 1960's method of apparent recruitment of the candidate for some other purposes which was based on concealing the real intend of the recruitment till the secret collaborator was already involved in cooperation and more ready to execute the tasks imposed on him or her.[55]

In 1960 it was concluded that apart from secret collaborator's moral satisfaction and emphasis on the value of the information supplied by him or her for the state equally positive impact on building cooperation attitude might have had some material benefits offered. The secret collaborators were to be rewarded for particular achievements, ardour and initiative, realisation of tasks that involved some hazards or were time consuming – if the offer of such reward would not hurt the feelings of the secret collaborator. Taking into account the mentality of the particular secret collaborator and the motives behind his or her taking up the cooperation with SB there were different kinds of rewards offered.[56] Beginning with the year 1956 most of the secret collaborators were recruited by offering them financial reward or some other material benefits.[57]

---

51 T. Ruzikowski, Instrukcje pracy operacyjnej Aparatu Bezpieczeństwa (1945–1989), s. 7.
52 Instrukcja nr 03/60 z dnia 2 lipca 1960 r. o podstawowych środkach i formach pracy operacyjnej Służby Bezpieczeństwa, s. 99.
53 T. Ruzikowski, Instrukcje pracy operacyjnej Aparatu Bezpieczeństwa (1945–1989), s. 9-10.
54 Instrukcja nr 03/60 z dnia 2 lipca 1960 r. o podstawowych środkach i formach pracy operacyjnej Służby Bezpieczeństwa, s. 101.
55 Ibidem, s. 101.
56 Ibidem, s. 105.
57 H. Dominiczak, Organy bezpieczeństwa PRL 1944-1990, s. 144.

At the beginning of 1960s some representatives of the governing elites would promote patriotic ideals to be included in communist propaganda. The directive of 1960 declared that security apparatus works for the benefit of the nation and with the support of its trust and help.[58] The process of adding some ideals of patriotism and service to the nation was meant for legitimising the system. The political system was more acceptable for the citizens of the country if it appealed to their patriotic sentiments, national identity or pride of being a Pole. Such ideals for those persons who were devoted to political realism were a sign of weakening the dependence on the USSR and at the same time a process which was beneficial and worth of support.[59] In the mid 1960s the authorities drew a picture of the nation united with the state and the ruling party by common interests – the society tightening its bounds with the Soviet Union and living in a constant alert because of the German threat.[60]

In 1970 a new directive entered into force stating that the Security Service was not only to expose the cases of hostile activities but also monitor any negative social trends and foresee the hazards of violating the safety and order.[61] The secret police would penetrate all the spheres of Polish people's life.[62] Prophylactic measures would include screening all the potential enemies of the communist system irrespective of their active participation in anti-state activities or staying away from such actions. That was a sign of return to commonly denounced Stalinist method of controlling the whole society justifying it by the increase of various threats for socialist system.[63] In the directive of 1970 the secret collaborators were understood to be persons who were recruited for the purpose of cooperation with the SB and executing the tasks pertaining to preventing, identifying and exposing anti-state activities.[64]

In 1970 there were four different recruitment basis mentioned: compromising materials, aggravating evidence, desire for material benefits, and

---

58 Instrukcja nr 03/60 z dnia 2 lipca 1960 r. o podstawowych środkach i formach pracy operacyjnej Służby Bezpieczeństwa, s. 94.

59 K. Tyszka, Nacjonalizm w komunizmie, s. 145-146 i 152 -157.

60 M. Zaremba, Komunizm, legitymizacja, nacjonalizm, s. 325.

61 See Instrukcja o pracy operacyjnej Służby Bezpieczeństwa resortu spraw wewnętrznych, załącznik do zarządzenia nr 006/70 Ministra Spraw Wewnętrznych z dnia 1 lutego 1970 r. w sprawie pracy operacyjnej Służby Bezpieczeństwa resortu spraw wewnętrznych [w:] T. Ruzikowski, Instrukcje pracy operacyjnej Aparatu Bezpieczeństwa (1945–1989), Warszawa: Materiały pomocnicze Biura Edukacji Publicznej IPN, T. 1, 2004, s. 124.

62 A. Albert, Najnowsza historia Polski 1914-1993, s. 565.

63 H. Dominiczak, Organy bezpieczeństwa PRL 1944-1990, s. 150.

64 See Instrukcja o pracy operacyjnej Służby Bezpieczeństwa resortu spraw wewnętrznych, załącznik do zarządzenia nr 006/70 Ministra Spraw Wewnętrznych z dnia 1 lutego 1970 r. w sprawie pracy operacyjnej Służby Bezpieczeństwa resortu spraw wewnętrznych, s. 127.

the sense of civic joint responsibility for public safety and order.[65] The statistics show that up till 1953 the most of the secret collaborators would be recruited on the basis of presenting to them some compromising materials. The recruitment based on juggling with some pseudo patriotic phraseology such as so called 'patriotic sentiments' which in 1970s and 1980s were addressed to with a term 'civic joint responsibility,' was an expression of voluntary willingness to cooperate. The experience showed that the most fruitful cooperation was guaranteed if the cooperators volunteered to cooperate. According to the data of the Ministry of Public Security only one third of the agent network were the volunteers. But it should be also mentioned that this 'volunteering' would sometimes be an effect of psychological manipulations and persistent attempts to convince the candidate.[66] After publishing the directive of 1960 these proportions were at least formally changed. The method of recruitment based on compromising materials was employed more sparsely because of low effectiveness of the recruited persons work and his or her organic unwillingness to cooperate.[67] The most often mentioned recruitment motive in the department's registers of 1970s and 1980s was the one of "civic joint responsibility" which often was just a cover up for the recruitment on the basis of proposing some material benefits.[68] The so called material rewards would take many varied forms ranging from a regular salary for information granted, all kinds of help including easy and fast receiving of passport, permit for starting professional or commercial activities, to receiving some rationed items or 'arranging' for family member's job.[69]

Each method of recruitment could be combined with another depending on the needs and conclusions based on candidate vetting.[70] The example of such activities were efforts taken up by the Department I (foreign intelligence) of the Ministry of Foreign Affairs during 1957–1960 to recruit for cooperation Franciszek Charpkiewicz, Polish biochemist who had been working as a scientist for the Institute of Atomic Energy in Saclay, France. The basis of recruitment were to be patriotic sentiments underpinned with some compromising materials. Initial plan was to accuse Charpkiewicz of escaping abroad with some public money and suggest that the Polish authorities possess some documents that were the evidence of his family having been collaborating

65 Ibidem, s. 127-128.
66 F. Musiał, Podręcznik bezpieki, s. 105-106.
67 T. Ruzikowski, Instrukcje pracy operacyjnej Aparatu Bezpieczeństwa (1945–1989), s. 16.
68 Ibidem, s. 9.
69 F. Musiał, Osobowe źródła informacji, Biuletyn Instytutu Pamięci Narodowej, Nr 10, 2006, s. 62
70 T. Ruzikowski, Instrukcje pracy operacyjnej Aparatu Bezpieczeństwa (1945–1989), s. 10.

with Germans during the world war II occupation. By scanning the letters the authorities knew that Chrapkiewicz had a strong bound with his sister who was living in Poland. She was arrested after having been accused of illegal foreign currency trading. The plan of May 1960 was to communicate Chrapkiewicz that the only way to free his sister was some contribution made by him on the grounds of technological and scientific help for Poland. Chrapkiewicz had never yielded to blackmail and his recruitment had never proved a success. SB came to a conclusion, that despite of his having declared to be a patriot he could not have been taken into consideration as a person who was ready to help Poland.[71]

Secret collaborators referred to as 'PRL's patriots' who desired to act in line with 'progressive policy of the state and the party' were recruited on the basis of loyalty backed with some rewards for the information supplied.[72] Some of the secret collaborators declared understanding for the secret police's need to gather information. Cooperation was taken up by them with an ease. Their 'patriotic attitude' was a result of conviction that staying in touch with the political police and all the benefits that came with it, e.g. arranging for the passports, were their at best interest and the integral part of their professional career.[73] I think that a good conclusion of the above elaboration would be quoting some suggestive words of the former secret police functionary:

Amongst them [secret collaborators] were patriotic feelings. But such a person would one day say: 'Do not bother me with that any more, I have had it.' Only those informants that were regularly paid were sure not to let down and refuse cooperation. The person materially dependent was ours."[74]

Translated by Iwona Szuwalska

---

71 Pozyskać „Dobrego" Wywiad PRL wobec Franciszka Chrapkiewicza i jego rodziny, pod red. A. Fary, P. Szopy, R. Witalca, s. 47-58.

72 P. Warot, Z pocztu olsztyńskich rektorów- współpracowników SB, Biuletyn Instytutu Pamięci Narodowej, Nr 8-9, 2008, s. 101-102

73 P. Warot, Patriota PRL czyli o współpracy z komunistycznym wywiadem Cypriana Krzysztofa Rogowskiego Cz. II, 2009, dostępne na stronie: http://debata.olsztyn.pl/ index.php?option=com_content&view=article&id=650:patriota-prl-czyli-o-wspopracy-z-komunistycznym-wywiadem-cypriana-krzysztofa-rogowskiego&catid=58:z-archiwum-ipn&Itemid=125 (10.02.2012)

74 Rzeczpospolita, 24.09.2005.

The image of the British secret services in the light of the ministerial monograph by Ryszard Gułkowski

Sebastian Michalak

Opening the archives of the communist repression apparatus for the researchers in Poland brought about in the last decade a rise in their interest in activities of the communist secret services. Many editions of documents, materials and study collections usually shed some light on the actions having been taken by the services against individual persons and circles.[1] The aim of this article is to present the image of the British secret services in the light of the monograph by Ryszard Gułkowski: *Brytyjskie służby specjalne: historia – organizacja – działalność* (*British Secret Services: History – Structure – Activities*) which appeared in 1987 as a release of the Department of Professional Training and Development of the Ministry of Internal Affairs (Ministerstwo Spraw Wewnętrznych), further referred to as the MSW, as well as reports, exclusive of operational documentation, by Department II of the MSW – the civilian counter-intelligence. The adequacy of this image was compared with the modern state of knowledge. For that purpose the work by Philip Davies, one of the leading British experts in the field of security studies, *Mi6 and the Machinery of Spring*, was looked into. This article is demonstrative in character and is an introduction to further, deeper studies on the image of the British services presented in the archives of the communist repression apparatus. The monograph by R. Gułkowski and documents used for this article are available at the Wrocław Branch of the Institute of National Remembrance.

In November 1956 the Central Committee of the Polish United Workers' Party reorganised the public security organs. Tasks pertaining to the protection of the political system and the interest of the country were commended to the MSW, which absorbed into its structures the central and local units of the security apparatus. On their basis the Security Service was created, further referred to us the SB, which until its dissolution in 1990 was one of the MSW sections. The counter-intelligence tasks of geographical profile were assigned to specialised departments of the civilian counter-intelligence. The officers of Department II were also occupied with exposing and dismantling the British intelligence. The counter-intelligence exposed the people suspected of intelligence activity, took up dismantling actions towards the intelligence

---

1   For the state of research and bibliography see A Handbook of the Communist Security Apparatus in East Central Europe (2005) eds. A. Dudek, A. Paczkowski, IPN, Warszawa, 276-280.

residences located at diplomatic posts and trade offices, operated in order to cover the individuals and places that were of Great Britain's interest. The surveillance of the British posts, diplomats, and citizens visiting Poland was conducted by Bureau "B" of the MSW. This bureau was also responsible for operational control over the hotels as well as for determining the contacts of the persons visiting the British embassy in Warsaw (Aparat bezpieczeństwa w Polsce, 2006, 13-15).

One of the first counter-intelligence reports on the British secret services was the study of 1959 signed by Department II of the MSW. The report was based on data collected by the Polish civilian counter-intelligence as per January 1953. Firstly the British system of classifying and assessing the information, and then the organisational structure of the Secret Intelligence Service, known also as MI6, were described. According to the research conducted by the Polish counter-intelligence the intelligence sections of MI6 organised recruitment and intelligence activities at the British diplomatic residences. This department was divided into 9 geographical sections marked with a section code and a following Arabic numeral; e.g. section P-5 was responsible for intelligence activities on the territories of Poland, USSR and Czechoslovakia. The information and research sections analysed intelligence data and passed on particular missions to operational sections. Special communication section organised and managed connections with the agents and residents. It was also responsible for smuggling intelligence agents through the borders. The Department also maintained connections with the intelligence services of other democratic states. The independent radio intelligence section decoded foreign telegrams and organised its own radio connections. As for exposing the foreign intelligence MI6 organised e.g. the recruitment of officers and agents of the foreign services. The agents were also recruited from the oppositionist circles of the territories under the SIS surveillance. Section "X-9" was to expose and dismantle communist parties and left-wing organisations (IPN Wr 054/1339, Wywiad Wielkicj Brytanii, Warszawa, 1959, 46-49). The image of the SIS, drawn in the above described report, shows substantial deficiencies. Indeed during 1946-1955 the SIS operational P Sections were numbered and grouped on geographical basis. Under this system P1 dealt with Belgium, France, Italy, and Iberia; P2 with Scandinavia, and Holland; P3 with Austria, Germany, and Switzerland; P4 with Middle East. The numeral designations of the P Sections operating in Far East have not been indicated. The SIS had also two regional headquarters, one in Middle East and one in Far East. In the report there was no mention of the system of four regional production controllers having been introduced in 1943. The operational sections were conforming to "controllerates" headed by controllers (Davies, 2004, 172). Section P5 handled Poland during 1941-1945,

Balkans during 1946-1966, and the Soviet bloc beginning with 1966. Since 1948 the Eastern Europe and Soviet bloc P Sections had been subordinated to the Controller Production Research (Davies, 2004, 207-208). The SIS's consumer liaison sections were briefly described in the report as R Sections with numerical designations. R1 was working on behalf of the Foreign Office, R2 was the Air Section, R3 was the Navy Section, R4 was the Military Section, R6 supplied industrial and commercial intelligence for a wide range of departments, R7 handled scientific intelligence and R8 was responsible for liaison with the GCHQ. R Sections were divided mainly along geographical lines. Some of them had geographical subsections. Section IX mentioned in the report was created in 1944. It was responsible for collection and interpretation of information on the Soviet and communist espionage as well as subversion in all parts of the world outside the British territory. In 1946 Section IX became the agency's counter-espionage unit and took on the designation R5. Section R5 was divided into two sub-sections. R5 Int was dealing with counter-intelligence and counter-espionage against Soviet bloc intelligence services. R5 Com studied Soviet ideological and subversion efforts and the clandestine efforts of the foreign communist parties and Comintern. Each of these was in turn subdivided into four regional sub-sections. Section R5 operated via the SIS's foreign stations (Davies, 2004, 199-201). The Radio Section mentioned in the report was hived off after the war from the SIS and turned into the Foreign Office's Diplomatic Wireless Service. This medium was used for secure wireless communications with the SIS stations abroad, and with agents using clandestine transceivers (Davies, 2004, 204-205).

Another British secret service described in the report of March 1959 was the Security Service known as MI5. According to the SB, MI5 was represented abroad by defence security officers, who advised on internal safety of chief officers of the services and civil authorities in British colonies and overseas territories. The MI5 branch marked with code "B" comprised of 6 operational sections marked with the department code and a following number. Section "B-1" was in charge of the activities of communist and socialist organisations. Section "B-2" exposed and dismantled foreign intelligence services operating on the territory of Great Britain. Section "B-3" controlled the counter-intelligence posts in British colonies and dominions. Section "B-4" recruited double agents and supervised their work. Section "B-5" was responsible for investigation works. Section "B-6" conducted the surveillance of persons and buildings. Section "A-1" of branch "A" was in charge of employing technical means in order to secretly obtain information including the content of phone connections (IPN Wr 054/1339, Wywiad Wielkiej Brytanii, Warszawa, 1959, 50-53). The image of MI5 presented in the SB report suggests the thesis that the Polish counter-intelligence was quite well acquainted with the structures of the British offensive counter-intelligence. P. Davies states that MI5 was internally divided into different branches and sections. MI5's B Branch handled investigations, D Branch comprised of counter-intelligence, and C Branch dealt with protective security. Administrative and supportive functions such as MI5's taps at foreign embassies were the responsibility of A Branch. The division of responsibilities between the MI6 and MI5 was formally established in 1931. The MI5 was assigned to British and Colonial territory. Britain's withdrawal from its possessions in Middle and Far East changed the former colonies into 'foreign' SIS targets as they were no more the object of 'domestic' Security Service concerns (Davies, 2004, 271-280).

Substantial increase in ministerial publications was observed in 1970s and 1980s. The MSW had published for internal use manuals and studies which were later used e.g. for the SB officers trainings. This was a result of research development by academic workers of the MSW schools as the ministry started employing researchers from the state-owned higher education institutions (Musiał, 2007, 13-15). The problem of the UK secret services' activity did not become a subject of a broader interest for the authors of the ministerial publications. The first work to comprehensively delineate the issue being discussed herein was the monograph by R. Gułkowski. The chronological span of the book covers the period of 1945-1980. The main source of information about the actions of the British intelligence on the territory of Poland was for him a report by a KGB officer Konon Trofimowicz Mołodyc, who during 1955-1961 was operating in Great Britain. Gułkowski had also drawn on some openly published works by Ellis M. Zachariasz, an American military intelligence officer of the world war II period who had access to the report archives of the Polish civilian counter-intelligence. (Gułkowski, 1980, 15)

The information gathered by Gułkowski was not sufficient to accurately identify all the different departments and branches of the British intelligence services. Therefore the term "British intelligence" in his work is being used both in the meaning of the military and civil intelligence services. Gułkowski uses the term "Intelligence Service" in relation to an independent political intelligence institution working under the British Ministry of Internal Affairs. Most probably he was relating to the British civilian intelligence. MI5 was given a much lesser attention in the monograph than the MI6. The organisational structure of MI6 described in Gułkowski's book was based on the data gathered by the Polish counter-intelligence of 1960s. According to Gułkowski in the London SIS headquarters functioned 4 operational branches dealing with a particular group of countries as well as the information and communication branches. The author listed also the branches such as sabotage, special technology, counter-intelligence, as well as inspection and security. The first SIS branch was responsible for the intelligence activity in Western Europe and running from that area the operations against the "socialist" countries. The branch comprised of the following sections: P-1 (France, Belgium), P-2 (Italy, Portugal, Greece), P-3 (FRG), P-4 (Denmark, Norway, Sweden, Finland), P-5 (Switzerland, Austria), P-6 (Holland). Each section delegated the operational and technical officers to different intelligence posts, and supervised the recruitment and work of the agents. The second branch gathered intelligence information in the Near and Middle East countries as well as in Africa. The third branch was in charge of Far East and Latin America. The forth branch organised intelligence operations against the USSR and the European countries in its influence zone. Information and operational strategy branch employed intelligence analysts who analysed data and assigned tasks to operational officers. The description indicates the author probably meant requirements sections working under SIS's Director of Requirements. Definitely harder is to ascertain the unit described by Gułkowski as the sabotage branch, the so called branch X which was in charge of "special political actions." Gułkowski most probably meant by it the actions related to disinformation and propaganda. This assumption is confirmed by the studies conducted on the matter. Somewhere on the turn of 1953 and 1954 a new non-operational special political activity sub-section was created and placed under the supervision of R1 section. The types of operations delegated to the new sub-section included coordinating the activities influencing the results of the elections, deceptive actions, and black propaganda. This unit was shut down in the mid-1970s (Davies, 2004, 244 and 305). The SIS Branch, as stated Gułkowski, dealt with exposing the officers, organisational structures, methods, and operational means of the socialist states' security services. Counter-intelligence MI6 cooperated with MI5 in exposing the citizens of the socialist states who temporarily visited Great Britain. The branch also took up offensive actions such as infiltrating the structures of the foreign intelligence services with its agents and preventing the similar actions on the side of its foreign counterparts. The personnel of the Security Inspection founded in 1956 was responsible for the protection of premises, repositories and SIS personnel. They were also in charge of contacts with the counter-intelligence services and police (Gułkowski, 1987, 130-134). The internal organisational structure of MI6 presented by Gułkowski in his book essentially adhered to the actual situation. Although the author did not avoid certain inconsistencies it could well be the result of the fact that at the time there was no access to the up to date counter-intelligence reports, which the Author mentions in his monograph (Gułkowski, 1987, 15). Gułkowski does not mention that in 1958 the regional chief controllerates were replaced by four regional Directorships of Production. The

Area Controllers were replaced with a single deputy under each director of production. In 1962 the Soviet bloc and Eastern Europe production sections were moved from under the supervision of the Production Research Controller to the Director for Western Europe and Soviet Bloc. As a result the reformed production side-organisation consisted of Director for Western Europe and Soviet Bloc, Director for Middle East and Africa, Director for Far East, and Director for Americas. Director for Americas also supervised the area under Deputy Director for Latin America (Davies, 2004, 281-282). In 1964 counter-intelligence and security mechanisms of the SIS were transferred from R5 section to the new directorate of counter-intelligence and security. Within this directorate counter-intelligence operations were overseen by a number of area counter-intelligence sections, including CI4 (Soviet Union) and CI7 (Eastern Europe) (Davies, 2004, 283-284). In 1966 under the new arrangements directorate of production was reinstituted and the seven area controllers were re-established. The Western Europe and Soviet bloc directorate broke up into controller for Europe and controller for the Soviet bloc. The Soviet bloc and Eastern Europe sections were placed under the supervision of the controller for the Soviet bloc. The production section of the SIS throughout the 1960s and 1970s was structured as follows: P1 (France), P2 (Scandinavia), P3 (Germany and Austria) and P6 (Greece, Turkey and Cyprus) under Controller for Europe; P4 (Eastern Europe), P5 (Soviet Union), P7 (USA, Canada), P8 (Latin America) and P10 (Caribbean), P9 (China), P11 (South East Asia, Australasia), P12 (Japan) and P13 (India and Pakistan), P16 and P17 (both different Middle East areas), four different African sections P14, P15, P18, P19 and P20 (UK). Since 1946 the Inspectorate of Security was responsible for MI6 protective security. In 1964 the inspectorate was absorbed by the counter-intelligence and security directorate (Davies, 2004, 284-287).

According to Gułkowski the British intelligence abroad operated mainly through intelligence residences working behind the facade of diplomatic agencies. In embassies apart from diplomats there were also regular intelligence officers employed. The British intelligence operated also within the structures of the United Nations agency in New York, the United Nations office in Geneva, and in the developing countries of Asia and Africa, where the specialists from the Middle and Eastern Europe had been employed. The Intelligence residency in Geneva was greatly interested in the employees of secretariat and the mission of the People's Republic of Poland (further referred to as PRL) at the United Nations European Office. Particularly vivid intelligence activity against the socialist states was present at the British intelligence residencies in the Federal Republic of Germany (Gułkowski, 1980, 132). In 1970s the Polish counter-intelligence assumed that the activity of the Middle and Eastern Europe residencies had been directed by the British intelligence station in Vienna. This assumption was based on the alleged frequent few days long visits to Austria by regular intelligence officers who were employed by the British embassy in Warsaw. Allegedly in the Austrian capital the meetings of intelligence officers with important agents operating in Poland had been taking place (Teczka IPN Wr 054/205, Karta nr 32-38). The above are the data confirmed by the source literature. In 1918–1939 the SIS's foreign stations operated under an official, but technically non-diplomatic, cover in the form of the Passport Control Organisation arranged for British diplomatic missions. The cover of a Passport Control Officer was abandoned after being compromised in 1939. As a result, the SIS officers took to more conventional diplomatic cover provided by the Foreign Office. They were typically given positions at embassies such as junior First Secretaries. The SIS's foreign residencies were prohibited from operating against their host country. The Soviet Union's consolidation of its occupied territories in Eastern Europe in years 1944-1946 left little or no opportunity for the SIS residential work. The opportunities to mount operations into the Soviet bloc were coming chiefly from the bordering states. The SIS's agents operating in Eastern Europe were using also covers provided by a British firm or organisation. MI6 was seeking assistance from UK citizens traveling to and from the USSR to mount operations against foreign trade delegations and embassies in the UK (Davies, 2004, 207-208). Station abroad operated mostly against neighbouring countries. This was later referred to as the 'Third Country Rule' and formalised as a standard operational doctrine in the SIS. The stations in Vienna and Berlin counted over 100 officers and staff in the 1950s. They were organised into four operational sections: political intelligence and Soviet penetration; Soviet and East German armed forces; scientific intelligence; and technical methods section. (Davies, 2004, 213) During the late 1950s the SIS was targeting and recruiting Soviet and Eastern European nationals in the UK with an eye to subsequently running them abroad in their home country. (Davies, 2004, 289) Agents who returned home were supervised by station officers. In 1956 the SIS's Soviet Union and Eastern Europe targeting sections were introduced to keep files on potential targets, monitor the movements of targeted foreign nationals abroad, and provide the necessary information for the station officers abroad who operated against these individuals. It was often an officer from the relevant targeting section, rather than a resident officer from the station, that would make the final approach to a Soviet bloc individuals being targeted for recruitment. Such officers came to be known as Visiting Case Officers. (Davies, 2004, 274) In December 1959 a SIS officer Colin Figures was delegated to Warsaw where he was acquainted with defection cases of the Polish SB intelligence officers.[2] (West, 2005, 182)

Gułkowski maintains that the British intelligence residency operating in Poland was quartered in the British embassy in Warsaw. Such resident agents were supervised by political affairs counsellor who performed the function of the vice-ambassador and the first secretary of the embassy. There was also a counter-intelligence vice-resident present at the residence. The remaining intelligence officers held the posts of I, II or III secretary of the embassy chiefly in the political, trade, administration or consular departments. The resident agents could be the intelligence officers who were not embassy employees and therefore were not shielded by diplomatic immunity. They could operate more freely than diplomats who were under the Polish counter-intelligence's surveillance. A resident diplomat was at times also supervising other intelligence employees or agents who were visiting Poland in order to pursue some clearly defined missions. The agents temporarily visiting Poland, taking up roles of businessmen or journalists, were supposed to reconnoitre the activities, structures, and personnel of the Polish enterprises. (Gułkowski, 1987, 129) Gułkowski ascertains that as per knowledge of the Polish counter-intelligence the resident agents were often attached to the British delegations visiting Poland. The estimations were made that during 1957-1970 a diplomatic "cover-up" had been used in the British embassy by eleven intelligence employees and co-operators. (Gułkowski, 1987, 322)

The British intelligence were interested in relations between the authorities of Poland and Soviet Union as well as in contacts between the communist parties of these countries. The aim was to gather information about strategic plans of the Polish military forces, distribution and weaponry of the regular shoreline defence forces, mobilisation plans of the land and air forces, organisational structure of the military formations and command systems, magazines and military depots, country air defence and the cooperation with its Russian counterpart, data about the distribution of the radar posts and airports. As for military issues they were also interested in missions, personal data, positions, activities and personal qualities of the officers holding ranks of major or higher in the officers corpses of all the Warsaw Pact member states. As for the science and technology intelligence the data on the works, as well as psychological profiles of the science and technology professionals working in the field of aviation were being gathered. That included data on Polish scientists cooperating with the USSR regarding defence technologies. The British

---

2   Department I officers of the Ministry of Internal Affairs (civilian intelligence) Capitain Władysław Mróz and Lieutenant Colonel Michał Goleniewski

intelligence gave special attention to the Russian scientists residing and working in Poland. The information was gathered on nuclear energy production is socialist countries, cooperation of these countries in that field, the direction of socio-political changes taking place in Poland, her coal mining, detailed information on her export activity, foreign loans, projects realised within the COMECON (Council for Mutual Economic Assistance) framework, factories' production potential, new enterprises, power engineering and automatics development. The British intelligence agents residing in Warsaw were also interested in the relations between the state and the Church, the attitude of different circles towards the policy of the Party as well as the activities of the opposition. (Gułkowski, 1987, 254-256)

In 1950 a famous show trial of a British embassy air attaché in Warsaw Henry Turner took place in Poland. The trial was to warn the Polish against spying activity of the British, American and Canadian diplomats. Turner was accused of an attempt to organise for his acquaintance Barbara Bobrowska an illegal trip to Great Britain. In the course of the trial the court disclosed alleged intelligence orders for the British attachés. Turner testified to have received the order to gather intelligence about the Polish and Soviet air forces. His informants were allegedly introduced to him through Irena Findaisen. The information on the air forces power and equipment had been provided to him by certain Skalski and Śliwiński. According to Gułkowski, Władysław Śliwiński's spy ring passed abroad the information and documents concerning deployment, number and arms of the Polish and Soviet military forces, especially the air and armoured units; the locations of military supply depots and liquid fuels storages; military transports and their destinations; programmes and methods of military and civil pilots trainings; activities of the Polish Workers' Party (PPR) as well as functionaries of the public security and judiciary organs; deployment and production profiles of the important industrial sites; electro-technical industry; condition of railways and rolling stock; transport facilities, roads and bridges construction; as well as uranium mining in Poland. Turner established contact with the Polish airlines LOT employee Aleksander Majewski through his assistant major Dobree-Bella, who received from Majewski the information about the Polish civil aviation. Another informant who gathered materials on the Aviation Institute and Warsaw industrial plants where the aircraft equipment was produced was Eugeniusz Dyga who worked at the British embassy as a mechanic. Turner testified before the court that diplomats travelled around Poland to gather information about the air forces (Gułkowski, 1987, 280-283). The motif of reconnaissance trips also appears in counter-intelligence reports. In 1970s the Polish counter-intelligence suspected that the military, naval, and air attachés accredited by the British embassy were officers of the military intelligence. They were responsible for verifying and supplementing intelligence gathered by the mother centres through their agents, radio intercept, as well as air and satellite photos. For these the attachés were to locate and monitor the military installations as well as other objects important for defence, e.g. arms industry plants, roads, railways and water transport. They were also interested in types of military forces, weapons, number of soldiers, and arms industry. The basic method of fulfilling this mission was reconnaissance tours comprising of going on a round by car. Usually they would start such tours early in the morning. There were always at least two persons in a car. Typically an attaché was accompanied by one of the four non-commissioned officers from the post, or by his wife (Teczka IPN Wr 054/205, Karta nr 24-29). In 1971 attachés went on 42 such tours. In 20 cases the companions were the wives. The behaviour of the ladies, according to the counter-intelligence officers, showed their active involvement in the intelligence activity. The tours would take average two days (Teczka IPN Wr 054/205, Karta nr 30-31). During these events they would sometimes eat and sleep in a car. The counter-intelligence did not have any proves of military attachés having been engaged in espionage activity. They assumed that the agents had been recruited through other embassy employees. Simultaneously they did not exclude the possibility that during the car tours, especially throughout the military trainings, the military attachés used the agents' connections with the embassy – and via the embassy with the command centre. (Teczka IPN Wr 054/205, Karta nr 24-29)

According to the estimations quoted by Gułkowski, during 1945-1956 there were 262 British intelligence agents active on the territory of Poland. The basis of these estimations were the data presented in the official *The Register of the Convicted in the People's Republic of Poland during 1944-1970* (*Informator o osobach skazanych w Polsce Rzeczpospolitej Ludowej za działalność szpiegowską w latach 1944-1970*). These data were in a greater part misinforming and unreliable, which Gułkowski himself was perfectly aware of. During 1944-1956 not only the real agents were accused of the crime of espionage but also the so-called enemies of "the people's fatherland", especially the members of the underground independence movement and Polish emigration. Gułkowski sensibly calculated that one third of the convicted had not taken any part in intelligence activities (Gułkowski, 1987, 262-266). In his opinion only in 18 cases the agents recruited might have had a direct contact with the British intelligence (Gułkowski, 1987, 276-277). This thesis is confirmed by the research sources. The NKVD immediately upon the liberation in 1944-1945 arrested special Operation Executive operators in Poland who worked with the resistance. (Davies, 2004, 174) Gułkowski maintained that apart from the Polish citizens the British intelligence used also Ukraine and

Belarus nationals residing in Poland. The resident agent was Zbigniew Kamiński aka Drapała who during 1946-1954 cooperated with the British Intelligence station in Munich. In 1950 Kamiński had undergone espionage training in London, and later on was provided with the false documents, radio transmitter, weapons, codes, instructions, chemical agents, poison, maps, and money, and then illegally entered Poland. He organised a large espionage ring comprised of Ukrainian nationalists, which gathered information on military units, Polish army weapon, airports, radar stations, military judicature and security organs. The training had been also taken up by Piotr Nojsan aka Zenon, who was transferred to Poland through Czechoslovakia. Nojsan organised his own intelligence sources, contacts, and dead letter boxes (dead drops). The spy kept in direct contact with Kamiński. The British Intelligence also sent from abroad Władysław Nyż, who had undergone a document forging training in Munich and a navigation course in London. He was equipped with a radio transmitter and document forging mill, 100 thousand rubles and some other means. He also brought letters for the spy rings of Kamiński and Nojsan. Nyż was smuggled into Poland by a balloon from Bornholm along with a messenger Józef Ptasznyk. The later allegedly transmitted the information gathered by the rings of Kamiński and Nojsan by an R/T radio. In order to support Kamiński's ring another agent-messenger Tomasz Sokołowski aka Bojczuk was transferred from Hanover and he was also equipped with an R/T radio. A former Belarusian chief police officer Wacław Zawadzki vel Jaworski's agent network was also involved in such cooperation. Zawadzki recruited agents for the British intelligence whose main task was in turn to recruit informants from amongst Belarusian nationals, who were the messengers and organisers of the recruitment channels from Poland to the Soviet Union. Informants gathered information on defence and economy of PRL as well as Belarusian nationalists living in Poland. (Gułkowski, 1980, 269-274) According to the data presented in the register, during 1957-1970 period 15 people had been convicted for cooperation with the British Intelligence. One of them was Czesław Cwinarowicz, who during the International Festival of Youth and Students in 1955 met a British woman and wanted to marry her. Two years later he went to Great Britain where he was recruited by MI6. In 1958 he was sentenced to 4 years in prison for espionage crime (Gułkowski, 1980, 296-298). In 1965 Adam Kaczmarzyk, a radiotelegraph operator at the Communications Regiment of the Ministry of National Defence, and then at the V Connections Regiment of the General Staff of the Polish Armed Forces offered its services and he took up cooperation with the British Intelligence. On the British side the agent Kaczmarek was supervised by intelligence officers Denis Alindon, and since 1967 Barrie Charles Gane. Both officers worked as II secretaries of trade at the UK embassy in Warsaw.

Kaczmarzyk passed information on radio-connection systems of the Ministry of National Defence, including the codenames of R/T radio units and the places they were located, call signs, code change time, day-night frequency transition time, frequency tables, types of transmitters and receivers installed in the ministry's communication centre, and materials on the organisational structure of a communication centre. He would also inform about the atmosphere amongst staff and their economical situation. He was also a source of information about the military communication system within the Warsaw Pact. He took up the cooperation for purely financial reasons. His sumptuous life-style, indulgence in women and alcohol attracted the attention of colleagues, neighbours, and superiors. He was apprehended by military intelligence officers in 1968. He was sentenced to death for espionage on behalf of the foreign intelligence. (Gułkowski, 1980, s. 307)

The agents of the British Intelligence forwarded intelligence in many different ways: by letters using encryptions addressed to a foreign contact; through a messenger network, a command centre located abroad, underground networks; through agent networks connected not only to the British intelligence service, but also French or American ones. For these purposes people travelling abroad, British embassies and consulates, as well as R/T radios were being used. Individually operating agents after having gathered the information would return to their command centres. For this purpose special hiding places were arranged in the wagons of trains travelling to Western Europe. (Gułkowski, 1980, 274) The SIS was using secret compartments built into suitcases, torches and cigarette lighters as places for cameras and microphones in boxes. (Davies, 2004, 226)

The counter-intelligence ascertained that the British intelligence recruited agents from amongst the people who had access to the information on matters pertaining to state defence, or the Polish secret services, diplomacy or foreign trade issues. They were interested in journalists, authors, radio and TV staff, as well as members of academic circles. The bases of the recruitment were financial interest, aversion to the political systems of the People's Republic of Poland and USSR, authentic or fabricated defamatory information and accusing materials obtained by provocation, more seldom by threat or blackmail. During 1957-1970 the counter-intelligence noted 10 cases of recruitment proposals on the part of British citizens who were former embassy employees in Poland or had been visiting the country for business purposes. The recruitment was taking place mainly abroad, also on the territory of the United Kingom (Gułkowski, 1987, 298-299). Information about the recruitment candidates was drawn from: the materials about scholarship holders sent to the British Council; data held by institutions and persons dealing with the tourist flow; conference, convention and symposium organisers; as well as institutions and companies which the Polish would visit on business. Under surveillance were also the families, friends and other persons related to the visitor invited to Poland. The information was gathered from the agents set at the hotels, pensions or flats where the rooms were rented to the Poles. They interrogated people employed at or visiting Polish community centres in London as well as those who worked with the inviting institutions. The British Intelligence followed Polish press and other official publications in order to gather some information on the life goals, attitudes, and views of persons who were of their interest. The Polish counter-intelligence maintained that the information was also pursued from the British Council personnel, as well as from British traders, technicians, and academic workers visiting Poland. On the basis of such reconnaissance the efforts were made to come in contact with a particular journalist, author or scientist in order to grant him or her a research visit to Great Britain. Accidental contacts with Polish citizens were limited to one conversation for the fear such a meeting might have been prearranged by the Polish counter-intelligence. Generally any effort to make contact on the part of the Polish citizens was treated with caution (Gułkowski, 1987, 314-322). The officers of the British Intelligence usually were not so much in a rush to reveal to the candidates their affiliation. Usually in the process of recruitment the agents would present themselves as citizens of some other countries than Great Britain working in the fields of industry, tourism, banking or some social organisations. Although in working with the agents special precautions were taken, personal meetings with them were not given up entirely even on the territories of the socialist states. The counter-intelligence suspected that the resident agents of the British intelligence cooperated with their counterparts from the Canadian and Australian embassies. They assumed that at those diplomatic posts the British citizens could have been meeting Polish citizens. (Gułkowski, 1987, 120)

British citizens were exposed to recruitment interviews and interrogations about official or personal matters. The interviews were pertaining to military, operational, socio-political, economical, as well as science and technology matters. The interrogation was more of a general procedure and the questions asked were rather related to socio-political, economical, or science and technology matters. Such interrogations could have been a part of a consular interview of the visa acquiring procedure. These were also pursued at border crossing, registering, visa extension or arranging for job permission. During 1969-1972 the counter-intelligence recorded 13 Polish citizen recruitment attempts pertaining to persons temporarily visiting Great Britain. Particularly interesting aim for the British intelligence were those Polish citizens who had been residing in the USSR for some longer period of time, or had some friends or relatives in that country. After the candidate's arrival to the United Kingdom he or she was given summons to the Home Office or a police office competent for a particular residence place. The police had interrogated the inviting party before the candidate's arrival, and often also during his or her stay. Depending on the needs the contact was initiated also through especially trained counter-intelligence agents of British or Polish origin who permanently resided in the United Kingdom. Sometimes the private meetings or "tea parties" were organised, on which apart from the family and friends of the person under surveillance there were also present secret intelligence officers. Direct encounters usually took place at hotels or while taking care of the customs and passport formalities. Part of this activity was interrogation of people applying for visa extension. Tape-recorded interviews were conducted at the Home Office, where most of the recruitment interviews took place during 1972-1975. The candidates were asked about the procedures involved with issuing passports in Poland, profiles of the SB employees, the People's Militia (pol. Milicja Obywatelska – abbr. MO), and the Passport Office, as well as description of the Voivodeship Command of the People's Militia (pol. Komenda Wojewódzka Milicji Obywatelskiej – abbr. KWMO) premises. The recruitment interviews were flexible, various arguments were used, and the interviewed was put under different forms of pressure according to his or her personality and identity. If the interviews were taking place during the official interrogations the interrogators usually asked many detailed questions requiring specific answers. In case of refusal or inexhaustible explanations the interrogator would resort to harassment and blackmail. (Teczka IPN Wr 054/205, Karta nr 32-38) Some interviews were conducted in room no. 055 at the Ministry of National Defence building. According to the Polish counter-intelligence in this place the people who wanted to pass information to MI5 had been interviewed or it was also the place where the Polish citizens had been sometimes recruited. (Wywiad Wielkiej Brytanii, Warszawa: MSW Dep. II 1959, IPN Wr 054/1339, 51-53) The answers given by the interrogated people were often registered in a sort of protocol that was to be signed by the Polish citizen after his or her having been interviewed. The interrogators warned the Polish about possible problems on the side of the Polish authorities if the fact of the interrogation was revealed. Interrogators were seeking to develop emotional contact with an interrogated. For that purpose they were trying to make a good impression on them, gave them presents, flattered them, and amply treated them to alcohol, offered small favours such as visa extension or money lending. Initially the questions asked were indirectly connected to issues of material interest for the intelligence service. The information about the situation in Poland was also pursued by searching the luggage at an airport or hotel, stealing the minutes taken by specialists, taking the person under individual surveillance by agents or with the use of technical means. For external scrutiny TV or photo cameras were used equipped with telephoto lenses. The methods such as provocation were resorted to (e.g. arrests and document checks); or they were trying to persuade the candidate not to go back to their country by offering them good financial conditions. (Gułkowski, 1987, 335-350)

MI5 was monitoring and controlling the Polish diplomatic, business and cultural institutions in the United Kingdom. The civil counter-intelligence exposed regular intelligence employees, qualified candidates for recruitment, organised and broke contacts of the Polish citizens with the British. The rule of early contact termination between institutions and the British citizens was applied. For that purpose talks discouraging the maintenance of such contacts were conducted, and sometimes cooperation proposals were put forward accompanied by heavy pressure methods and threatening. A range of special investigative techniques was applied beginning with an open external surveillance, which put a psychological pressure on the person observed with an increasing fear of defamation. The information on behaviour, contacts, and life-style of the persons under surveillance was collected. It concerned the persons, cars, institutions, contacts, and organisations. For that purpose permanent concealed observation posts were used. Mobile observation teams comprised of five or six counter-intelligence officers travelling with two to four cars, as they conducted a continuous observation, that means from one to three days a week, and from three to fifteen days a month. Secret searches in houses and cars of the Polish posts' employees were performed. Phones and rooms were tapped, letters monitored, the agents recruited from amongst the Polish community in Great Britain were also involved. Compromising and incriminating materials were collected to be used for recruitment. Sometimes open cooperation proposals were put forward. Such proposals were not always aimed at recruiting. These also constituted a method for disposing of inconvenient people who upon having informed their authorities about the recruitment attempts were immediately recalled from their posts back home. The British counter-intelligence used some British companies, which kept in contact with Polish trade institutions as a cover-up for their operations. The efforts were made to pursue some agents from amongst the British personnel at the Polish posts. With their help Polish employees were provoked to involve themselves in compromising behaviour. (Gułkowski, 1987, 352-360) The British Intelligence widely used phone tapping for information gathering. The centre of recording for the national connections was based in London in a building known as Chantrey House. The recording centre for international phone calls was located in Caroone House. (Nowak, 1989, 187)

At a single glance the image of the British secret services drawn in the monograph by R. Gułkowski is an interesting evidence of a fairly good intelligence. In all likelihood the most important reason behind it was information the KGB was provided by the Soviet agents who penetrated the structures of the SIS. In years 1953-1963 George Blake and Kim Philby had compromised many operations against Soviet nationals. (Davies, 2004, 283) Deeper verification of the means and methods of the British secret services operational activities, including the motif of reconnaissance trips mentioned by Gułkowski, is not possible without referring to the very archives of the secret services. Such materials are not available though.

The work by Gułkowski was written during the period of cold-war struggle. Therefore it was also a propaganda and disinformation tool. The author claims that the British secret services had inspired espionage-mania campaigns in the mass-medias. Publicity was to compromise the "socialist" countries and inspire the citizens and thus provide the secret services some additional information about persons from the communist countries visiting Great Britain. An explicit example of such activities was the 1971 expulsion of 105 Soviet diplomats, employees of various trade agencies and their family members from Great Britain. Information, as stated by Gułkowski, about an alleged USSR and other communist countries intelligence activities against Great Britain appeared in the British press at the beginning of w 1970. (Gułkowski, 140-142) In fact the information provided by KGB's defector was a vital part of the evidence that led to the expulsion of 90 Soviet diplomats from the UK under spying suspicion. Another 15 officials were barred from re-entry. The expulsions put the KGB's residency in difficulty to collect high-grade intelligence in London. (Davies, 2004, 294)

Translated by Iwona Szuwalska

Bibliography

A Handbook of the Communist Security Apparatus in East Central Europe (2005). eds. A. Dudek, A. Paczkowski, IPN, Warszawa.

Aparat bezpieczeństwa w Polsce, Kadra kierownicza 1956-1975 (2006). red. P. Piotrowski, Warszawa: Instytut Pamięci Narodowej Komisja Ścigania Zbrodni przeciwko Narodowi Polskiemu.

Charakterystyka polityczno-operacyjna Wielkiej Brytanii, Warszawa: Akademia Spraw Wewnętrznych 1989, IPN Wr 0148/103.

Davies, P. (2004). *MI6 and the machinery of spying*, Taylor & Francis e-Library.

Gułkowski, R (1987). *Brytyjskie służby specjalne: historia-organizacja-działalność*, Departament szkolenia i doskonalenia zawodowego MSW, Warszawa, IPN Wr 0148/179

Musiał, F. (2007). *Podręcznik bezpieki. Teoria pracy operacyjnej Służby Bezpieczeństwa w świetle wydawnictw resortowych Ministerstwa Spraw Wewnętrznych PRL (1970-1989)*, Kraków: IPN.

Nowak, W. (1989). *Charakterystyka polityczno-operacyjna Wielkiej Brytanii*, Warszawa: Akademia Spraw Wewnętrznych, IPN Wr 0148/103

West, N. (2005). *Historical Dictionary of British Intelligence*, The Scarecrow Press.

Wroga działalność pracowników placówek dyplomatycznych i konsularnych państw kapitalistycznych akredytowanych w Polsce, IPN WR 053/3372.

Wywiad Wielkiej Brytanii, IPN Wr 054/1339.

The situation of a transsexual person in Poland after a sex determining court order having come into force. Sex change in practice.

Joanna Matczuk

Introduction

The identification: „I – a woman", „I – a man" present in commonplace everyday life situations of more than 99% of society[1] does not constitute any problem and is generally unconscious. For the remaining members of the society it is not as obvious. Such is the case of transsexuals, people who experience discrepancy between physical sex and actual gender identity.

Although in Poland sex changes have occurred since 1960s,[2] transsexual people are still waiting for a proper legal act to regulate their status. In course of sex change practice in Poland a court proceeding path has been developed.[3] Completing a court proceeding on determining one's sex is just a beginning of a long way transsexual people have to go before being able to start their new life in a society. A complex sex reassignment process becomes even more complicated because of the lack of proper rules of law. Therefore there are still many doubts as for what steps should be taken by transsexuals in order to unambiguously clear their situation.

Civil status registers

After a court has issued an order satisfying for a transsexual person, the case falls under the administrative law jurisdiction. Determining the gender of a transsexual person according to Article 189 of the Civil Procedure Code is the basis of entering an additional reference in the civil status registers. After having obtained the order determining a transsexual person to belong to the gender opposite to the one stated in a birth certificate, the person must apply to the head of registry office where the birth certificate is stored to enter an appropriate amendment in civil status registers.

---

1   According to M. Filar the frequency of transgender identity of MTF type is 1:20,000, and FTM type is 1:50,000, see: M. Filar: *Prawne i społeczne aspekty transseksualizmu*, Państwo i Prawo, No. 7/1987, p. 67.

2   K. Gładych: *Odzwierciedlenie transseksualizmu w polskim akcie urodzenia*, Technika i USC, nr 1 (26)/2001.

3   The issues related to court proceedings involved with sex change exceed the scope of this discussion.

The basis of such amendment is Article 21 of the Act of 29 September 1986 of the Law on Certificates of Civil Status. The article provides that any changes that are material as per validity or content occurring after a record have been entered in civil status registers shall be annexed as an additional mention.

Transsexual people must attach an extract decree of an effective court order to their application for entering such additional mention.[4] The head of registry office having examined the application shall enter the additional mention in a birth certificate stating that in accordance with the order of the court the person for whom the certificate was issued is, accordingly, a man or a woman.

It is worth to mention that despite of the decision issued by the Supreme Court in extended composition of 7 judges,[5] which is a legally binding rule of law, stating that the occurrence of transsexualism is not the basis for the correction of the entry concerning a gender, the standpoint of the courts on this issue is not uniform. For the courts still adhere to Article 31 of the Law on Certificates of Civil Status and on its basis they order for changes to the legal designations of sex.[6] Fortunately a lack of consistent courts opinion does not determine the situation of transsexual people. It is because for the head of the registry office it is an order of a court that is binding and not the rule of law this order was based on. Therefore – when an "incorrect" order stating that the amendment concerning gender shall be entered in a birth certificate is filed with the registry office, the head of registry office must execute this order.[7]

Personal identification number (PESEL) and other documents change

A positive court decision on sex change is also a legal basis for altering the PESEL number[8] of a transsexual person. Such change is based on regulations of

---

4   According to Article 21 section 2 of the Act of 29 September 1986 of the Law on Certificates of Civil Status, the basis of entering an additional mention, as described in section 1, are the final and binding decisions of the court, copy of the record from the civil status registers, as well as other documents which affect the content or validity of the Act.

5   The resolution by seven judges of the Supreme Court of 22 June 1989, files No. III CZP 37/89, OSNCP 1989/12 item 188 OSPiKA 1991/3, item 3.

6   See the court order attached to a discussion by K. Gładych: *Odzwierciedlenie transseksualizmu…*, p.12. This order was issued on 30 May 1997 – that is 8 years after the resolution was passed by the panel of seven judges (pol. uchwała "siódemkowa").

7   K. Gładych: *Odzwierciedlenie transseksualizmu…*, p. 14.

8   According to Article 31a section 1 of the Act of 10 June 1974 on population records and identity cards the number of the Universal Electronic System for Registration of the Population (pol. Numer Powszechnego Elektronicznego Systemu Ewidencji Ludności) in

the Act of 10 April 1974 on population records and identity cards.[9] The provisions of the Act state that the PESEL number shall be changed in cases of designation correction or sex change of a person who it was issued for (Article 31b section 5 item 2 of the Act).

The sex is indicated by the 10th (last but one) digit of the PESEL number. Digits 0, 2, 4, 6, 8 – denote female gender, whereas digits 1, 3, 5, 7, 9 – denote male gender.[10] Having the "appropriate" PESEL number is not at all unimportant for transsexual people. A problem for transsexuals before and during the change of the PESEL number procedure is e.g. acquiring discounted prices for medicines that are refundable only for a particular sex. For example a MTF transsexual in the process of sex reassignment who is taking estrogens is not entitled to 3% discount which is given for that hormone to women, because the PESEL number denotes the male sex which is not entitled to any refunds for this medicine.[11] In such situations the explanations do not help much, neither do the prescriptions from a physician.

Change of name and surname

After entering the amendments in a birth certificate and changing a PESEL number a transsexual person takes up further steps towards changing a name and, if needed, also a surname. The legal basis for this change is Article 4 section 1 of the Act on change of name and surname,[12] which provides that such a change can be arranged for important reasons.

For such change of name and/or surname a transsexual person must file an application with a head (or a deputy head) of registry office competent as for the address of permanent residence of an applicant, and in case there is none, the application shall be filed with the head of registry office competent as for the last address of permanent residence (Article 12 section 1 of the Act). The application as a rule is filed personally, yet the applicants who stay abroad may

---

this act referred to as "PESEL number", is an 11-digit, permanent numerical symbol identifying a natural person. The first six digits indicate the birth date (YYMMDD), the following four digits stand for personal identification number and the sex of a person, the last one is a control digit which is used for computer verification of a given number.

9   Journal of Laws No. 14/1974, item 85.

10   The official website of the Ministry of Interior and Administration: http://www.mswia.gov.pl/portal/pl/381/32/#jakie%20informacje; verified as per 12 August 2010.

11   Information obtained courtesy of a person representing the Tran s-Fuzja Foundation.

12   The Act of 17 October 2008 on change of name and surname, Journal of Laws No. 220/2008, item 1414.

apply through the consul of the Republic of Poland. The Act allows to file the application for changing the name without adhering to the above mentioned requirements providing the applicant will do it in writing with a signature certified by a notary (Article10 section 3 of the Act on change of name and surname).

To this application a person undergoing a sex change procedure must attach, apart from some other documents, a full copy of a birth certificate with the appropriate amendment entered in it after the sex reassignment (Article 11 section 2 item 1, and Article 11 section 3 item 1 of the Act on change of name and surname) as well as the sex determining order of the court (see also Article 11 section 2 item 4, and Article11 section 3 item 3 of the Act on change of name and surname). The above mentioned documents should be for a head of registry office a sufficient basis for the change of the name and the surname of a transsexual person which is an administrative decision procedure (Article 12 section 1 of the Act on change of name and surname).

Change of identity card

After having changed the name and/or surname and a PESEL number a transsexual person can apply for changing an identity card. Having acquired a new ID card all the other documents such as driving license, passport, and so forth can be changed.

The process of sex reassignment – pertaining both to physical body transformation as well as legal issues going along with it – often takes many years. Before a transsexual person changes all the required documents using those still revealing the sex assigned at birth cannot be avoided. Such situations are very often awkward as the person is forced to give explanations for the discrepancy between the appearance and the documents being used. In such situation a medical certificate can be helpful and many physicians issue these for their transsexual patients. Unfortunately transsexuals usually do not possess such a document that would allow them to quickly, and relatively unembarrassingly, straighten out the inconsistency between the way they look and the documents they hold.

It seems reasonable to solve this problem by issuing some special identity cards proving that a person is currently undergoing a process of sex reassignment.[13] Such documents would contain two pictures of the transsexual –

---

13 According to information given by a person representing the Trans-Fuzja Foundation such ID cards are being used by transsexual people in Holland, France and Denmark. These ID cards prove useful in everyday situations – especially in contact with the state

one featuring the person "before" and the other "during" the process of sex reassignment. The Trans-Fuzja Foundation took up even some steps to issue such documents for transgender people.[14] The Foundation turned to the Minister of Interior and Administration with the request to educate the functionaries authorised to check citizens' documents about the fact of transgender people using such ID cards. The idea met with an initial approval of the Ombudsman, yet he ultimately changed this earlier positive approach when faced with an unfavourable opinion of the Minister of Interior and Administration.[15]

Change of other documents

Apart from a regular identity card a transsexual person may decide to change also some other documents, e.g. membership cards, certificates, diplomas, etc., which in many cases turns out to be very complicated. The hardships in this regard await transsexual people in their workplaces. The former employers refuse them to correct work certificates on the grounds of no legal basis to oblige them to do so (this matter will be elaborated more broadly further in this discussion).

Praiseworthy is a solution for documents, certificates in the resolution of the Minister of Culture of 6 April 2005 on the rules of issuing certificates, national diplomas and other school documents and their models, the procedure of their corrections and duplicates, and the rules of legalising the documents intended for legal transactions abroad as well as the fees for executing these formalities.[16] This resolution directly addresses the issue of a transsexual person's changing personal data in a diploma or certificate.

Section 16 item 1 of this regulation provides that the name or surname of the graduate on certificate, diploma or any other school document shall not be amended unless the name or surname have been altered on the basis of a court order issued as a result of sex change case. In the later situation a certificate, diploma or any other school document shall be reissued with the new name and/or surname. If such reissuance is not possible a duplicate of a certificate, diploma or any other school document shall be issued upon returning the

---

organs or the police saving the transsexual people awkwardness and trouble with describing the reasons for the discrepancy between their appearance and the data featured in their documents.

14   W. Dynarski, A. Grodzka, L. Podobińska: *Tożsamość płciowa – zagadnienia medyczne, społeczne i prawne* [w:] *Prawa osób transseksualnych. Rozwiązania modelowe a sytuacja w Polsce*, Warszawa 2010, p. 27 and 26.

15   *Ibidem*, p.26.

16   Journal of Law No. 60/2005, item 523.

certificate, diploma or any other school document issued for the previous name and surname.

According to section 16 item 2 of the regulation, in case the change of name and surname took place before the graduation, in the all the documentation kept by the school the previous name shall be crossed out, and the new name shall be written in red. Then at the bottom of the page shall be written a note: *The name/surname has been changed* followed by a date and signature of the person authorised to sign the documentation of a teaching course. The new name and/or surname of a transsexual person shall be written in on the basis of a court order.

In case a name and/or surname took place after the graduation, but before the maturity exam (section 16 item 3) the maturity exam certificate shall be issued for the new name and/or surname, and the note indicating the change of the name and/or surname shall be made in the official grade transcript.

Financing the treatment of transsexualism

The right to health as a state of physical, mental and social wellbeing is considered to be one of the fundamental human rights.[17] If accepting transsexualism to be a disorder the right of the transsexual people to protect their health should be respected as per Article 68 of the Constitution of the Republic of Poland,[18] and consequently also the right to health care services financed from public funds.

Transsexualism must be treated on several levels – social, legal and medical. Medical care comprises of surgical operation, hormonal treatment as well as number of other necessary medical procedures.

FTM transsexuals usually undergo breast reduction and female gonads removal surgeries. Sometimes the reconstruction of the penis is also performed. As for MTF transsexuals the necessary surgical interventions are breasts modeling or enlarging, removal of male gonads, vagina reconstruction, and if needed reduction of thyroid cartilage, hair removal by laser method or collagen lips injections.[19] Important is also FFS (facial feminisation surgery).

---

17 See the Preamble to the *Constitution of the World Health Organization*. Health, as per definition given in that document, is a state of complete physical, mental and social wellbeing and not merely the absence of disease or infirmity.

18 Article 68 sections 1 and 2 of the Constitution of the Republic of Poland provides that, "Everyone shall have the right to have his health protected" (section 1), and above that "equal access to health care services, financed from public funds, shall be ensured by public authorities to citizens irrespective of their material situation. The conditions for, and scope of, the provision of services shall be established by statute" (section 2).

19 *Ibid.*

The aforementioned surgical procedures, including the reconstruction of the sex organs, fall under the category of plastic surgery. As such they tend to be considered esthetic procedures, although for accident patients and those with congenital defects such surgeries play a reconstructive and corrective role (e.g. fused toes and fingers, cleft palate). But also in case of transsexuals such surgical procedures allow them to regain healthy condition.[20]

Presently health care financing regulates the Act of 27 August 2004 on health care services financed from public funds (the so-called Act on the basket of guaranteed medical services; pol. *ustawa koszykowa*) as amended.[21] Yet it is worth mentioning[22] what the legal situation directly before the amendment to the Act of 2009 on the basket of guaranteed medical services was.[23]

The system of financing health care services financed form public funds was based at that time on two "baskets" of guaranteed medical services – "positive basket" described in the Article 15 of the Act on health care services financed form public funds and the "negative basket" described in the Appendix to this Act issued on the basis of Article 17 of this Act. The Appendix specified health care services not financed from public funds regardless of the extent of their applying. Among these the legislator directly mentioned sex reassignment surgeries.

The amendment to the Act on the basket of guaranteed medical services excluded the above mentioned negative list of health care services (both the Appendix to the Act as well as Article 17 of the Act which was the basis for issuing this Appendix) and preserved (but amended) the positive catalog (Article 15 of the Act). After the amendment it is the Minister of Health who by means of resolution specifies the scope of guaranteed medical services. In the resolutions issued on the basis of the Act the treatment of transsexualism was not explicitly mentioned.

The present legal situation does not explicitly define whether transsexualism treatment shall be financed from the public funds, and even if accepted that it shall be refunded – still the scope of the refund is not clear.

Many of the general health care services specified in the positive "basket" definitely fall under the scope of procedure involved with sex reassignment therapy. Examples of these are psychiatric consultations, EEG, USG, blood

---

20 Cited in W. Dynarski, A. Grodzka, L. Podobińska: *Tożsamość płciowa...*, p. 33.
21 Journal of Laws No. 164/2008, item 1027, as amended.
22 More elaborately on that topic: N. Łojko: *Finansowanie zabiegów związanych z dostosowaniem płci psychicznej do płci fizycznej w Polsce* [w:] *Prawa osób transseksualnych...*, as above.
23 The Act of 25 June 2009 changing the Act on health care services financed form public funds and the Act on prices, Journal of Laws, No. 118/2009, item 989.

tests, hormone therapy. There are no basis to refuse financing the above mentioned medical care services just by the fact of their being the elements of sex reassignment therapy. It seems then that there are no contraindications to accept these as general health care services to be financed from public funds.

In practice though financing these medical care services depends in most cases on the physician. Therefore because of the lack of clear legal regulation the questions of financing sex reassignment treatments are not standardised. The physician should decide on financing health care based on Article 31a of the Act being discussed. Unfortunately a limited knowledge of the health care personnel about the transsexualism results in poor qualifying of health care procedures specified in the aforementioned resolutions involved in sex assignment treatment.[24]

Among the "set" of resolutions a special attention should be given to the one issued by the Minister of Health on 29 August 2009 on guaranteed hospital health care.[25] Big controversy involves Article 3 section 2 of the resolution which states that "plastic surgery or cosmetic treatments fall under the category of guaranteed services specified in part I of the Appendix no. 1 only in cases of congenital defect, injury, illness or the result of its treatment." Unfortunately, the experience of transsexual people shows, that the physicians often do not recognise, that plastic surgery in case of a transsexual does not play a role of a beautifying procedure but rather a corrective one and that, just like in cases of people with congenital defects, it is the only chance for a transsexual person to regain healthy condition.

Similar is the situation in case of medicines used for the therapy. Public funds cover medicines for main diseases, supplementary medicines and prescribed medicines (Article 36 section 5 of the Act on health care services financed from public funds), medicines for infectious and mental diseases, medicines for mentally disabled, suffering for some chronic, congenital or acquired diseases (Article 37 section 1). The Minister of Health by issuing resolutions assigns a particular medicine to the appropriate category. And thus for example[26] – the medicines based on active ingredient *Cyproteronum* were assigned as supplementary medications and distributed with 50% discount.[27] The purpose for which the medicines containing this substance are given out is

---

24 Information obtained courtesy of a person representing the Trans-Fuzja Foundation.
25 Journal of Laws No. 140/2009, item 1143 as amended.
26 Cit. in. N. Łojko: *Finansowanie zbiegów związanych z dostosowaniem płci psychicznej do płci fizycznej w Polsce*, [w:] Prawa osób transseksualnych..., do., p.56.
27 See Appendix no. 3 to the resolution of the Minister of Health of 23 February 2009 on the list of core and supplementary medicines and payments for supplementary medicines, Journal of Laws No. 35/2009, item 275.

not essential for public funds financing. Therefore from the legal point of view *Cyproteronum* containing medicines should be given out to the transsexual people who are undergoing a hormonal therapy on the same basis as to people suffering from other conditions.

As one can see, in the present legal situation there are no premise against transsexual people having refunded many of their treatments, medical examinations and medicines. In case of sex reassignment therapy public funds can be thus employed on general basis if the physician decides it is necessary.

Therefore it seems that the problem with refunding the treatments for transsexual people is factual rather than legal in nature.[28] In practice however unclear content of the resolutions results in excluding sex reassignment therapy treatments from the range of medical care services to be financed from public funds. As the study literature shows,[29] in Poland most of the medical procedures related to transsexualism treatment are not financed from public funds.

Transsexualism and marriage

In the Polish legal system marriage is a relationship between a man and woman.[30] At the same time the Polish law does not accept marriage of people of the same sex. Therefore the question arises how to classify the marriages of transsexual people before and after their having undergone a transition. A lack of legal regulation of this issue results in many controversies around the legal family relations of transsexual people.

It seems that in the Polish law the status of a transsexual person in legal matters should be considered based on the sex defined in civil status registers.[31] On this basis a transsexual person after having undergone legal sex change procedure in all legal situations shall be treated as a male or female according to the mention in the birth certificate.

If the above is to be accepted there are no legal obstacles for a transsexual to marry a person of the sex opposite to the one that is stated in the transsexuals civil status registers even if a sex reassignment surgery was not performed.

Much more complicated is a situation of a transsexual person who is already married. Such situations are not rare. A transsexual person often for different

---

28   As justly pointed out by N. Łojko: *Finansowanie zabiegów...*, do.
29   Cited in W. Dynarski, A. Grodzka, L. Podobińska: *Tożsamość płciowa...*, p. 32.
30   See Article 18 of the Constitution of the Republic of Poland and Article 1 section 1 of the Family and Guardianship Code.
31   See also K. Osajda: *Cywilnoprawne aspekty zmiany płci u transseksualistów*, in *Orientacja seksualna...*, do., p. 195.

reasons takes up sex reassignment therapy in mature age, and before that leads „normal" life – which includes getting married, having children. Theoretically the fact of being married should not interfere with the possibility of legal sex change. Because the sex is part of personal state of being about which nobody but the individual concerned can decide. Nevertheless a question arises as for the status of the marriage after one of the spouses had legally changed the sex while still remaining in marriage. The law presently in force does not clearly answer this question.

The status of such a marriage was relevantly commented by K. Osajda.[32] He put attention to Article 2 of the Family and Guardianship Code which provides a possibility of accepting the nonexistence of the marriage. This provision is declarative in character and therefore leads to an assertion that the marriage has never been entered into. Article 2 of the Family and Guardianship Code provides that in order to consider the nonexistence of the marriage it is necessary to prove the non-compliance of the provisions which state under what conditions the marriage should be entered into, and one of them is that it shall occur between the opposite sexes. However K. Osajda argues, it pertains to the non-compliance of the provisions in the moment of entering into marriage. Therefore as per presently effective provisions there is no legal basis to declare a marriage nonexistent on the grounds that one of the spouses has changed the sex during its course.

The issue looks similar in case of annulment of marriage – there are no legal basis to cancel a marriage after the legal sex change by one of the spouses. Article 17 of the Family and Guardianship Code contains a closed catalogue of premises to be fulfilled in order to annul a marriage. Yet there is no mention concerning spouses being of the same sex.

Still in the course of analysis of the above mentioned provisions one should not forget the content of Article 18 of the *Constitution of the Republic of Poland.* This article provides that the spouses must be of opposite sex under pain of nullity of the marriage as such. That means the condition must be fulfilled not only in the moment of entering into marriage but also during its course. Hence the above given interpretation of Article 2 of the Family and Guardianship Code can lead to an assumption that this provision is inconsistent with the *Constitution* within a scope of its accepting the validity of the same sex marriage. On the other hand by interpreting Article 2 of the Family and Guardianship Code in consistence with Article 18 of the *Constitution* one can assume that the circumstances allowing to consider the marriage nonexistent shall be extended to the whole period of marriage. That would mean the spouses

---

32   See K. Osajda: *Cywilnoprawne aspekty...*, do.

not being of the opposite sex is the basis to consider the marriage nonexistent regardless of the circumstances having occurred while entering into marriage or later during its course.

In one sense it is also possible to accept that a marriage is terminated *ex lege* with a legal sex change.[33] Since after this change the marriage of two persons does not fulfill the conditions for the existence of constitutionally specified marriage, it cannot be considered a marriage.

A lack of clear status of the marriage of transsexual people not only does not allow them to preserve any specified role in a family, but it also leads to an inconsistence with an accepted legal order. It is because present regulations with simultaneous legal sex change possible introduce into the legal system marriage of the same sex people.[34]

The above deliberations are rather theoretical in character. Legal family issues are usually solved by life itself. In practice it is seen that transsexual people who decided to change sex first apply for a divorce decree.[35] Legal order is at times protected by the courts ordering in cases of legal sex change. In one case the court dismissed the action on the grounds that changing sex by the transsexual person remaining in the marriage would cause a situation of existing a marriage of the same sex people which is unacceptable by the Polish law.[36] Furthermore there are very few cases of transsexual people who file a sex determining case while still remaining in marriage. It is already at the stage of medical advice and preparing for the court case that transsexual people are being informed their legal sex will not be changed unless they get divorced.[37]

Typically though a divorce case is filed by a spouse of a transsexual person. And usually such divorce summons include a petition for dissolution of marriage by the sole fault of a transsexual spouse. It is not at all uncommon for the courts to order in compliance with these summons.[38]

---

33 This possibility is presented by K. Osajda: *Cywilnoprawne aspekty...*, do., p. 192.

34 This pertains a situation when a person changes sex in a course of marriage and no party involved as per Article 2 of the Family and Guardianship Code applies to annul the marriage.

35 W. Dynarski, A. Grodzka, L. Podobińska argues that in order to change one's legal sex it is obligatory to obtain a divorce, see W. Dynarski, A. Grodzka, L. Podobińska: *Tożsamość płciowa...*, do., p. 29.

36 Information obtained courtesy of a person representing the Trans-Fuzja Foundation.

37 Information obtained courtesy of a person representing the Trans-Fuzja Foundation.

38 Information obtained courtesy of a person representing the Trans-Fuzja Foundation.

Transsexual parents

Equally problematic is settling parental status of a transsexual person. As it has been mentioned above legal sex change is possible without undergoing a sex reassignment surgery. In this situation there are no obstacles for a FTM transsexual to bear a child. Therefore the question arises – who should be written in a child's birth certificate as a biological mother?[39] Unfortunately the existing regulations do not give any answer to this question, and their present content – which includes the content of the Family and Guardianship Code – does not allow separating the institution of a mother from female sex.[40]

"Simpler" is a situation of a child born before a legal sex change by a transsexual parent. In practice birth certificate of a transsexual person's child does not change after the parent's legal sex change. In this case administrative organs completely ignore the fact that the consequence in this case is an inconsistence with the actual legal situation presented in civil status registers.[41]

Furthermore one can imagine a situation of FTM transsexual who after a legal sex change and sex reassignment surgery (SRS) enters into a marriage with a woman. In this case it is not possible for a child to be born from that couple since the transsexual after SRS is sterile. Yet his spouse can still become pregnant and in this situation FTM transsexual who in legal terms is a man may apply to a court for an acknowledgement of paternity. As K. Osajda rightly argues, such an acknowledgement is not supported by the rules of law since an acknowledgement of a child's parentage is a declaration of knowledge not a declaration of will.[42] On the other hand, what about a situation when a transsexual enters into marriage with his female spouse and she gives birth to a

---

39   Possibility of occurring of such situation may be an important argument for the supporters of conducting a legal sex change only after the sex reassignment surgery has taken place.

40   For example the Civil Procedure Code provides a possibility of court proceedings to establish maternity or paternity and to admit or deny paternity – these two terms are clearly differentiated (there is no general proceeding regarding e.g. establishing parenthood). Also K. Pietrzykowski notes that the Family and Guardianship Code concerning parents uses term "both" (pol. *oboje*) in the meaning of parents, in a grammatical form which according to the rules of the Polish language indicates that they are of opposite sexes. See K. Pietrzykowski, in Kodeks rodzinny i opiekuńczy. Komentarz, p. 111.

41   According to information obtained courtesy of a MTF transsexual person who had changed her legal sex after having fathered a child in a marriage that was entered into before the transition, despite of the parent's sex change and amendment entered in the civil status register, the birth certificate of the child remained unchanged.

42   See K. Osajda: *Cywilnoprawne aspekty...*, do., p. 195.

child in a course of marriage? In such cases presumption of paternity by marriage described in Article 62 section 1 of the Family and Guardianship Code shall apply. This presumption according to Article 62 section 3 can be dismissed only as a result of bringing an action for denial of paternity. But if no legitimate party brings such an action a transsexual will rather be able to execute all his rights and duties of a child's father.

Transsexual on the labour market

The whole transformation process usually lasts a few years. In this period a transsexual visually transforms to be a different person. At that time a new face has to be presented to others, a new place has to be found in a society and work environment.

During the transformation process transsexual people are often dismissed from work even though the whole process does not influence their ability to work. Apart from surgery and recuperation time there are no medical contradictions as for Professional activity of a transsexual undergoing the process of transition. Of course an "official" reason for dismissal is not the fact of changing sex but all kinds of other confabulated reasons an employer can think of.

Obtaining so much awaited court order and changing documents unfortunately are not sufficient to overcome the difficulties created by employers. The transsexuals are often refused correcting or issuing new documents, e.g. a certificate of employment featuring new personal data.[43] The employers argue that a given document such as certificates of employment should feature data complying with the gender a transsexual person was in the moment of issuing the document. The advocates of this approach argue that sex change takes place only with the moment of issuing the order by a court and that for example if an employee was previously a man there is no basis to enter woman's data in a certificate.[44] In such situation a transsexual person is forced to simultaneously use the uncorrected certificate of employment and birth certificate with a mention of sex change on it. But this forces a transsexual person even after full transformation to reveal the previous sex every time a job is being changed which exposes such person to further acts of discrimination.

---

43   It does not concern certificates, national diplomas and other school documents mentioned in the resolution of the Minister of Culture of 6 April 2005, see p. 9 of this discussion.

44   M. Gadomska: *Zmiana płci nie ma wpływu na świadectwo pracy*, Rzeczpospolita 19 VI 2009, http://finanse.wp.pl/kat,7026,title,Zmiana-plci-nie-ma-wplywu-na-swiadectwo-pracy, wid,11235164,wiadomosc_prasa.html

In face of unfavourable for transsexuals, although justified, legal argument the question arises whether having corrected by an employer a certificate of employment without a legal basis would mean an attestation of an untruth, and in consequence would be considered as an offence according to Article 271 of the Penal Code.[45] Some authors say that such a situation does not show any features of criminal offence since the action is not an intentional or socially dangerous act. Therefore Article 271 of the Penal Code is not applicable thereto.[46] The above interpretation seems correct, however a lack of data pertaining to the case concerned makes it hard to predict the prosecution office's actions or possible decision of the criminal court in this regard.

Despite of conviction that there is no necessity to correct the certificates of employment the labour law experts point that such practice creates discomfort for a transsexual person and apart from that may become grounds for discrimination.[47]

Discrimination of transsexuals is frequently seen at working places or in a very process of recruitment. Generally such discrimination is concealed but at times it is openly displayed. Transsexual people rarely take any legal actions in order to protect their rights. One of the reasons is a lack of solid legal basis to support their claims. Article 11 section 3 of the Labour Code forbids discrimination against sex or sex preferences, yet there is no mention of discrimination against gender identity or sex change. This situation could be corrected by extending the scope of this regulation and applying it per analogy in a way it precludes sex or sex preferences discrimination. On this basis the European Court of Justice (ECJ) ruled in case of P. against Sand Cornwall County Council.[48] The case pertained to dismissal of a transsexual for a reason related to her decision of gender reassignment. The British High Court considering the case forwarded it to the ECJ to decide whether discrimination for a reason related to a gender reassignment is to be considered a discrimination on grounds of sex in violation of Council Directive 76/207/EEC of 9 February 1976 on the implementation of the principle of equal treatment for men and women. The ECJ ruled that the provisions of the Directive preclude dismissal of a transsexual for a reason related to a gender reassignment and that P. was discriminated against on grounds of sex.

---

45 Article 271 section 1 of the Penal Code provides that: A public official or other person authorised to issue a document who attests therein an untruth regarding circumstances of legal consequences shall be subject to the penalty of the deprivation of liberty for a term of between 3 months and 5 years.

46 M. Gadomska: *Zmiana płci...*

47 As argued by an expert S. Paruch in M. Gadomska, *Zmiana płci...*, do.

48 Decision of the European Court of Justice of 30 June 1996 on *P. v. Cornwall County Council*, Case number C-13/94.

A transsexual person in the army

Transsexual people experience discrimination on the grounds of sex reassignment not only on the job market. Although after legal sex change a transsexual should be considered a gender sex "amended" in the birth certificate, the reality shows otherwise.

One of the examples of discrimination on the grounds of sex is refusing the transsexual people to serve in the military. In evaluation of physical and psychological ability to fulfill military service the diseases and lamenesses listed in the regulation of the Minister of National Defense of 25 June 2004 on qualifying for active military service and method of proceeding of army medical advisory boards in those matters are taken under consideration.[49] Transsexualism and hermaphroditism are directly mentioned in Appendix 2 and Appendix 3 containing the index of diseases and lamenesses taken into consideration in physical and psychological evaluation of ability to be admitted to military service.[50] According to Appendix 2 transsexuals belong to E category in groups I and II, and N category in groups III and IV. But according to Appendix 3 transsexuals should be assigned to N category in all the three groups mentioned in this Appendix. It should be noted that transsexualism is mentioned in Chapter I of the Resolution – Body habitus. Such structure of the regulations is undoubtedly a result of perceiving sex of an individual solely in terms of biological sex. It can be then assumed that – an "ill" transsexual before the legal sex change and undergoing the surgery could be admitted to military service, whereas "healed" transsexual would be treated just the opposite, that means as incapable to fulfill military service according to the Resolution of 25 June 2004.

Excluding transsexual people from the military service is probably meant for protecting them against trouble and discrimination on the part of e.g. other soldiers or superiors. Yet in the light of resolutions of the European Court of Human Rights in cases of refusing the admission or expelling from the service homosexual people this argument seems to be inadequate.[51] Moreover it should

---

49 Journal of Laws No. 151/2004, item 1595 as amended.

50 Appendix 2 – The index of diseases and lamenesses taken into consideration in evaluation of physical and psychological ability to be admitted to active military service and to perform such a service abroad.

Appendix 3 – The index of diseases and lamenesses taken into consideration in evaluation of physical and psychological ability to be admitted to air service, ground based air traffic control and air-engineering services.

51 See the ECHR judgement of 27 September 1999 on *Lustig-Prean & Beckett v. UK*, case no. 31417/96, the ECHR judgement on *Smith & Grady v. UK* of 29 September 1999, case nos. 33985/96 and 33986/96.

be mentioned that despite of the above mentioned Regulation being in force, in practice military service is not an uncommon thing among transsexual people.[52]

Conclusion

The above analysis of the chosen aspects of transsexualism leads to an obvious and frequently repeated by researchers of this matter conclusion: the situation of transsexual people requires extensive rearrangement.

The experience of transsexual people shows that the lack of adequate rules of law becomes a formally founded reason for refusing them services that are important for their normal functioning in the society (e.g. refusal of correcting a certificate of employment). A transsexual who does not find any support in the rules of law is in consequence forced to depend on the goodwill of a clerk, employer or physician.

It is true that introducing certain regulations could mean destroying the basis of the present law system. This problem is particularly noticeable in family legal relations in which determining the unambiguous status of a transsexual person creates controversies. However in many aspects introducing needed regulations would not interfere with the present legal system (like e.g. correcting school certificates according to the above mentioned resolution of the Minister of Culture of 6 June 2005). Nevertheless one should remember that introducing necessary regulations requires from a legislator a deeper understanding of the problem as well as proper balancing the situation not to "force anybody into happiness" as it is presently done in case of evaluating the ability to take up an active military service.

The need for changes, at least in basic scope, is obvious. However the demands of the persons representing the doctrine and appeals of LGBT circles for years have remained unanswered.

Translated by Iwona Szuwalska

---

52 See *Polscy transseksualiści będą walczyć o miejsce w wojsku* – the article available at http://wiadomosci.wp.pl/kat,1342,title,Polscy-transseksualisci-beda-walczyc-o-miejsce-w-wojsku,wid,13004410,wiadomosc.html

Contributors

A. Sybill Bidwell, of Warsaw School of Social Sciences and Humanities, Poland, previuosly worked for many years at the Wrocław University. In her reaserch concentrates on historical studies of the Polish Parliament, European parliamentary systems, interdependence between national administration and European Union institutions and 20th century British history. Author of: Unia Europejska, Udział państw członkowskich w podejmowaniu decyzji. (European Union, the member states participation in the decision making proces) (Wrocław, UP, 1999). Drogi i bezdroża brytyjskiego parlamentaryzmu (History of the procedures in British parliament) (Warszawa, Trio, 2003). Dzieje Wielkiej Brytanii w XX wieku (The twentith century history of Great Britain) (Warszawa, Academica, 2008).

Monika Łukasik-Duszyńska – doctor of humanities in the field of history. Tutor at the Warsaw School of Social Sciences and Humanities, Poland (Chair of European Studies, Faculty in Wroclaw). Focuses in her research on Polish-British relations, history of the Diplomatic Service in the XX century UK, and the information and communication policy in the European Union.

Joanna Matczuk – graduated from University of Wroclaw, Faculty of Law, Administration and Economics. Worked for several years on the legal aspects of transgender issues. The author of the articles focused on problems concerning transsexual people. Currently, a barrister's trainee at the District Bar Council in Warsaw, (in the fourth year of the training).

Sebastian Michalak – holds a doctorate in Humanities from the Faculty of Historical and Pedagogical Sciences at the Wroclaw University. Studied at the International Relations Faculty at University in Aberystwyth. He is a researcher in the filed of classified information exchange, intelligence history and etiology of espionage. Among others published in Studia Europejskie and Polish Psychological Bulletin. As well as translated five books from English into Polish.

Przemysław Paradowski – has a PhD in humanities in the field of history. His PhD thesis was awarded a prize by the Aurea Demokratia Foundation. In his research focuses on problems of European parliamentarism. The author of "The functioning of the parliaments of Central Europe in comparative perspective", a research project financed by the Polish Ministry of Science and Higher Education (2010-2013).